The Romantic Period Literature

ABOUT THE BOOK

Romantic ideas centered around art as inspiration, the spiritual and aesthetic dimension of nature, and metaphors of organic growth. Art, rather than science, Romantics argued, could best express universal truth. The Romantics underscored the importance of expressive art for the individual and society. Major political and social charges at the end of the 18th century, particularly the French Revolution, prompted a new breed of writing know as Romanticism. William Wordsworth and Samuel Taylor Coleridge began the trend for bringing emotionalism and introspection to English literature, with a new concentration on the individual and the common man. The reaction to urbanism and industrialization prompted poets to explore nature, for example the Lake poets. The changing landscape of Britain brought about by the steam engine has two major outcomes: the boom of industrialism with the expansion of the city, and the consequent depopulation of the countryside as a result of the enclosures, or privatisation of pastures. Most peasants poured into the city to work in the new factories. This period of Romantic Triumph, or of the lives of its authors, coincides in time, and not by mere accident, with the period of the success of the French Revolution, the prolonged struggle of England and all Europe against Napoleon, and the subsequent years when in Continental Europe despotic government reasserted itself and sternly suppressed liberal hopes and uprisings, while in England liberalism and democracy steadily and doggedly gathered force until by the Reform Bill of 1832 political power was largely transferred from the former small governing oligarchy to the middle class. This book is devised as a compact handbook of reference for students, researchers and teachers of English literature besides general readers.

ABOUT THE AUTHOR

Dr. Aprajita Sharma (b. 1964) is a professor of English at Govt. Hamidia Arts and Commerce P.G. College Bhopal. She obtained her doctorate in English from Barkatullah University Bhopal. She has presented a number of articles and research papers at international and national conferences and seminars in India. She has been teaching for the last 26 years. She has produced 22 research scholars who are working in India and abroad. She has published books namely 'A Semiotic Approach to H.D. Thoreau's Walden; [A book on American literature], 'Unspoken feelings' [A collection of short stories], 'Feelings of the Heart' [A collection of poems] and 'Introduction to linguistics' which provides a brief introduction to the subject.

The Romantic Period Literature

Dr. Aprajita Sharma

AMIGA PRESS. INC
Delhi -110051

AMIGA PRESS INC.

H.O :- 28-A, Indra Park,

Chander Nagar, Delhi :- 110051 (India)

Tel :- 011-22504028, +91-98736-57000

Email :- amigapress@gmail.com
amigaeditorial@gmail.com
amigapub@gmail.com

Website :- www.amigapress.co.in

This edition is published by Amiga Press Inc.

ISBN : 978-93-84533-48-9

First Published 2019

Printed and bound by Replika Press Pvt. Ltd.

Preface

Romanticism was affirmative and appropriate for most American poets and creative essayists. America's vast mountains, deserts, and tropics embodied the sublime. The Romantic spirit seemed particularly suited to American democracy: It stressed individualism, affirmed the value of the common person, and looked to the inspired imagination for its aesthetic and ethical values. Certainly the New England Transcendentalists — Ralph Waldo Emerson, Henry David Thoreau, and their associates — were inspired to a new optimistic affirmation by the Romantic movement. In New England, Romanticism fell upon fertile soil.

Major political and social charges at the end of the 18th century, particularly the French Revolution, prompted a new breed of writing know as Romanticism. William Wordsworth and Samuel Taylor Coleridge began the trend for bringing emotionalism and introspection to English literature, with a new concentration on the individual and the common man. The reaction to urbanism and industrialization prompted poets to explore nature, for example the Lake poets.

The poets Wordsworth and Coleridge are of special interest not only from the primary fact that they are among the greatest of English authors, but also secondarily because in spite of their close personal association each expresses one of the two main contrasting or complementary tendencies in the Romantic movement; Coleridge the delight in wonder and mystery, which he has the power to express with marvelous poetic suggestiveness, and Wordsworth, in an extreme degree, the belief in the simple and quiet forces, both of human life and of Nature.

William Wordsworth was born in 1770 in Cumberland, in the 'Lake Region,' which, with its bold and varied mountains as well as its group of charming lakes, is the most picturesque part of England proper. He had the benefit of all the available formal education, partly at home, partly at a 'grammar' school a few miles away, but his genius was formed chiefly by the influence of Nature, and, in a qualified degree, by that of the simple peasant people of the region. Already as a boy, though normal and active, he began to be sensitive to the Divine Power in Nature which in his mature years he was to express with deeper sympathy than any poet before him.

Realism would be one of the great artistic movements of the era. In politics a widespread commitment to economic and personal freedom was, nonetheless, accompanied by a steady growth in the power of the state. The prudery for which the Victorian Age is notorious in fact went hand in hand with an equally violent immoralism, seen, for example, in Algernon Charles Swinburne's poetry or the writings of the Decadents. Most fundamentally of all, the rapid change that many writers interpreted as progress inspired in others a fierce nostalgia. Enthusiastic rediscoveries of ancient Greece, Elizabethan England, and, especially, the Middle Ages by writers, artists, architects, and designers made this age of change simultaneously an age of active and determined historicism.

This period of Romantic Triumph, or of the lives of its authors, coincides in time, and not by mere accident, with the period of the success of the French Revolution, the prolonged struggle of England and all Europe against Napoleon, and the subsequent years when in Continental Europe despotic government reasserted itself and sternly suppressed liberal hopes and uprisings, while in England liberalism and democracy steadily and doggedly gathered force until by the Reform Bill of 1832 political power was largely transferred from the former small governing oligarchy to the middle class. How all these events influenced literature we shall see as we proceed. The beginning of the Romantic triumph is found, by general consent, in the publication in 1798 of the little volume of 'Lyrical Ballads' which contained the first significant poetry of Wordsworth and Coleridge. Even during this its greatest period, however, Romanticism had for a time a hard battle to fight, and a chief literary fact of the period was the founding and continued success of the first two important English literary and political quarterlies, 'The Edinburgh Review' and 'The Quarterly Review,' which in general stood in literature for the conservative eighteenth century tradition and violently attacked all, or almost all, the Romantic poets.

This is a reference book. All the matter is just compiled and edited in nature, taken from the various sources which are in public domain.

This book is devised as a compact handbook of reference for students, researchers and teachers of English literature besides general readers.

—Editor

Contents

1

Introduction

The changing landscape of Britain brought about by the steam engine has two major outcomes: the boom of industrialism with the expansion of the city, and the consequent depopulation of the countryside as a result of the enclosures, or privatisation of pastures. Most peasants poured into the city to work in the new factories.

This abrupt change is revealed by the change of meaning in five key words: industry (once meaning "creativity"), democracy (once disparagingly used as "mob rule"), class (from now also used with a social connotation), art (once just meaning "craft"), culture (once only belonging to farming).

But the poor condition of workers, the new class-conflicts and the pollution of the environment causes a reaction to urbanism and industrialisation prompting poets to rediscover the beauty and value of nature. Mother earth is seen as the only source of wisdom, the only solution to the ugliness caused by machines.

The superiority of nature and instinct over civilisation had been preached by Jean Jacques Rousseau and his message was picked by almost all European poets. The first in England were the Lake Poets, a small group of friends including William Wordsworth and Samuel Taylor Coleridge. These early Romantic Poets brought a new emotionalism and introspection, and their emergence is marked by the first romantic Manifesto in English literature, the "Preface to the Lyrical Ballads". This collection was mostly contributed by Wordsworth, although Coleridge must be credited for his long and impressive Rime of the Ancient Mariner, a tragic ballad about the survival of one sailor through a series of supernatural events on his voyage through the south seas which involves the slaying of an albatross, the death of the rest of the crew, a visit from Death and his mate, Life-in-Death, and the eventual redemption of the Mariner.

Coleridge and Wordsworth, however, understood romanticism in two entirely different ways: while Coleridge sought to make the supernatural "real" (much like sci-fi movies use special effects to make unlikely plots believable), Wordsworth sought to stir the imagination of readers through his down-to-earth characters taken from real life (for e.g. in "The Idiot Boy"), or the beauty of the Lake District that largely inspired his production (as in "Lines Composed a Few Miles Above Tintern Abbey").

SECOND GENERATION ROMANTICISM

The "Second generation" of Romantic poets includes Lord Byron, Percy Bysshe Shelley, Mary Shelley and John Keats. Byron, however, was still influenced by 18th-century satirists and was, perhaps the least 'romantic' of the three. His amours with a number of prominent but married ladies was also a way to voice his dissent on the hypocrisy of a high society that was only apparently religious but in fact largely libertine, the same that had derided him for being physically impaired. His first trip to Europe resulted in the first two cantos of Childe Harold's Pilgrimage, a mock-heroic epic of a young man's adventures in Europe but also a sharp satire against London society. Despite Childe Harold's success on his return to England, accompanied by the publication of The Giaour and The Corsair his alleged incestuous affair with his half-sister Augusta Leigh in 1816 actually forced him to leave England for good and seek asylum on the continent. Here he joined Percy Bysshe Shelley, his wife Mary, with his secretary Dr. John Polidori on the shores of Lake Geneva during the 'year without a summer' of 1816.

Although his is just a short story, Polidori must be credited for introducing The Vampyre, conceived from the same competition which spawned Mary Shelley's Frankenstein, to English literature. Percy, like Mary, had much in common with Byron: he was an aristocrat from a famous and ancient family, had embraced atheism and free-thinking and, like him, was fleeing from scandal in England.

Shelley had been expelled from college for openly declaring his atheism. He had married a 16-year-old girl, Harriet Westbrook whom he had abandoned soon after for Mary (Harriet took her own life after that). Harriet did not embrace his ideals of free love and anarchism, and was not as educated as to contribute to literary debate. Mary was different: the daughter of philosopher and revolutionary William Godwin, she was intellectually more of an equal, shared some of his ideals and was a feminist like her late mother, Mary Wollstonecraft, author of Vindication of the Rights of Women.

One of Shelley's best works is the Ode to the West Wind. Despite his apparent refusal to believe in God, this poem is considered a homage to pantheism, the recognition of a spiritual presence in nature.

Mary Shelley did not go down in history for her poetry, but for giving birth to science fiction: the plot for the novel is said to have come from a nightmare during stormy nights on Lake Geneva in the company of Percy Shelley, Lord Byron, and John Polidori. Her idea of making a body with human parts stolen from different corpses and then animating it with electricity was perhaps influenced by Alessandro Volta's invention and Luigi Galvani's experiments with dead frogs. Frankenstein's chilling tale also suggests modern organ transplants, tissue regeneration, reminding us of the moral issues raised by today's medicine. But the creature of Frankenstein is incredibly romantic as well. Although "the monster" is intelligent, good and loving, he is shunned by everyone because of his ugliness and deformity, and the desperation and envy that result from social exclusion turn him against the very man who created him.

John Keats did not share Byron's and Shelley's extremely revolutionary ideals, but his cult of pantheism is as important as Shelley's. Keats was in love with the ancient stones of the Parthenon that Lord Elgin had brought to England from Greece, also known as the Elgin Marbles). He celebrates ancient Greece: the beauty of free, youthful love couples here with that of classical art. Keats's great attention to art, especially in his Ode on a Grecian Urn is quite new in romanticism, and it will inspire Walter Pater's and then Oscar Wilde's belief in the absolute value of art as independent from aesthetics.

The most popular novelist of the era was Sir Walter Scott, whose grand historical romances inspired a generation of painters, composers, and writers throughout Europe. By contrast, Jane Austen wrote novels about the life of the landed gentry, seen from a woman's point of view, and wryly focused on practical social issues, especially marriage and money.

RESTORATION LITERATURE

Restoration literature includes both Paradise Lost and the Earl of Rochester's Sodom, the high spirited sexual comedy of The Country Wife and the moral wisdom of Pilgrim's Progress. It saw Locke's Treatises on Government, the founding of the Royal Society, the experiments of Robert Boyle and the holy meditations of Boyle, the hysterical attacks on theaters from Jeremy Collier, the pioneering of literary criticism from Dryden, and the first newspapers. The official break in literary culture caused by censorship and radically moralist standards under Cromwell's Puritan regime created a gap in literary tradition, allowing a seemingly fresh start for all forms of literature after the Restoration. During the Interregnum, the royalist forces attached to the court of Charles I went into exile with the twenty-year old Charles II. The nobility who travelled with Charles II were therefore lodged for over a decade in the midst of the continent's literary scene. Charles spent his time attending plays in France, and he developed a taste for Spanish plays. Those nobles living in Holland began to learn about mercantile exchange as well as the tolerant, rationalist prose debates that circulated in that officially tolerant nation.

The largest and most important poetic form of the era was satire. In general, publication of satire was done anonymously. There were great dangers in being associated with a satire. On the one hand, defamation law was a wide net, and it was difficult for a satirist to avoid prosecution if he were proven to have written a piece that seemed to criticize a noble. On the other hand, wealthy individuals would respond to satire as often as not by having the suspected poet physically attacked by ruffians. John Dryden was set upon for being merely suspected of having written the Satire on Mankind. A consequence of this anonymity is that a great many poems, some of them of merit, are unpublished and largely unknown.

Prose in the Restoration period is dominated by Christian religious writing, but the Restoration also saw the beginnings of two genres that would dominate later periods: fiction and journalism. Religious writing often strayed into political and economic writing, just as political and economic writing implied or directly addressed religion. Thomas Sprat wrote his The Dead Poet's Society in 1667 and set forth, in a single document, the goals of empirical science ever after. The Restoration was also the time when John Locke wrote many of his philosophical works. Locke's empiricism was an attempt at understanding the basis of human understanding itself and thereby devising a proper manner for making sound decisions. These same scientific methods led Locke to his three Treatises on Government, which later inspired the thinkers in the American Revolution.

As with his work on understanding, Locke moves from the most basic units of society toward the more elaborate, and, like Thomas Hobbes, he emphasizes the plastic nature of the social contract. For an age that had seen absolute monarchy overthrown, democracy attempted, democracy corrupted, and limited monarchy restored, only a flexible basis for government could be satisfying. The Restoration moderated most of the more strident sectarian writing, but radicalism persisted after the Restoration. Puritan authors such as John Milton were forced to retire from public life or adapt, and those Digger, Fifth Monarchist, Leveller, Quaker, and Anabaptist authors who had preached against monarchy and who had participated directly in the regicide of Charles I were partially suppressed. Consequently, violent writings were forced underground, and many of those who had served in the Interregnum attenuated their positions in the Restoration.

John Bunyan stands out beyond other religious authors of the period. Bunyan's The Pilgrim's Progress is an allegory of personal salvation and a guide to the Christian life. Instead of any focus on eschatology or divine retribution, Bunyan instead writes about how the individual saint can prevail against the temptations of mind and body that threaten damnation. The book is written in a straightforward narrative and shows influence from both drama and biography, and yet it also shows an awareness of the grand allegorical tradition found in Edmund Spenser. During the Restoration period, the most common manner of getting news would have been a broadsheet publication.

A single, large sheet of paper might have a written, usually partisan, account of an event. However, the period saw the beginnings of the first professional and periodical (meaning that the publication was regular) journalism in England. Journalism develops late, generally around the time of William of Orange's claiming the throne in 1689. Coincidentally or by design, England began to have newspapers just when William came to court from Amsterdam, where there were already newspapers being published.

First Edition of Oroonoko, 1688

It is impossible to satisfactorily date the beginning of the novel in English. However, long fiction and fictional biographies began to distinguish themselves from other forms in England during the Restoration period. An existing tradition of Romance fiction in France and Spain was popular in England. The "Romance" was considered a feminine form, and women were taxed with reading "novels" as a vice. One of the most significant figures in the rise of the novel in the Restoration period is Aphra Behn. She was not only the first professional female novelist, but she may be among the first professional novelists of either sex in England. Behn's most famous novel was Oroonoko in 1688. This was a biography of an entirely fictional African king who had been enslaved in Suriname. Behn's novels show the influence of tragedy and her experiences as a dramatist.

As soon as the previous Puritan regime's ban on public stage representations was lifted, the drama recreated itself quickly and abundantly. The most famous plays of the early Restoration period are the unsentimental or "hard" comedies of John Dryden, William Wycherley, and George Etherege, which reflect the atmosphere at Court, and celebrate an aristocratic macho lifestyle of unremitting sexual intrigue and conquest. After a sharp drop in both quality and quantity in the 1680s, the mid-90s saw a brief second flowering of the drama, especially comedy. Comedies like William Congreve's Love For Love (1695) and The Way of the World (1700), and John Vanbrugh's The Relapse (1696) and The Provoked Wife (1697) were "softer" and more middle-class in ethos, very different from the aristocratic extravaganza twenty years earlier, and aimed at a wider audience. The playwrights of the 1690s set out to appeal to more socially mixed audiences with a strong middle-class element, and to female spectators, for instance by moving the war between the sexes from the arena of intrigue into that of marriage. The focus in comedy is less on young lovers outwitting the older generation, more on marital relations after the wedding bells.

Diarists John Evelyn and Samuel Pepys depicted everyday London life and the cultural scene of the times.

Augustan Literature

The term Augustan literature derives from authors of the 1720's and 1730's themselves, who responded to a term that George I of England preferred for himself. While George I meant the title to reflect his might, they instead saw in it a reflection of Ancient Rome's transition from rough and ready literature to highly political and highly polished literature. Because of the aptness of the metaphor, the period from 1689-1750 was called "the Augustan Age" by critics throughout the 18th century (including Voltaire and Oliver Goldsmith). The literature of the period is overtly political and thoroughly aware of critical dictates for literature. It is an age of exuberance and scandal, of enormous energy and inventiveness and outrage, that reflected an era when English, Scottish, and Irish people found themselves in the midst of an expanding economy, lowering barriers to education, and the stirrings of the Industrial Revolution.

The most outstanding poet of the age is Alexander Pope, but Pope's excellence is partially in his constant battle with other poets, and his serene, seemingly neo-Classical approach to poetry is in competition with highly idiosyncratic verse and strong competition from such poets as Ambrose Philips. It was during this time that James Thomson produced his melancholy The Seasons and Edward Young wrote Night Thoughts. It is also the era that saw a serious competition over the proper model for the pastoral. In criticism, poets struggled with a doctrine of decorum, of matching proper words with proper sense and of achieving a diction that matched the gravity of a subject. At the same time, the mock-heroic was at its zenith. Pope's Rape of the Lock and The Dunciad are still the greatest mock-heroic poems ever written.

In prose, the earlier part of the period was overshadowed by the development of the English essay. Joseph Addison and Richard Steele's The Spectator established the form of the British periodical essay, inventing the pose of the detached observer of human life who can meditate upon the world without advocating any specific changes in it. However, this was also the time when the English novel, first emerging in the Restoration, developed into a major art form. Daniel Defoe turned from journalism and writing criminal lives for the press to writing fictional criminal lives with Roxana and Moll Flanders. He also wrote a fictional treatment of the travels of Alexander Selkirk called Robinson Crusoe (1719). The novel would benefit indirectly from a tragedy of the stage, and in mid-century many more authors would begin to write novels.

If Addison and Steele overawed one type of prose, then Jonathan Swift did another. Swift's prose style is unmannered and direct, with a clarity that few contemporaries matched. He was a profound skeptic about the modern world, but he was similarly profoundly distrustful of nostalgia. He saw in history a record of lies and vanity, and he saw in the present a madness of vanity and lies. Core Christian values were essential, but these values had to be muscular and assertive and developed by constant rejection of the games of confidence men and their gullies. Swift's A Tale of a Tub announced his skeptical analysis of the claims of the modern world, and his later prose works, such as his war with Patridge the astrologer, and most of all his derision of pride in Gulliver's Travels left only the individual in constant fear and humility safe.

After his "exile" to Ireland, Swift reluctantly began defending the Irish people from the predations of colonialism. His A Modest Proposal and the Drapier Letters provoked riots and arrests, but Swift, who had no love of Irish Roman Catholics, was outraged by the abuses and barbarity he saw around him.

Drama in the early part of the period featured the last plays of John Vanbrugh and William Congreve, both of whom carried on the Restoration comedy with some alterations. However, the majority of stagings were of lower farces and much more serious and domestic tragedies. George Lillo and Richard Steele both produced highly moral forms of tragedy, where the characters and the concerns of the characters were wholly middle class or working class. This reflected a marked change in the audience for plays, as royal patronage was no longer the important part of theatrical success. Additionally, Colley Cibber and John Rich began to battle each other for greater and greater spectacles to present on stage. The figure of Harlequin was introduced, and pantomime theater began to be staged.

This "low" comedy was quite popular, and the plays became tertiary to the staging. Opera also began to be popular in London, and there was significant literary resistance to this Italian incursion. This trend was broken only by a few attempts at a new type of comedy. Pope and John Arbuthnot and John Gay attempted a play entitled Three Hours After Marriage that failed. In 1728, however, John Gay returned to the playhouse with The Beggar's Opera. Gay's opera was in English and retold the story of Jack Sheppard and Jonathan Wild. However, it seemed to be an allegory for Robert Walpole and the directors of the South Sea Company, and so Gay's follow up opera was banned without performance. In 1737, 18th century drama almost ends, for that was the year of the Licensing Act. At that point, there was official state censorship of all plays.

An effect of the Licensing Act was to cause more than one aspiring playwright to switch over to writing novels. Henry Fielding began to write prose satire and novels after his plays could not pass the censors. Henry Brooke also turned to novels. In the interim, Samuel Richardson had produced a novel intended to counter the deleterious effects of novels in Pamela, or Virtue Rewarded (1749). Henry Fielding attacked the absurdity of this novel with two of his own works, Joseph Andrews and Shamela, and then countered Richardson's Clarissa with Tom Jones. Brooke wrote The Man of Feeling and indirectly began the sentimental novel.

Laurence Sterne attempted a Swiftian novel with a unique perspective on the impossibility of biography (the model for most novels up to that point) and understanding with Tristram Shandy, even as his detractor Tobias Smollett elevated the picaresque novel with his works. Each of these novels represents a formal and thematic divergence from the others. Each novelist was in dialogue and competition with the others, and, in a sense, the novel established itself as a diverse and open-formed genre in this explosion of creativity. The most lasting effects of the experimentation would be the psychological realism of Richardson, the bemused narrative voice of Fielding, and the sentimentality of Brooke.

18th Century During the Age of Sensibility, literature reflected the worldview of the Age of Enlightenment (or Age of Reason)-a rational and scientific approach to religious, social, political, and economic issues that promoted a secular view of the world and a general sense of progress and perfectibility. Led by the philosophers who were inspired by the discoveries of the previous century (Newton) and the writings of Descartes, Locke and Bacon. They sought to discover and to act upon universally valid principles governing humanity, nature, and society. They variously attacked spiritual and scientific authority, dogmatism, intolerance, censorship, and economic and social restraints. They considered the state the proper and rational instrument of progress. The extreme rationalism and skepticism of the age led naturally to deism; the same qualities played a part in bringing the later reaction of romanticism.

The Encyclopédie of Denis Diderot epitomized the spirit of the age.

Increased emphasis on instinct and feeling, rather than judgment and restraint. A growing sympathy for the Middle Ages during the Age of Sensibility sparked an interest in medieval ballads and folk literature.

THE GREAT WRITERS OF 1798-1830

As we look back to-day over the literature of the last three quarters of the eighteenth century, here just surveyed, the progress of the Romantic Movement seems the most conspicuous general fact which it presents. But at the, death of Cowper in 1800 the movement still remained tentative and incomplete, and it was to arrive at full maturity only in the work of the great writers of the following quarter century, who were to create the finest body of literature which England had produced since the Elizabethan period. All the greatest of these writers were poets, wholly or in part, and they fall roughly into two groups: first, William Wordsworth, Samuel Taylor Coleridge, Robert Southey, and Walter Scott; and second, about twenty years younger, Lord Byron, Percy Bysshe Shelley, and John Keats.

This period of Romantic Triumph, or of the lives of its authors, coincides in time, and not by mere accident, with the period of the success of the French Revolution, the prolonged struggle of England and all Europe against Napoleon (above, page 233), and the subsequent years when in Continental Europe despotic government reasserted itself and sternly suppressed liberal hopes and uprisings, while in England liberalism and democracy steadily and doggedly gathered force until by the Reform Bill of 1832 political power was largely transferred from the former small governing oligarchy to the middle class.

How all these events influenced literature we shall see as we proceed. The beginning of the Romantic triumph is found, by general consent, in the publication in 1798 of the little volume of 'Lyrical Ballads' which contained the first significant poetry of Wordsworth and Coleridge.

Even during this its greatest period, however, Romanticism had for a time a hard battle to fight, and a chief literary fact of the period was the founding and continued success of the first two important English literary and political quarterlies, 'The Edinburgh Review' and 'The Quarterly Review,' which in general stood in literature for the conservative eighteenth century tradition and violently attacked all, or almost all, the Romantic poets.

These quarterlies are sufficiently important to receive a few words in passing. In the later eighteenth century there had been some periodicals devoted to literary criticism, but they were mere unauthoritative booksellers' organs, and it was left for the new reviews to inaugurate literary journalism of the modern serious type.

'The Edinburgh Review,' suggested and first conducted, in 1802, by the witty clergyman and reformer Sydney Smith, passed at once to the hands of Francis (later Lord) Jeffrey, a Scots lawyer who continued to edit it for nearly thirty years. Its politics were strongly liberal, and to oppose it the Tory 'Quarterly Review' was founded in 1808, under the editorship of the satirist William Gifford and with the cooperation of Sir Walter Scott, who withdrew for the purpose from his connection with the 'Edinburgh.' These reviews were followed by other high-class periodicals, such as 'Blackwood's Magazine,' and most of the group have maintained their importance to the present day.

SAMUEL TAYLOR COLERIDGE

The poets Wordsworth and Coleridge are of special interest not only from the primary fact that they are among the greatest of English authors, but also secondarily because in spite of their close personal association each expresses one of the two main contrasting or complementary tendencies in the Romantic movement; Coleridge the delight in wonder and mystery, which he has the power to express with marvelous poetic suggestiveness, and Wordsworth, in an extreme degree, the belief in the simple and quiet forces, both of human life and of Nature.

To Coleridge, who was slightly the younger of the two, attaches the further pathetic interest of high genius largely thwarted by circumstances and weakness of will. Born in Devonshire in 1772, the youngest of the many children of a self-made clergyman and schoolmaster, he was a precocious and abnormal child, then as always a fantastic dreamer, despised by other boys and unable to mingle with them. After the death of his father he was sent to

Christ's Hospital, the 'Blue-Coat' charity school in London, where he spent nine lonely years in the manner briefly described in an essay of Charles Lamb, where Coleridge appears under a thin disguise. The very strict discipline was no doubt of much value in giving firmness and definite direction to his irregular nature, and the range of his studies, both in literature and in other fields, was very wide.

Through the aid of scholarships and of contributions from his brothers he entered Cambridge in 1791, just after Wordsworth had left the University; but here his most striking exploit was a brief escapade of running away and enlisting in a cavalry troop. Meeting Southey, then a student at Oxford, he drew him into a plan for a 'Pantisocracy' (a society where all should be equal), a community of twelve young couples to be founded in some 'delightful part of the new back settlements' of America on the principles of communistic cooperation in all lines, broad mental culture, and complete freedom of opinion. Naturally, this plan never past beyond the dream stage.

Coleridge left the University in 1794 without a degree, tormented by a disappointment in love. He had already begun to publish poetry and newspaper prose, and he now attempted lecturing. He and Southey married two sisters, whom Byron in a later attack on Southey somewhat inaccurately described as 'milliners of Bath'; and Coleridge settled near Bristol. After characteristically varied and unsuccessful efforts at conducting a periodical, newspaper writing, and preaching as a Unitarian (a creed which was then considered by most Englishmen disreputable and which Coleridge later abandoned), he moved with his wife in 1797 to Nether Stowey in Somersetshire.

Expressly in order to be near him, Wordsworth and his sister Dorothy soon leased the neighboring manor-house of Alfoxden, and there followed the memorable year of intellectual and emotional stimulus when Coleridge's genius suddenly expanded into short-lived but wonderful activity and he wrote most of his few great poems, 'The Ancient Mariner,' 'Kubla Khan,' and the First Part of 'Christabel.' 'The Ancient Mariner' was planned by Coleridge and Wordsworth on one of their frequent rambles, and was to have been written in collaboration; but as it proceeded, Wordsworth found his manner so different from that of Coleridge that he withdrew altogether from the undertaking. The final result of the incident, however, was the publication in 1798 of 'Lyrical Ballads,' which included of Coleridge's work only this one poem, but of Wordsworth's several of his most characteristic ones.

Coleridge afterwards explained that the plan of the volume contemplated two complementary sorts of poems. He was to present supernatural or romantic characters, yet investing them with human interest and semblance of truth; while Wordsworth was to add the charm of novelty to everyday things and to suggest their kinship to the supernatural, arousing readers from their accustomed blindness to the loveliness and wonders of the world around us. No better description could be given of the poetic spirit and the whole poetic work of the two men.

Like some other epoch-marking books, 'Lyrical Ballads' attracted little attention. Shortly after its publication Coleridge and the Wordsworths sailed for Germany, where for the greater part of a year Coleridge worked hard, if irregularly, at the language, literature, and philosophy.

The remaining thirty-five years of his life are a record of ambitious projects and fitful efforts, for the most part turned by ill-health and lack of steady purpose into melancholy failure, but with a few fragmentary results standing out brilliantly. At times Coleridge did newspaper work, at which he might have succeeded; in 1800, in a burst of energy, he translated Schiller's tragedy 'Wallenstein' into English blank verse, a translation which in the opinion of most critics surpasses the original; and down to 1802, and occasionally later, he wrote a few more poems of a high order. For a few years from 1800 on he lived at Greta Hall in the village of Keswick (pronounced Kesick), in the northern end of the Lake Region (Westmoreland), fifteen miles from Wordsworth; but his marriage was incompatible (with the fault on his side), and he finally left his wife and children, who were thenceforward supported largely by Southey, his successor at Greta Hall. Coleridge himself was maintained chiefly by the generosity of friends; later, in part, by public pensions.

It was apparently about 1800, to alleviate mental distress and great physical suffering from neuralgia, that he began the excessive use of opium (laudanum) which for many years had a large share in paralyzing his will. For a year, in 1804-5, he displayed decided diplomatic talent as secretary to the Governor of Malta. At several different times, also, he gave courses, of lectures on Shakspere and Milton; as a speaker he was always eloquent; and the fragmentary notes of the lectures which have been preserved rank very high in Shaksperean criticism.

His main interest, however, was now in philosophy; perhaps no Englishman has ever had a more profoundly philosophical mind; and through scattered writings and through his stimulating though prolix talks to friends and disciples he performed a very great service to English thought by introducing the viewpoint and ideas of the German transcendentalists, such as Kant, Schelling, and Fichte. During his last eighteen years he lived mostly in sad acceptance of defeat, though still much honored, in the house of a London physician. He died in 1834.

As a poet Coleridge's first great distinction is that which we have already pointed out, namely that he gives wonderfully subtile and appealing expression to the Romantic sense for the strange and the supernatural, and indeed for all that the word 'Romance' connotes at the present day. He accomplishes this result partly through his power of suggesting the real unity of the inner and outer worlds, partly through his skill, resting in a large degree on vivid impressionistic description, in making strange scenes appear actual, in securing from the reader what he himself called 'that willing suspension of disbelief which constitutes poetic faith.' Almost every one has felt the weird charm of 'The Ancient Mariner,' where all the unearthly story centers about a moral and religious idea, and where we are dazzled by a constant succession of such pictures as these:

And ice, mast-high, came floating by,
As green as emerald.
We were the first that ever burst Into that silent sea.
The western wave was all aflame:
The day was well nigh done:
Almost upon the western wave
Rested the broad, bright sun;
When that strange shape drove suddenly
Betwixt us and the sun.

'Christabel' achieves what Coleridge himself described as the very difficult task of creating witchery by daylight; and 'Kubla Khan,' worthy, though a brief fragment, to rank with these two, is a marvelous glimpse of fairyland.

In the second place, Coleridge is one of the greatest English masters of exquisite verbal melody, with its tributary devices of alliteration and haunting onomatopoeia. In this respect especially his influence on subsequent English poetry has been incalculable. The details of his method students should observe for themselves in their study of the poems, but one particular matter should be mentioned. In 'Christabel' and to a somewhat less degree in 'The Ancient Mariner' Coleridge departed as far as possible from eighteenth century tradition by greatly varying the number of syllables in the lines, while keeping a regular number of stresses. Though this practice, as we have seen, was customary in Old English poetry and in the popular ballads, it was supposed by Coleridge and his contemporaries to be a new discovery, and it proved highly suggestive to other romantic poets. From hearing 'Christabel' read (from manuscript) Scott caught the idea for the free-and-easy meter of his poetical romances.

With a better body and will Coleridge might have been one of the supreme English poets; as it is, he has left a small number of very great poems and has proved one of the most powerful influences on later English poetry.

WILLIAM WORDSWORTH, 1770-1850

William Wordsworth was born in 1770 in Cumberland, in the 'Lake Region,' which, with its bold and varied mountains as well as its group of charming lakes, is the most picturesque part of England proper. He had the benefit of all the available formal education, partly at home, partly at a 'grammar' school a few miles away, but his genius was formed chiefly by the influence of Nature, and, in a qualified degree, by that of the simple peasant people of the region. Already as a boy, though normal and active, he began to be sensitive to the Divine Power in Nature which in his mature years he was to express with deeper sympathy than any poet before him.

Early left an orphan, at seventeen he was sent by his uncles to Cambridge University. Here also the things which most appealed to him were rather the new revelations of men and life than the formal studies, and indeed the torpid instruction of the time offered little to any thoughtful student. On leaving Cambridge he was uncertain as to his life-work. He said that he did not feel himself 'good enough' for the Church, he was not drawn toward law, and though he fancied that he had capacity for a military career, he felt that 'if he were ordered to the West Indies his talents would not save him from the yellow fever.' At first, therefore, he spent nearly a year in London in apparent idleness, an intensely interested though detached spectator of the city life, but more especially absorbed in his mystical consciousness of its underlying current of spiritual being.

After this he crossed to France to learn the language. The Revolution was then (1792) in its early stages, and in his 'Prelude' Wordsworth has left the finest existing statement of the exultant anticipations of a new world of social justice which the movement aroused in himself and other young English liberals. When the Revolution past into the period of violent bloodshed he determined, with more enthusiasm than judgment, to put himself forward as a leader of the moderate Girondins. From the wholesale slaughter of this party a few months later he was saved through the stopping of his allowance by his more cautious uncles, which compelled him, after a year's absence, to return to England.

For several years longer Wordsworth lived uncertainly. When, soon after his return, England, in horror at the execution of the French king, joined the coalition of European powers against France, Wordsworth experienced a great shock--the first, he tells us, that his moral nature had ever suffered--at seeing his own country arrayed with corrupt despotisms against what seemed to him the cause of humanity. The complete degeneration of the Revolution into anarchy and tyranny further served to plunge him into a chaos of moral bewilderment, from which he was gradually rescued partly by renewed communion with Nature and partly by the influence of his sister Dorothy, a woman of the most sensitive nature but of strong character and admirable good sense.

From this time for the rest of her life she continued to live with him, and by her unstinted and unselfish devotion contributed very largely to his poetic success. He had now begun to write poetry (though thus far rather stiffly and in the rimed couplet), and the receipt of a small legacy from a friend enabled him to devote his life to the art. Six or seven years later his resources were several times multiplied by an honorable act of the new Lord Lonsdale, who voluntarily repaid a sum of money owed by his predecessor to Wordsworth's father.

In 1795 Wordsworth and his sister moved from the Lake Region to Dorsetshire, at the other end of England, likewise a country of great natural beauty. Two years later came their change (of a few miles) to Alfoxden, the association with Coleridge, and 'Lyrical Ballads,' containing nineteen of Wordsworth's poems (above, page 267). After their winter in Germany the Wordsworths settled permanently in their native Lake Region, at first in 'Dove Cottage,' in the village of Grasmere.

This simple little stone house, buried, like all the others in the Lake Region, in brilliant flowers, and opening from its second story onto the hillside garden where Wordsworth composed much of his greatest poetry, is now the annual center of pilgrimage for thousands of visitors, one of the chief literary shrines of England and the world. Here Wordsworth lived frugally for several years; then after intermediate changes he took up his final residence in a larger house, Rydal Mount, a few miles away. In 1802 he married Mary Hutchinson, who had been one of his childish schoolmates, a woman of a spirit as fine as that of his sister, whom she now joined without a thought of jealousy in a life of self-effacing devotion to the poet.

Wordsworth's poetic inspiration, less fickle than that of Coleridge, continued with little abatement for a dozen years; but about 1815, as he himself states in his fine but pathetic poem 'Composed upon an Evening of Extraordinary Splendour,' it for the most part abandoned him. He continued, however, to produce a great deal of verse, most of which his admirers would much prefer to have had unwritten. The plain Anglo-Saxon yeoman strain which was really the basis of his nature now asserted itself in the growing conservatism of ideas which marked the last forty years of his life. His early love of simplicity hardened into a rigid opposition not only to the materialistic modern industrial system but to all change--the Reform Bill, the reform of education, and in general all progressive political and social movements. It was on this abandonment of his early liberal principles that Browning based his spirited lyric 'The Lost Leader.'

During the first half or more of his mature life, until long after he had ceased to be a significant creative force, Wordsworth's poetry, for reasons which will shortly appear, had been met chiefly with ridicule or indifference, and he had been obliged to wait in patience while the slighter work first of Scott and then of Byron took the public by storm. Little by little, however, he came to his own, and by about 1830 he enjoyed with discerning readers that enthusiastic appreciation of which he is certain for all the future. The crowning mark of recognition came in 1843 when on the death of his friend Southey he was made Poet Laureate. The honor, however, had been so long delayed that it was largely barren. Ten years earlier his life had been darkened by the mental decay of his sister and the death of Coleridge; and other personal sorrows now came upon him. He died in 1850 at the age of eighty.

Wordsworth, as we have said, is the chief representative of some (especially one) of the most important principles in the Romantic Movement; but he is far more than a member of any movement; through his supreme poetic expression of some of the greatest spiritual ideals he belongs among the five or six greatest English poets. First, he is the profoundest interpreter of Nature in all poetry. His feeling for Nature has two aspects. He is keenly sensitive, and in a more delicately discriminating way than any of his predecessors, to all the external beauty and glory of Nature, especially inanimate Nature--of mountains, woods and fields, streams and flowers, in all their infinitely varied aspects. A wonderfully joyous and intimate sympathy with them is one of his controlling impulses.

But his feeling goes beyond the mere physical and emotional delight of Chaucer and the Elizabethans; for him Nature is a direct manifestation of the Divine Power, which seems to him to be everywhere immanent in her; and communion with her, the communion into which he enters as he walks and meditates among the mountains and moors, is to him communion with God.

He is literally in earnest even in his repeated assertion that from observation of Nature man may learn (doubtless by the proper attuning of his spirit) more of moral truth than from all the books and sages. To Wordsworth Nature is man's one great and sufficient teacher.

It is for this reason that, unlike such poets as Keats and Tennyson, he so often views Nature in the large, giving us broad landscapes and sublime aspects. Of this mystical semi-pantheistic Nature-religion his 'Lines composed above Tintern Abbey' are the noblest expression in literature. All this explains why Wordsworth considered his function as a poet a sacred thing and how his intensely moral temperament found complete satisfaction in his art.

It explains also, in part, the limitation of his poetic genius. Nature indeed did not continue to be to him, as he himself says that it was in his boyhood, absolutely 'all in all'; but he always remained largely absorbed in the contemplation and interpretation of it and never manifested, except in a few comparatively short and exceptional poems, real narrative or dramatic power (in works dealing with human characters or human life).

In the second place, Wordsworth is the most consistent of all the great English poets of democracy, though here as elsewhere his interest is mainly not in the external but in the spiritual aspect of things. From his insistence that the meaning of the world for man lies not in the external events but in the development of character results his central doctrine of the simple life. Real character, he holds, the chief proper object of man's effort, is formed by quietly living, as did he and the dalesmen around him, in contact with Nature and communion with God rather than by participation in the feverish and sensational struggles of the great world. Simple country people, therefore, are nearer to the ideal than are most persons who fill a larger place in the activities of the world.

This doctrine expresses itself in a striking though one-sided fashion in his famous theory of poetry--its proper subjects, characters, and diction. He stated his theory definitely and at length in a preface to the second edition of 'Lyrical Ballads,' published in 1800, a discussion which includes incidentally some of the finest general critical interpretation ever made of the nature and meaning of poetry. Wordsworth declared: 1. Since the purpose of poetry is to present the essential emotions of men, persons in humble and rustic life are generally the fittest subjects for treatment in it, because their natures and manners are simple and more genuine than those of other men, and are kept so by constant contact with the beauty and serenity of Nature. 2. Not only should artificial poetic diction (like that of the eighteenth century) be rejected, but the language of poetry should be a selection from that of ordinary people in real life, only purified of its vulgarities and heightened so as to appeal to the imagination. (In this last modification lies the justification of rime.) There neither is nor can be any essential difference between the language of prose and that of poetry.

This theory, founded on Wordsworth's disgust at eighteenth century poetic artificiality, contains a very important but greatly exaggerated element of truth. That the experiences of simple and common people, including children, may adequately illustrate the main spiritual aspects of life Wordsworth unquestionably demonstrated in such poems as 'The Reverie of Poor Susan,' 'Lucy Gray,' and 'Michael.' But to restrict poetry largely to such characters and subjects would be to eliminate not only most of the external interest of life, which certainly is often necessary in giving legitimate body to the spiritual meanings, but also a great range of significant experiences which by the nature of things can never come to lowly and simple persons.

That the characters of simple country people are on the average inevitably finer and more genuine than those of others is a romantic theory rather than a fact, as Wordsworth would have discovered if his meditative nature had, allowed him to get into really direct and personal contact with the peasants about him. As to the proper language of poetry, no one to-day (thanks partly to Wordsworth) defends artificiality, but most of Wordsworth's own best work, as well as that of all other poets, proves clearly that there is an essential difference between the language of prose and that of poetry, that much of the meaning of poetry results from the use of unusual, suggestive, words and picturesque expressions, which create the essential poetic atmosphere and stir the imagination in ways distinctly different from those of prose. Wordsworth's obstinate adherence to his theory in its full extent, indeed, produced such trivial and absurd results as 'Goody Blake and Harry Gill,' 'The Idiot Boy,' and 'Peter Bell,' and great masses of hopeless prosiness in his long blank-verse narratives.

This obstinacy and these poems are only the most conspicuous result of Wordsworth's chief temperamental defect, which was an almost total lack of the sense of humor. Regarding himself as the prophet of a supremely important new gospel, he never admitted the possibility of error in his own point of view and was never able to stand aside from his poetry and criticise it dispassionately. This somewhat irritating egotism, however, was perhaps a necessary element in his success; without it he might not have been able to live serenely through the years of misunderstanding and ridicule which would have silenced or embittered a more diffident spirit.

The variety of Wordsworth's poetry deserves special mention; in addition to his short lyric and narrative poems of Nature and the spiritual life several kinds stand out distinctly. A very few poems, the noble 'Ode to Duty,' 'Laodamia,' and 'Dion,' are classical in inspiration and show the finely severe repression and finish of classic style. Among his many hundreds of sonnets is a very notable group inspired by the struggle of England against Napoleon. Wordsworth was the first English poet after Milton who used the sonnet powerfully and he proves himself a worthy successor of Milton. The great bulk of his work, finally, is made up of his long poems in blank-verse. 'The Prelude,' written during the years 1799-1805, though not published until after his death, is the record of the development of his poet's mind, not an outwardly stirring poem, but a unique and invaluable piece of spiritual autobiography. Wordsworth intended to make this only an introduction to another work of enormous length which was to have presented his views of Man, Nature, and Society. Of this plan he completed two detached parts, namely the fragmentary 'Recluse' and 'The Excursion,' which latter contains some fine passages, but for the most part is uninspired.

Wordsworth, more than any other great English poet, is a poet for mature and thoughtful appreciation; except for a very small part of his work many readers must gradually acquire the taste for him. But of his position among the half dozen English poets who have made the largest contribution to thought and life there can be no question; so that some acquaintance with him is a necessary part of any real education.

THE DRAMA

The history of the drama may be divided into two classes, the Christian, which began with the Mystery and Morality plays; and the Greek, which was eminently classic. These two types were the foundation of all that came after them.

The first dawn of the drama was in Greece; for although the Hindus also had dramatic poetry, it did not arise until there had been a lengthened intercourse between Greece and India, so that the latter undoubtedly borrowed from the former. The learned writers of ancient times agree that both tragedy and comedy were originally choral song. It has been said that poetry and song are divided into three periods of a nation's history, that the Epic has to do with the first awakening of a people, telling of their legends, or of some great deeds in remote antiquity. This is followed by the second stage, which embraces elegiac and lyric poetry and arose in stirring and martial times, during the development of new forms of government, when each individual wanted to express his own thoughts and wishes; and the third is the drama, which can only be born in a period of civilization, and which, it has been said, implies a nation.

Hence Greek drama arose at the height of Grecian civilization and splendor. It originated in the natural love of imitation, of dancing and singing, especially at the Bacchic feasts. The custom at these feasts of taking the guise of nymphs and satyrs, and of wearing masks while they danced and sang in chorus, seems to have been the beginnings of the Greek drama.

Ancient tragedy was ideal, and had nothing to do with ordinary life; it arose from the winter feasts of Bacchus, while comedy was the outcome of the harvest feasts, and the accompanying Bacchanalian processions, which were more in the nature of a frolic than of real acting. The influence of the Middle and New Greek comedy, especially, that of Menander, on the Roman comedy of Terence is well defined. Under Ennius and Plautus the Roman comedy was fairly original; but Terence wrote for the fashionable set, like Caecilius and Scipio Africanus, and consequently imitated Greek models very carefully. The drama in Rome never attained any noteworthy height although the French tragic poets took Seneca for their model.

In the time of Lorenzo the Magnificent there was a great revival in Italy of the ancient classic drama, of which Poliziano was the most successful exponent. Both he and the later writers, however, made no attempt to found any National Italian drama—their works are entirely an imitation of the tragedies of Sophocles and Euripides, and the comedies of Plautus and Terence.

The Melodrama, which arose in the seventeenth century, is distinctly Italian and national, and has been extensively produced all over the civilized world. Alfieri, in the eighteenth century, is the greatest and most patriotic of the Italian tragedians, and he did as much to revive the national character in modern times as Dante did in the fourteenth century.

In France we have the dramatic representation of the Mysteries in the twelfth and thirteenth centuries, introduced by the pilgrims who had returned from the Crusades. At first these performances were given in the street, but later a company was formed, called the "Confraternity of the Passion," the suffering of Christ being its chief representation. This Mystery is the most ancient dramatic work of modern Europe, and gives the whole Gospel narrative from the birth of our Saviour until His death. Being too long for a play of one act, it was continued from day to day. What would seem irreverent on a modern stage was regarded as perfectly simple and natural in the Middle Ages, and it was a potent factor in teaching the masses the truths of their faith.

Following these Mysteries of the Passion came a host of other plays taken from the Old Testament, or from the lives of the Saints. The earliest "Miracle" on record is the Play of St. Catherine, which was represented at Dunstable about 1119, written in French; it was in all probability a rude picture of the miracles and martyrdom of the saint.

The stage was divided into three different floors, with Heaven on top, hell on the ground floor, and the earth between. Frequently the play would proceed in all three divisions at once, with angels and devils ascending and descending by means of ladders, as their help was needed in the different worlds.

The Devil generally played the part of clown or jester. The modern puppet play of Punch is a tradition handed down from these ancient miracles, in which the Evil One was alternately the conqueror or victim of the human Buffoon; who was also called by the names of Jester or Vice.

These early miracle plays were generally written in mixed prose and verse.

The oldest manuscript of a miracle play in English is The Harrowing of Hell, believed to have been written in 1350.

The Morality plays were the outcome of the Mysteries; they were either allegorical or else taken from the Parables, or from the historical events in the Bible. The chief Moralities were Everyman, Lusty Juventus, Good Counsel, and Repentance. The oldest English Morality play now extant is The Castle of Perseverance, written about 1450. It is a dramatic allegory of human life representing the many conflicting influences that surround man on his way through the world. Lusty Juventus depicts in a vivid and humorous way the extravagances and follies of a young heir surrounded by the virtues and vices, and the misery which follows a departure from the path of religion and virtue. Gradually these Moralities were corrupted and became mixed with a species of comedy called Interludes, a merry and farcical dialogue.

The Four P's, one of the best of these early Interludes, was written by John Heywood, an entertainer at the Court of Henry VIII. It turns upon a dispute between a Peddler, a Palmer, a Pardoner and a Poticary, in which each tries to tell the greatest lie; plays of this kind are seen in France at the present day. In the fifteenth century the drama in France became more secularized and included political events and satire, but the French were undoubtedly the fathers of drama in the Middle Ages. Their plays were known a whole century before Spain or Italy had any theater, while the romantic drama in other countries of Europe was founded on the early French drama. Modern drama in France during the time of Corneille, Racine and Voltaire was almost entirely classic. The French regarded the Greek standard as the highest art; and sought to imitate it faithfully, so much so that the French Academy, criticizing a tragedy of Corneille, said "that the poet, from the fear of sinning against the rules of art, had chosen rather to sin against the rules of nature."

Comic drama in France from the end of the sixteenth to the middle of the seventeenth century was borrowed from Spain, and had to do with a multiplication of trap doors, dark lanterns, intrigues, and puzzling disguises, until Moliere, in his "Precieuses Ridicules" successfully attacked these follies of his age.

The Romantic drama, which arose in the second quarter of the nineteenth century, holds at present the first place in France. Its chief exponents have been Victor Hugo, the two Dumases, Sardou and Octave Feuillet. Between them and the followers of the Classic School there was for some time a lively war. The latter wanted to exclude the Romanticists from the Theatre Francais, but without success. In spite of the beauty of its French, and the polish of its style, this latest form of the drama in France frequently offends strongly against morality. In Spain the drama was at all times thoroughly national. Even when they introduced mythological, Greek or Roman characters, it was always in a Castilian dress. In this respect Spain stands alone among the nations of Europe, as it borrowed nothing from France, Italy or England. Its earliest plays were the Mysteries, which it is supposed to have obtained from Constantinople, where the ancient theatre of Greece and Rome was kept up, in a grosser form, far into the Middle Ages. In later times this Eastern drama became so corrupt that the Christian Church tried to offset it by introducing the Mysteries, and it became a common custom every year at Christmas, for the Manger at Bethlehem, the Worship of the Shepherds, and the Adoration of the Magi, to be exhibited before the Altar, just as the Mysteries of the Passion were introduced during Lent. The Passion Play at Oberammergau and the Creche, representing the Manger at Bethlehem, as seen in Catholic Churches at Christmas, are the sole survivals of these ancient Mysteries.

The second dramatic period in Spain was pastoral and satirical. Nothing worthy of note adorns this period in the fifteenth century. In the sixteenth century de Rueda and Lope de Vega founded the true national drama of Spain. It was unlike anything of an earlier period, and yet, resting faithfully on tradition, it gave a vivid picture of the National Spanish life in all classes of society. From the gallantries of the "dramas of the Cloak and Sword," to the historical plays in which Dings and Princes figure; down to the manners and incidents of common life, all is essentially Spanish. A fourth class still represented Scriptural and sacred scenes. Calderon wrote at the height of the Spanish drama during the reign of Philip II; and after his time the drama in Spain declined until, in the eighteen century, it was at its lowest ebb. At this time plays were still held in open courtyards, and in the daytime, as in the earlier ages. Efforts were made to subject it to French and Italian rule, but this had only a limited success; stiff, cold translation from the French could not please a people who always found in the Spanish drama an essentially popular entertainment.

In Germany traces of the drama first appeared in the thirteenth century, when rude attempts to imitate the Mystery plays were conducted in churches by the priests. But when the populace tried to introduce the Burlesque, the performances were banished to the open fields. Students in the universities took part in them, and they continued until after the Reformation. Brought into Europe from Constantinople by the Crusaders and pilgrims, the Mystery plays became the chief amusement of an illiterate age. Christianity was first thoroughly impressed on the mind of Northern Europe by means of them; and the first missionaries familiarized the rude Goths and Huns with Biblical incidents at a time when reading was unknown outside of the Cloister. No change in German drama occurred until the seventeenth century, when operas after the Italian superseded the Mysteries and Moralities. The production of this age, however, were characterized by bad taste and pedantry; and it was not until Goethe brought his genius to bear on the subject, that the Germans acquired any drama worthy of the name. Whether in his national play Gotz von Berlichingen or in his classical drama of Iphigenia, this great German master stands at the summit of his art. Lessing attacked French drama as enacted in Germany prior to Goethe, and brought forward the Shakespearian plays as a model.

Schiller's Wallenstein obtained a worldwide reputation, and among the Romantic dramatists Werner's Attila and Grillparzer's Ancestress are the best examples of the extravagant and fertile mind of the German romanticist.

Modern German drama has found the highest art it has ever attained in the compositions of Richard Wagner, whose operas are entirely German and National, and mostly founded on the old German legends. Tannhauser is taken from the epic poem of "Parzifal," written by Wolfram von Eschenbach in the Middle Ages. Lohengrin, which is touched on in the "Parzifal," Wagner also found in the poem of an obscure Bavarian poet; and a more complete account of the celebrated "Swan Knight" appears in a collection of stories edited by the brothers Grimm. Lohengrin is a Knight of the Holy Grail, so part of the legend is borrowed from ancient Britain.

All dramatic effort in England before the sixteenth century was so rude as to be of little account. The Miracle and Mystery plays were introduced into England in the reign of Henry VI, and many of them had a personage called "Iniquity," a coarse buffoon, whose object was to amuse the audience.

After the Reformation the Protestant Bishop Bale wrote plays on the same plan as the Mysteries, intended to instruct the people in the supposed errors of Popery. These plays, which deal largely in satire, became popular and after the era of Henry VIII were known as Interludes.

In the beginning of the sixteenth century real comedy and tragedy began to exist in a rude form. The oldest known English comedy, Ralph Royster Doyster, was written by Nicholas Udall, and describes a character whose comic misadventures are somewhat akin to Don Quixote.

The earliest tragedy, Gorboduc, known also Ferrex and Porrex, was played in the Lower Temple.

It is founded on the legends of fabulous British history. The tragedies of Marlowe and the legendary plays of Greene come next in order, followed by the golden age of English drama, from the dawn of the Shakespeare plays in 1585 until the closing of the theatre in 1645 on the breaking out of the Civil war in England.

For a period of sixty years the splendid genius of the world's greatest dramatist gave to mankind a series of plays that have no equal in the literature of any country or age.

Contemporaneous with Shakespeare, or coming after him, were Beaumont and Fletcher, Ben Jonson, Massinger, Ford, and Shirley; these Elizabethan dramatists took their subjects from the stories and legends of all countries and ages—or else they depicted the national life. For this reason English drama has been called Irregular, in contrast to the Greek, which is called the Regular, and that of modern France, founded upon the Greek. The chief rule of the Regular is the Unity of Time, Place and Action. In the Greek, the time of action was allowed to extend to twenty-four hours, and the scene to change from place to place in the same city; but Shakespeare and his contemporaries acknowledged no fixed limit either of time, place or action. The operation of their plays covered many different countries, and the time extended over many years; but the rule that laid down in the Greek drama the principle that there should be unity of action (everything being subordinate to a series of events, which form the thread of the plot), was adopted by Shakespeare and his contemporaries. It has been called "unity of impression," as opposed to unity of time and place.

ENGLISH LITERATURE

The term English literature refers to literature written in the English language, including literature composed in English by writers not necessarily from England; Joseph Conrad was Polish, Robert Burns was Scottish, James Joyce was Irish, Dylan Thomas was Welsh, Edgar Allan Poe was American, Salman Rushdie is Indian, V.S. Naipaul is Trinidadian. In other words, English literature is as diverse as the varieties and dialects of English spoken around the world. In academia, the term often labels departments and programmes practising English studies in secondary and tertiary educational systems.

Middle Ages

The first works in English, written in the Anglo-Saxon dialect now called Old English, appeared in the early Middle Ages (the oldest surviving text is Cædmon's Hymn). The oral tradition was very strong in early British culture and most literary works were written to be performed. Epic poems were thus very popular and many, including Beowulf, have survived to the present day in the rich corpus of Anglo-Saxon literature.

These are languages that closely resemble today's Norwegian or, better yet, Icelandic, though much Anglo-Saxon verse in the extant manuscripts is probably a "milder" adaptation of the earlier Viking and German war poems from the continent. When such poetry was brought to England it was still being handed down orally from one generation to another, and the constant presence of alliterative verse, or consonant rhyme (today's newspaper headlines and marketing abundantly use this technique such as in Big is Better) helped the Anglo-Saxon peoples remember it. Such rhyme is a feature of Germanic languages and is opposed to vocalic or end-rhyme of Romance languages. But the first written literature dates to the early Christian monasteries founded by St. Augustine of Canterbury and his disciples and it is reasonable to believe that it was somehow adapted to suit to needs of Christian readers. Even without their crudest lines, Viking war poems still smell of blood feuds and their consonant rhymes sound like the smashing of swords under the gloomy northern sky: there is always a sense of imminent danger in the narratives. Sooner or later, all things must come to an end, as Beowulf eventually dies at the hands of the huge monster he spends his life fighting.

The feelings of Beowulf that nothing lasts, that youth and joy will turn to death and sorrow entered Christianity and were to dominate the future landscape of English fiction. The "ubi sunt" theme is, for example, recurrent in Hamlet ("Alas, poor Yorick"), not to mention much Jacobean poetry. With the exception of the relatively light-hearted and optimistic Restoration and the Augustan Age, melancholia and angst remain a favorite theme with English-speaking writers, through the Gothic novel and Pre-romanticism to the birth of modern romantic sensibility. When William the Conqueror makes England a part of the Anglo-Norman realm in 1066 bringing Norman, there is a period of Anglo-Norman literature, though Old English poetry continues to be read and its language widely spoken. It was not until the early 13th century when Albion becomes independent and severs its relations to France that the language really changes.

As the Normans are assimilated into mainstream culture, their French penetrates the lower orders of society changing much of the grammar and lexicon of Old English. Though it does not become a Romance language, Chaucer's English is much closer to present-day English than the language that people spoke a century before. The average English-speaker cannot read Chaucer (Middle English) without difficulty but can nonetheless grasp the gist of the story, while he needs to read Beowulf in modern English—in translation.

In the late medieval period (1200-1500), the ideals of courtly love entered England and authors began to write romances, either in verse or prose. Especially popular were tales of King Arthur and his court. The poem Sir Gawain and the Green Knight shows many of the key features of literature at this time: a setting in the legendary time of King Arthur, an emphasis on chivalry and knightly behavior, and religious overtones.

English drama at this time was overtly religious. Mystery plays were enacted in cities and towns to celebrate major holidays, and the less formal mummers plays also conveyed Christian themes.

England's first great author, Geoffrey Chaucer (1340-1400), wrote in Middle English. His most famous work is The Canterbury Tales, a collection of stories in a variety of genres, ostensibly told by a group of pilgrims on their way to Canterbury. Remarkably, they are from all walks of life, which is reflected as much in the language they use as in the content of their stories. But, though Shakespeare is most certainly an English author, he was inspired by literary developments taking place elsewhere in Europe, especially in Italy. Chaucer's The Canterbury Tales are quite indebted to Giovanni Boccaccio's Decameron. The Renaissance was making its way to Britain.

Early Modern (Renaissance)

Following the introduction of a printing press into England by William Caxton in 1476, vernacular literature flourished. The Reformation inspired the production of vernacular liturgy which led to the Book of Common Prayer, a lasting influence on literary English language. The poetry, drama, and prose produced under both Queen Elizabeth I and King James I constitute what is today labelled as Early modern (or Renaissance). This is noted for its interest in the human being as a worthy subject (due in large part to the importation of humanism from Italy). Unlike the literature of Medieval England, which was almost entirely religious in nature, Early modern literature offered readers a more secular literature; though it should be noted, Early modern literature does appear overtly religious in many ways when compared with modern secularism.

Elizabethan Literature

The Elizabethan era saw a great flourishing of literature, especially in the field of drama. The Italian Renaissance had rediscovered the ancient Greek and Roman theatre, which was then beginning to evolve apart from the old mystery and miracle plays of the Middle Ages. The Italians were particularly inspired by Seneca (a major tragic playwright and philosopher, the tutor of Nero) and Plautus (its comic clichés, especially that of the boasting soldier had a powerful influence on the Renaissance and after). However, the Italian tragedies embraced a principle contrary to Seneca's ethics: showing blood and violence on the stage.

In Seneca's plays such scenes were only acted by the characters. But the English playwrights were intrigued by Italian model: a conspicuous community of Italian actors had settled in London and Giovanni Florio had brought much of the Italian language and culture to England. It is also true that the Elizabethan Era was a very violent age and that the high incidence of political assassinations in Renaissance Italy (embodied by Niccolò Machiavelli's The Prince) did little to calm fears of popish plots. As a result, representing that kind of violence on the stage was probably more cathartic for the Elizabethan spectator. Following earlier Elizabethan plays such as Gorboduc by Sackville & Norton and The Spanish Tragedy by Kyd that was to provide much material for Hamlet, William Shakespeare stands out in this period as a poet and playwright as yet unsurpassed. Shakespeare was not a man of letters by profession, and probably had only some grammar school education.

He was neither a lawyer, nor an aristocrat as the "university wits" that had monopolised the English stage when he started writing. But he was very gifted and incredibly versatile, and he surpassed "professionals" as Greene who mocked this "shake-scene" of low origins. Though most dramas met with great success, it is in his later years (marked by the early reign of James I) that he wrote what have been considered his greatest plays: Hamlet, Othello, King Lear, Macbeth, Antony and Cleopatra, and The Tempest, a tragicomedy that inscribes within the main drama a brilliant pageant to the new king. This 'play within a play' takes the form of a masque, an interlude with music and dance colored by the novel special effects of the new indoor theaters. Critics have shown that this masterpiece, which can be considered a dramatic work in its own right, was written for James's court, if not for the monarch himself.

The magic arts of Prospero, on which depend the outcome of the plot, hint at the fine relationship between art and nature in poetry. Significantly for those times (the arrival of the first colonists in America), The Tempest is (though not apparently) set on a Bermudan island, as research on the Bermuda Pamphlets (1609) has shown, linking Shakespeare to the Virginia Company itself. The "News from the New World", as Frank Kermode points out, were already out and Shakespeare's interest in this respect is remarkable. Shakespeare also popularized the English sonnet which made significant changes to Petrarch's model.

The sonnet was introduced into English by Thomas Wyatt in the early 16th century. Poems intended to be set to music as songs, such as by Thomas Campion, became popular as printed literature was disseminated more widely in households. See English Madrigal School. Other important figures in Elizabethan theatre include Christopher Marlowe, Thomas Dekker, John Fletcher and Francis Beaumont. Had Marlowe (1564-1593) not been stabbed at twenty-nine in a tavern brawl, says Anthony Burgess, he might have rivalled, if not equalled Shakespeare himself for his poetic gifts. Remarkably, he was born only a few weeks before Shakespeare and must have known him well. Marlowe's subject matter, though, is different: it focuses more on the moral drama of the renaissance man than any other thing. Marlowe was fascinated and terrified by the new frontiers opened by modern science.

Drawing on German lore, he introduced Dr. Faustus to England, a scientist and magician who is obsessed by the thirst of knowledge and the desire to push man's technological power to its limits. He acquires supernatural gifts that even allow him to go back in time and wed Helen of Troy, but at the end of his twenty-four years' covenant with the devil he has to surrender his soul to him. His dark heroes may have something of Marlowe himself, whose untimely death remains a mystery. He was known for being an atheist, leading a lawless life, keeping many mistresses, consorting with ruffians: living the 'high life' of London's underworld. But many suspect that this might have been a cover-up for his activities as a secret agent for Elizabeth I, hinting that the 'accidental stabbing' might have been a premeditated assassination by the enemies of The Crown. Beaumont and Fletcher are less-known, but it is almost sure that they helped Shakespeare write some of his best dramas, and were quite popular at the time. It is also at this time that the city comedy genre develops. In the later 16th century English poetry was characterised by elaboration of language and extensive allusion to classical myths. The most important poets of this era include Edmund Spenser and Sir Philip Sidney.

Jacobean Literature

After Shakespeare's death, the poet and dramatist Ben Jonson was the leading literary figure of the Jacobean era (The reign of James I). However, Jonson's aesthetics hark back to the Middle Ages rather than to the Tudor Era: his characters embody the theory of humors. According to this contemporary medical theory, behavioral differences result from a prevalence of one of the body's four "humors" (blood, phlegm, black bile, and yellow bile) over the other three; these humors correspond with the four elements of the universe: air, water, fire, and earth. This leads Jonson to exemplify such differences to the point of creating types, or clichés.

Jonson is a master of style, and a brilliant satirist. His Volpone shows how a group of scammers are fooled by a top con-artist, vice being punished by vice, virtue meeting its reward.

Others who followed Jonson's style include Beaumont and Fletcher, who wrote the brilliant comedy, The Knight of the Burning Pestle, a mockery of the rising middle class and especially of those nouveau riches who pretend to dictate literary taste without knowing much literature at all. In the story, a couple of grocers wrangle with professional actors to have their illiterate son play a leading role in a drama. He becomes a knight-errant wearing, appropriately, a burning pestle on his shield. Seeking to win a princess's heart, the young man is ridiculed much in the way Don Quixote was. One of Beaumont and Fletcher's chief merits was that of realising how feudalism and chivalry had turned into snobbery and make-believe and that new social classes were on the rise.

Another popular style of theatre during Jacobean times was the revenge play, popularized by John Webster and Thomas Kyd. George Chapman wrote a couple of subtle revenge tragedies, but must be remembered chiefly on account of his famous translation of Homer, one that had a profound influence on all future English literature, even inspiring John Keats to write one of his best sonnets.

The King James Bible, one of the most massive translation projects in the history of English up to this time, was started in 1604 and completed in 1611.

It represents the culmination of a tradition of Bible translation into English that began with the work of William Tyndale. It became the standard Bible of the Church of England, and some consider it one of the greatest literary works of all time. This project was headed by James I himself, who supervised the work of forty-seven scholars. Although many other translations into English have been made, some of which are widely considered more accurate, many aesthetically prefer the King James Bible, whose meter is made to mimic the original Hebrew verse.

Besides Shakespeare, whose figure towers over the early 1600s, the major poets of the early 17th century included John Donne and the other Metaphysical poets. Influenced by continental Baroque, and taking as his subject matter both Christian mysticism and eroticism, metaphysical poetry uses unconventional or "unpoetic" figures, such as a compass or a mosquito, to reach surprise effects. For example, in one of Donne's Songs and Sonnets, the points of a compass represent two lovers, the woman who is home, waiting, being the center, the farther point being her lover sailing away from her. But the larger the distance, the more the hands of the compass lean to each other: separation makes love grow fonder. The paradox or the oxymoron is a constant in this poetry whose fears and anxieties also speak of a world of spiritual certainties shaken by the modern discoveries of geography and science, one that is no longer the center of the universe.

Apart from the metaphysical poetry of Donne, the 17th century is also celebrated for its Baroque poetry. Baroque poetry served the same ends as the art of the period; the Baroque style is lofty, sweeping, epic, and religious. Many of these poets have an overtly Catholic sensibility (namely Richard Crashaw) and wrote poetry for the Catholic counter-Reformation in order to establish a feeling of supremacy and mysticism that would ideally persuade newly emerging Protestant groups back toward Catholicism.

Caroline and Cromwellian Literature

The turbulent years of the mid-17th century, during the reign of Charles I and the subsequent Commonwealth and Protectorate, saw a flourishing of political literature in English. Pamphlets written by sympathisers of every faction in the English civil war ran from vicious personal attacks and polemics, through many forms of propaganda, to high-minded schemes to reform the nation. Of the latter type, Leviathan by Thomas Hobbes would prove to be one of the most important works of British political philosophy. Hobbes's writings are some of the few political works from the era which are still regularly published while John Bramhall, who was Hobbes's chief critic, is largely forgotten. The period also saw a flourishing of news books, the precursors to the British newspaper, with journalists such as Henry Muddiman, Marchamont Needham, and John Birkenhead representing the views and activities of the contending parties. The frequent arrests of authors and the suppression of their works, with the consequence of foreign or underground printing, led to the proposal of a licensing system. The Areopagitica, a political pamphlet by John Milton, was written in opposition to licensing and is regarded as one of the most eloquent defenses of press freedom ever written.

Specifically in the reign of Charles I (1625-42), English Renaissance theatre experienced its concluding efflorescence. The last works of Ben Jonson appeared on stage and in print, along with the final generation of major voices in the drama of the age: John Ford, Philip Massinger, James Shirley, and Richard Brome. With the closure of the theatres at the start of the English Civil War in 1642, drama was suppressed for a generation, to resume only in the altered society of the English Restoration in 1660.

Other forms of literature written during this period are usually ascribed political subtexts, or their authors are grouped along political lines. The cavalier poets, active mainly before the civil war, owed much to the earlier school of metaphysical poets. The forced retirement of royalist officials after the execution of Charles I was a good thing in the case of Izaak Walton, as it gave him time to work on his book The Compleat Angler. Published in 1653, the book, ostensibly a guide to fishing, is much more: a meditation on life, leisure, and contentment. The two most important poets of Oliver Cromwell's England were Andrew Marvell and John Milton, with both producing works praising the new government; such as Marvell's An Horatian Ode upon Cromwell's Return from Ireland. Despite their republican beliefs they escaped punishment upon the Restoration of Charles II, after which Milton wrote some of his greatest poetical works (with any possible political message hidden under allegory). Thomas Browne was another writer of the period; a learned man with an extensive library, he wrote prolifically on science, religion, medicine and the esoteric.

2

Fiction of Romantic Period

Walt Whitman, Nathaniel Hawthorne, Herman Melville, Edgar Allan Poe, Emily Dickinson, and the Transcendentalists represent the first great literary generation produced in the United States. In the case of the novelists, the Romantic vision tended to express itself in the form Hawthorne called the "Romance," a heightened, emotional, and symbolic form of the novel. Romances were not love stories, but serious novels that used special techniques to communicate complex and subtle meanings. Instead of carefully defining realistic characters through a wealth of detail, as most English or continental novelists did, Hawthorne, Melville, and Poe shaped heroic figures larger than life, burning with mythic significance. The typical protagonists of the American Romance are haunted, alienated individuals. Hawthorne's Arthur Dimmesdale or Hester Prynne in *The Scarlet Letter*, Melville's Ahab in *Moby-Dick*, and the many isolated and obsessed characters of Poe's tales are lonely protagonists pitted against unknowable, dark fates that, in some mysterious way, grow out of their deepest unconscious selves. The symbolic plots reveal hidden actions of the anguished spirit.

One reason for this fictional exploration into the hidden recesses of the soul is the absence of settled, traditional community life in America. English novelists — Jane Austen, Charles Dickens (the great favourite), Anthony Trollope, George Eliot, William Thackeray — lived in a complex, well-articulated, traditional society and shared with their readers attitudes that informed their realistic fiction. American novelists were faced with a history of strife and revolution, a geography of vast wilderness, and a fluid and relatively classless democratic society. American novels frequently reveal a revolutionary absence of tradition. Many English novels show a poor main character rising on the economic and social ladder, perhaps because of a good marriage or the discovery of a hidden aristocratic past. But this buried plot does not challenge the aristocratic social structure of England. On the contrary, it confirms it. The rise of the main character satisfies the wish fulfillment of the mainly middle-class readers.

In contrast, the American novelist had to depend on his or her own devices. America was, in part, an undefined, constantly moving frontier populated by immigrants speaking foreign languages and following strange and crude ways of life. Thus the main character in American literature might find himself alone among cannibal tribes, as in Melville's *Typee*, or exploring a wilderness like James Fenimore Cooper's Leatherstocking, or witnessing lonely visions from the grave, like Poe's solitary individuals, or meeting the devil walking in the forest, like Hawthorne's Young Goodman Brown. Virtually all the great American protagonists have been "loners. " The democratic American individual had, as it were, to invent himself.

The serious American novelist had to invent new forms as well hence the sprawling, idiosyncratic shape of Melville's novel *Moby-Dick* and Poe's dreamlike, wandering *Narrative of Arthur Gordon Pym*. Few American novels achieve formal perfection, even today. Instead of borrowing tested literary methods, Americans tend to invent new creative techniques. In America, it is not enough to be a traditional and definable social unit, for the old and traditional gets left behind; the new, innovative force is the centre of attention.

THE ROMANCE

T he Romance form is dark and forbidding, indicating how difficult it is to create an identity without a stable society. Most of the Romantic heroes die in the end: All the sailors except Ishmael are drowned in Moby-Dick, and the sensitive but sinful minister Arthur Dimmesdale dies at the end of The Scarlet Letter. The self-divided, tragic note in American literature becomes dominant in the novels, even before the Civil War of the 1860s manifested the greater social tragedy of a society at war with itself.

Herman Melville (1819-1891)

Herman Melville, like Nathaniel Hawthorne, was a descendant of an old, wealthy family that fell abruptly into poverty upon the death of the father. Despite his patrician upbringing, proud family traditions, and hard work, Melville found himself in poverty with no college education. At 19 he went to sea. His interest in sailors' lives grew naturally out of his own experiences, and most of his early novels grew out of his voyages. In these we see the young Melville's wide, democratic experience and hatred of tyranny and injustice. His first book, *Typee*, was based on his time spent among the supposedly cannibalistic but hospitable tribe of the Taipis in the Marquesas Islands of the South Pacific. The book praises the islanders and their natural, harmonious life, and criticizes the Christian missionaries, who Melville found less genuinely civilized than the people they came to convert. *Moby-Dick; or, The Whale,* Melville's masterpiece, is the epic story of the whaling ship *Pequod* and its "ungodly, god-like man," Captain Ahab, whose obsessive quest for the white whale Moby-Dick leads the ship and its men to destruction. This work, a realistic adventure novel, contains a series of meditations on the human condition. Whaling, throughout the book, is a grand metaphor for the pursuit of knowledge. Realistic catalogues and descriptions of whales and the whaling industry punctuate the book, but these carry symbolic connotations. "The Right Whale's Head," the narrator says that the Right Whale is a Stoic and the Sperm Whale is a Platonian, referring to two classical schools of philosophy. Although Melville's novel is philosophical, it is also tragic. Despite his heroism, Ahab is doomed and perhaps damned in the end. Nature, however beautiful, remains alien and potentially deadly. In Moby-Dick, Melville challenges Emerson's optimistic idea that humans can understand nature. *Moby-Dick,* the great white whale, is an inscrutable, cosmic existence that dominates the novel, just as he obsesses Ahab. Facts about the whale and whaling cannot explain Moby-Dick; on the contrary, the facts themselves tend to become symbols, and every fact is obscurely related in a cosmic web to every other fact. This idea of correspondence does not, however, mean that humans can "read" truth in nature, as it does in Emerson. Behind Melville's accumulation of facts is a mystic vision — but whether this vision is evil or good, human or inhuman, is never explained.

The novel is modern in its tendency to be self-referential, or reflexive. In other words, the novel often is about itself. Melville frequently comments on mental processes such as writing, reading, and understanding. One chapter, for instance, is an exhaustive survey in which the narrator attempts a classification but finally gives up, saying that nothing great can ever be finished ("God keep me from ever completing anything. This whole book is but a draught — nay, but the draught of a draught. O Time, Strength, Cash and Patience"). Melvinne's notion of the literary text as an imperfect version or an abandoned draft is quite contemporary.

Ahab insists on imaging a heroic, timeless world of absolutes in which he can stand above his men. Unwisely, he demands a finished text, an answer. But the novel shows that just as there are no finished texts, there are no final answers except, perhaps, death.

Certain literary references resonate throughout the novel. Ahab, named for an Old Testament king, desires a total, Faustian, god-like knowledge. Like Oedipus in Sophocles' play, who pays tragically for wrongful knowledge, Ahab is struck blind before he is wounded in the leg and finally killed. *Moby-Dick* ends with the word "orphan. " Ishmael, the narrator, is an orphan-like wanderer. The name Ishmael emanates from the Book of Genesis in the Old Testament — he was the son of Abraham and Hagar (servant to Abraham's wife, Sarah). Ishmael and Hagar were cast into the wilderness by Abraham.

Other examples exist. Rachel (one of the patriarch Jacob's wives) is the name of the boat that rescues Ishmael at book's end. Finally, the metaphysical whale reminds Jewish and Christian readers of the biblical story of Jonah, who was tossed overboard by fellow sailors who considered him an object of ill fortune. Swallowed by a "big fish," according to the biblical text, he lived for a time in its belly before being returned to dry land through God's intervention. Seeking to flee from punishment, he only brought more suffering upon himself.

Historical references also enrich the novel. The ship *Pequod* is named for an extinct New England Indian tribe; thus the name suggests that the boat is doomed to destruction. Whaling was in fact a major industry, especially in New England: It supplied oil as an energy source, especially for lamps. Thus the whale does literally "shed light" on the universe. Whaling was also inherently expansionist and linked with the idea of manifest destiny, since it required Americans to sail round the world in search of whales (in fact, the present state of Hawaii came under American domination because it was used as the major refuelling base for American whaling ships). The *Pequod's* crew members represent all races and various religions, suggesting the idea of America as a universal state of mind as well as a melting pot. Finally, Ahab embodies the tragic version of democratic American individualism. He asserts his dignity as an individual and dares to oppose the inexorable external forces of the universe.

The novel's epilogue tempers the tragic destruction of the ship. Throughout, Melville stresses the importance of friendship and the multicultural human community. After the ship sinks, Ishmael is saved by the engraved coffin made by his close friend, the heroic tattooed harpooner and Polynesian prince Queequeg. The coffin's primitive, mythological designs incorporate the history of the cosmos. Ishmael is rescued from death by an object of death. From death life emerges, in the end.

Moby-Dick has been called a "natural epic" — a magnificent dramatization of the human spirit set in primitive nature — because of its hunter myth, its initiation theme, its Edenic island symbolism, its positive treatment of pre-technological peoples, and its quest for rebirth. In setting humanity alone in nature, it is eminently American. The French writer and politician Alexis de Tocqueville had predicted, in the 1835 work *Democracy in America,* that this theme would arise in America as a result of its democracy:

The destinies of mankind, man himself taken aloof from his country and his age and standing in the presence of Nature and God, with his passions, his doubts, his rare propensities and inconceivable wretchedness, will become the chief, if not the sole, theme of (American) poetry.

Tocqueville reasons that, in a democracy, literature would dwell on "the hidden depths of the immaterial nature of man" rather than on mere appearances or superficial distinctions such as class and status. Certainly both *Moby-Dick* and *Typee,* like *Adventures of Huckleberry Finn* and *Walden,* fit this description. They are celebrations of nature and pastoral subversions of class-oriented, urban civilization.

Edgar Allan Poe (1809-1849)

Edgar Allan Poe, a southerner, shares with Melville a darkly metaphysical vision mixed with elements of realism, parody, and burlesque. He refined the short story genre and invented detective fiction. Many of his stories prefigure the genres of science fiction, horror, and fantasy so popular today.

Poe's short and tragic life was plagued with insecurity. Like so many other major 19th-century American writers, Poe was orphaned at an early age. Poe's strange marriage in 1835 to his first cousin Virginia Clemm, who was not yet 14, has been interpreted as an attempt to find the stable family life he lacked.

Poe believed that strangeness was an essential ingredient of beauty, and his writing is often exotic. His stories and poems are populated with doomed, introspective aristocrats (Poe, like many other southerners, cherished an aristocratic ideal). These gloomy characters never seem to work or socialize; instead they bury themselves in dark, mouldering castles symbolically decorated with bizarre rugs and draperies that hide the real world of sun, windows, walls, and floors. The hidden rooms reveal ancient libraries, strange art works, and eclectic oriental objects. The aristocrats play musical instruments or read ancient books while they brood on tragedies, often the deaths of loved ones. Themes of death-in-life, especially being buried alive or returning like a vampire from the grave, appear in many of his works, including "The Premature Burial," "Ligeia," "The Cask of Amontillado," and "The Fall of the

House of Usher. " Poe's twilight realm between life and death and his gaudy, Gothic settings are not merely decorative. They reflect the over civilized yet deathly interior of his characters disturbed psyches. They are symbolic expressions of the unconscious, and thus are central to his art.

Poe's verse, like that of many Southerners, was very musical and strictly metrical. His best-known poem, in his own lifetime and today, is "The Raven" (1845). In this eerie poem, the haunted, sleepless narrator, who has been reading and mourning the death of his "lost Lenore" at midnight, is visited by a raven (a bird that eats dead flesh, hence a symbol of death) who perches above his door and ominously repeats the poem's famous refrain, "nevermore. " The poem ends in a frozen scene of death-in-life:

And the Raven, never flitting, still
is sitting, still *is sitting*
On the pallid bust of Pallas just
above my chamber door;
And his eyes have all the seeming of
a demon's that is dreaming,
And the lamp-light o'er him
streaming throws his shadow on the floor;
And my soul from out that shadow
that lies floating on the floor
Shall be lifted — nevermore!

Poe's stories — such as those cited above — have been described as tales of horror. Stories like "The Gold Bug" and "The Purloined Letter" are more tales of ratiocination, or reasoning. The horror tales prefigure works by such American authors of horror fantasy as H. P. Lovecraft and Stephen King, while the tales of ratiocination are harbingers of the detective fiction of Dashiell Hammett, Raymond Chandler, Ross Macdonald, and John D. MacDonald. There is a hint, too, of what was to follow as science fiction. All of these stories reveal Poe's fascination with the mind and the unsettling scientific knowledge that was radically secularizing the 19th-century world view.

In every genre, Poe explores the psyche. Profound psychological insights glint throughout the stories. "Who has not, a hundred times, found himself committing a vile or silly action, for no other reason than because he knows he should not," we read in "The Black Cat. " To explore the exotic and strange aspect of psychological processes, Poe delved into accounts of madness and extreme emotion. The painfully deliberate style and elabourate explanation in the stories heighten the sense of the horrible by making the events seem vivid and plausible. Poe's combination of decadence and romantic primitivism appealed enormously to Europeans, particularly to the French poets Stephane Mallarme, Charles Baudelaire, Paul Valery, and Arthur Rimbaud. But Poe is not un-American, despite his aristocratic disgust with democracy, preference for the exotic, and themes of dehumanization. On the contrary, he is almost a textbook example of Tocqueville's prediction that American democracy would produce works that lay bare the deepest, hidden parts of the psyche. Deep anxiety and psychic insecurity seem to have occurred earlier in America than in Europe, for Europeans at least had a firm, complex social structure that gave them psychological security. In America, there was no compensating security; it was every man for himself. Poe accurately described the underside of the American dream of the self-made man and showed the price of materialism and excessive competition — loneliness, alienation, and images of death-in-life.

Poe's "decadence" also reflects the devaluation of symbols that occurred in the 19th century — the tendency to mix art objects promiscuously from many eras and places, in the process stripping them of their identity and reducing them to merely decorative items in a collection. The resulting chaos of styles was particularly noticeable in the United States, which often lacked traditional styles of its own. The jumble reflects the loss of coherent systems of thought as immigration, urbanization, and industrialization uprooted families and traditional ways. In art, this confusion of symbols fuelled the grotesque, an idea that Poe explicitly made his theme in his classic collection of stories, *Tales of the Grotesque and Arabesque* (1840).

Nathaniel Hawthorne (1804-1864)

Nathaniel Hawthorne, a fifth-generation American of English descent, was born in Salem, Massachusetts, a wealthy seaport north of Boston that specialized in East India trade. One of his ancestors had been a judge in an earlier century, during trials in Salem of women accused of being witches. Hawthorne used the idea of a curse on the family of an evil judge in his novel *The House of the Seven Gables*. Many of Hawthorne's stories are set in Puritan New England, and his greatest novel, *The Scarlet Letter* (1850), has become the classic portrayal of Puritan America. It tells of the passionate, forbidden love affair linking a sensitive, religious young man, the Reverend Arthur Dimmesdale, and the sensuous, beautiful townsperson, Hester Prynne. Set in Boston around 1650 during early Puritan colonization, the novel highlights the Calvinistic obsession with morality, sexual repression, guilt and confession, and spiritual salvation.

For its time, *The Scarlet Letter* was a daring and even subversive book. Hawthorne's gentle style, remote historical setting, and ambiguity softened his grim themes and contented the general public, but sophisticated writers such as Ralph Waldo Emerson and Herman Melville recognized the book's "hellish" power. It treated issues that were usually suppressed in 19th-century America, such as the impact of the new, liberating democratic experience on individual behaviour, especially on sexual and religious freedom.

The book is superbly organized and beautifully written. Appropriately, it uses allegory, a technique the early Puritan colonists themselves practiced.

Hawthorne's reputation rests on his other novels and tales as well. In *The House of the Seven Gables* (1851), he again returns to New England's history. The crumbling of the "house" refers to a family in Salem as well as to the actual structure. The theme concerns an inherited curse and its resolution through love. As one critic has noted, the idealistic protagonist Holgrave voices Hawthorne's own democratic distrust of old aristocratic families: "The truth is, that once in every half-century, at least, a family should be merged into the great, obscure mass of humanity, and forget about its ancestors. "

Hawthorne's last two novels were less successful. Both use modern settings, which hamper the magic of romance. *The Blithedale Romance* (1852) is interesting for its portrait of the socialist, utopian Brook Farm community. In the book, Hawthorne criticizes egotistical, power-hungry social reformers whose deepest instincts are not genuinely democratic. *The Marble Faun* (1860), though set in Rome, dwells on the Puritan themes of sin, isolation, expiation, and salvation.

These themes, and his characteristic settings in Puritan colonial New England, are trademarks of many of Hawthorne's best-known shorter stories: "The Minister's Black Veil," "Young Goodman Brown," and "My Kinsman, Major Molineux. " In the last of these, a Naive young man from the country comes to the city — a common route in urbanizing 19th-century America — to seek help from his powerful relative, whom he has never met. Robin has great difficulty finding the major, and finally joins in a strange night riot in which a man who seems to be a disgraced criminal is comically and cruelly driven out of town. Robin laughs loudest of all until he realizes that this "criminal" is none other than the man he sought — a representative of the British who has just been overthrown by a revolutionary American mob. The story confirms the bond of sin and suffering shared by all humanity. It also stresses the theme of the self-made man: Robin must learn, like every democratic American, to prosper from his own hard work, not from special favours from wealthy relatives.

"My Kinsman, Major Molineux" casts light on one of the most striking elements in Hawthorne's fiction: the lack of functioning families in his works. Although Cooper's *Leather-Stocking Tales* manage to introduce families into the least likely wilderness places, Hawthorne's stories and novels repeatedly show broken, cursed, or artificial families and the sufferings of the isolated individual.

The ideology of revolution, too, may have played a part in glorifying a sense of proud yet alienated freedom. The American Revolution, from a psychohistorical viewpoint, parallels an adolescent rebellion away from the parent-figure of England and the larger family of the British Empire. Americans won their independence and were then faced with the bewildering dilemma of discovering their identity apart from old authorities. This scenario was played out countless times on the frontier, to the extent that, in fiction, isolation often seems the basic American condition of life. Puritanism and its Protestant offshoots may have further weakened the family by preaching that the individual's first responsibility was to save his or her own soul.

WOMEN WRITERS AND REFORMERS IN ROMANTIC PERIOD

American women endured many inequalities in the 19th century: They were denied the vote, barred from professional schools and most higher education, forbidden to speak in public and even attend public conventions, and unable to own property. Despite these obstacles, a strong women's network sprang up. Through letters, personal friendships, formal meetings, women's newspapers, and books, women furthered social change. Intellectual women drew parallels between themselves and slaves. They courageously demanded fundamental reforms, such as the abolition of slavery and women's suffrage, despite social ostracism and sometimes financial ruin. Their works were the vanguard of intellectual expression of a larger women's literary tradition that included the sentimental novel. Women's sentimental novels, such as Harriet Beecher Stowe's *Uncle Tom's Cabin*, were enormously popular. They appealed to the emotions and often dramatized contentious social issues, particularly those touching the family and women's roles and responsibilities.

Abolitionist Lydia Child (1802-1880), who greatly influenced Margaret Fuller, was a leader of this network. Her successful 1824 novel *Hobomok* shows the need for racial and religious toleration. Its setting — Puritan Salem, Massachusetts — anticipated Nathaniel Hawthorne. An activist, Child founded a private girls' school, founded and edited the first journal for children in the United States, and published the first anti-slavery tract, *An Appeal in Favour of that Class of Americans Called Africans*, in 1833. This daring work made her notorious and ruined her financially. Her *History of the Condition of Women in Various Ages and Nations* (1855) argues for women's equality by pointing to their historical achievements. Angelina Grimke (1805-1879) and Sarah Grimke (1792-1873) were born into a large family of wealthy slaveowners in elegant Charleston, South Carolina. These sisters moved to the North to defend the rights of blacks and women. As speakers for the New York Anti-Slavery Society, they were the first women to publicly lecture to audiences, including men. In letters, essays, and studies, they drew parallels between racism and sexism.

Elizabeth Cady Stanton (1815-1902), abolitionist and women's rights activist, lived for a time in Boston, where she befriended Lydia Child. With Lucretia Mott, she organized the 1848 Seneca Falls Convention for Women's rights; she also drafted its *Declaration of Sentiments*. Her "Woman's Declaration of Independence" begins "men and women are created equal" and includes a resolution to give women the right to vote. With Susan B. Anthony, Elizabeth Cady Stanton campaigned for suffrage in the 1860s and 1870s, formed the anti-slavery Women's Loyal National League and the National Woman Suffrage Association, and co-edited the weekly newspaper *Revolution*. President of the Woman Suffrage Association for 21 years, she led the struggle for women's rights. She gave public lectures in several states, partly to support the education of her seven children.

After her husband died, Cady Stanton deepened her analysis of inequality between the sexes. Her book *The Woman's Bible* (1895) discerns a deep-seated anti-female bias in Judaeo-Christian tradition. She lectured on such subjects as divorce, women's rights, and religion until her death at 86, just after writing a letter to President Theodore Roosevelt supporting the women's vote. Her numerous works — at first pseudonymous, but later under her own name — include three co-authored volumes of *History of Woman Suffrage* (1881-1886) and a candid, humorous autobiography.

Sojourner Truth (c. 1797-1883) epitomized the endurance and charisma of this extraordinary group of women. Born a slave in New York, she grew up speaking Dutch. She escaped from slavery in 1827, settling with a son and daughter in the supportive Dutch-American Van Wagener family, for whom she worked as a servant. They helped her win a legal battle for her son's freedom, and she took their name. Striking out on her own, she worked with a preacher to convert prostitutes to Christianity and lived in a progressive communal home. She was christened "Sojourner Truth" for the mystical voices and visions she began to experience. To spread the truth of these visionary teachings, she sojourned alone, lecturing, singing gospel songs, and preaching abolitionism through many states over three decades. Encouraged by Elizabeth Cady Stanton, she advocated women's suffrage. Her life is told in the *Narrative of Sojourner Truth* (1850), an autobiographical account transcribed and edited by Olive Gilbert. Illiterate her whole life, she spoke Dutch-accented English. Sojourner Truth is said to have bared her breast at a women's rights convention when she was accused of really being a man. Her answer to a man who said that women were the weaker sex has become legendary:

I have ploughed and planted, and gathered into bars, and no man could head me! And ain't I a woman? I could work as much and eat as much as a man — when I could get it — and bear the lash as well! And ain't I a woman? I have borne thirteen children, and seen them most all sold off to slavery, and when I cried out with my mother's grief, none but Jesus heard me! And ain't I a woman?

This humorous and irreverent orator has been compared to the great blues singers. Harriet Beecher Stowe and many others found wisdom in this visionary black woman, who could declare, "Lord, Lord, I can love even de white folk!"

Harriet Jacobs (1818-1896)

Born a slave in North Carolina, Harriet Jacobs was taught to read and write by her mistress. On her mistress's death, Jacobs was sold to a white master who tried to force her to have sexual relations. She resisted him, finding another white lover by whom she had two children, who went to live with her grandmother. "It seems less degrading to give one's self than to submit to compulsion," she candidly wrote. She escaped from her owner and started a rumour that she had fled North.

Terrified of being caught and sent back to slavery and punishment, she spent almost seven years hidden in her master's town, in the tiny dark attic of her grandmother's house. She was sustained by glimpses of her beloved children seen through holes that she drilled through the ceiling. She finally escaped to the North, settling in Rochester, New York, where Frederick Douglass was publishing the anti-slavery newspaper *North Star* and near which (in Seneca Falls) a women's rights convention had recently met. There Jacobs became friends with Amy Post, a Quaker feminist abolitionist, who encouraged her to write her autobiography. *Incidents in the Life of a Slave Girl*, published under the pseudonym "Linda Brent" in 1861, was edited by Lydia Child. It out spokenly condemned the sexual exploitation of black slave women. Jacobs's book, like Douglass's, is part of the slave narrative genre extending back to Olauda Equiano in colonial times.

Harriet Wilson (c. 1807-1870)

Harriet Wilson was the first African-American to publish a novel in the United States — *Our Nig: or, Sketches from the life of a Free Black, in a two-storey white house, North showing that Slavery's Shadows Fall Even There* (1859). The novel realistically dramatizes the marriage between a white woman and a black man, and also depicts the difficult life of a black servant in a wealthy Christian household. Formerly thought to be autobiographical, it is now understood to be a work of fiction.

Like Jacobs, Wilson did not publish under her own name (*Our Nig* was ironic), and her work was overlooked until recently. The same can be said of the work of most of the women writers of the era. Noted African-American scholar Henry Louis Gates, Jr. — in his role of spearheading the black fiction project — reissued *Our Nig* in 1983.

Frederick Douglass (1817-1895)

The most famous black American anti-lavery leader and orator of the era, Frederick Douglass was born a slave on a Maryland plantation. It was his good fortune to be sent to relatively liberal Baltimore as a young man, where he learned to read and write. Escaping to Massachusetts in 1838, at age 21, Douglass was helped by abolitionist editor William Lloyd Garrison and began to lecture for anti-lavery societies.

In 1845, he published his *Narrative of the Life of Frederick Douglass, An American Slave* (second version 1855, revised in 1892), the best and most popular of many "slave narratives. " Often dictated by illiterate blacks to white abolitionists and used as propaganda, these slave narratives were well-known in the years just before the Civil War. Douglass's narrative is vivid and highly literate, and it gives unique insights into the mentality of slavery and the agony that institution caused among blacks.

The slave narrative was the first black literary prose genre in the United States. It helped blacks in the difficult task of establishing an African-American identity in white America, and it has continued to exert an important influence on black fictional techniques and themes throughout the 20th century. The search for identity, anger against discrimination, and sense of living an invisible, hunted, underground life unacknowledged by the white majority have recurred in the works of such 20th-century black American authors as Richard Wright, James Baldwin, Ralph Ellison, and Toni Morrison.

Harriet Beecher Stowe (1811-1896)

Harriet Beecher Stowe's novel *Uncle Tom's Cabin; or, Life Among the Lowly* was the most popular American book of the 19th century. First published serially in the *National Era* magazine (1851-1852), it was an immediate success. Forty different publishers printed it in England alone, and it was quickly translated into 20 languages, receiving the praise of such authors as Georges Sand in France, Heinrich Heine in Germany, and Ivan Turgenev in Russia. Its passionate appeal for an end to slavery in the United States inflamed the debate that, within a decade, led to the U. S. Civil War (1861-1865).

Reasons for the success of *Uncle Tom's Cabin* are obvious. It reflected the idea that slavery in the United States, the nation that purportedly embodied democracy and equality for all, was an injustice of colossal proportions.

Stowe herself was a perfect representative of old New England Puritan stock. Her father, brother, and husband all were well-known, learned Protestant clergymen and reformers. Stowe conceived the idea of the novel — in a vision of an old, ragged slave being beaten — as she participated in a church service. Later, she said that the novel was inspired and "written by God. " Her motive was the religious passion to reform life by making it more godly. The Romantic period had ushered in an era of feeling: The virtues of family and love reigned supreme. Stowe's novel attacked slavery precisely because it violated domestic values.

Uncle Tom, the slave and central character, is a true Christian martyr who labours to convert his kind master, St. Clare, prays for St. Clare's soul as he dies, and is killed defending slave women. Slavery is depicted as evil not for political or philosophical reasons but mainly because it divides families, destroys normal parental love, and is inherently un-Christian. The most touching scenes show an agonized slave mother unable to help her screaming child and a father sold away from his family. These were crimes against the sanctity of domestic love.

Stowe's novel was not originally intended as an attack on the South; in fact, Stowe had visited the South, liked southerners, and portrayed them kindly. Southern slaveowners are good masters and treat Tom well. St. Clare personally abhors slavery and intends to free all of his slaves. The evil master Simon Legree, on the other hand, is a nrtherner and the villain. Ironically, the novel was meant to reconcile the North and South, which were drifting toward the Civil War a decade away. Ultimately, though, the book was used by abolitionists and others as a polemic against the South.

3

The Age of the Romantic Period Revival

(1)

APPROACHING THE PERIODS OF CHANGE AND NEW BIRTH IN LITERATURE

There are two ways of approaching the periods of change and new birth in literature. The commonest and, for all the study which it entails, the easiest, is that summed up in the phrase, literature begets literature. Following it, you discover and weigh literary influences, the influence of poet on poet, and book on book. You find one man harking back to earlier models in his own tongue, which an intervening age misunderstood or despised; another, turning to the contemporary literatures of neighbouring countries; another, perhaps, to the splendour and exoticism of the east. In the matter of form and style, such a study carries you far.

You can trace types of poetry and metres back to curious and unsuspected originals, find the well-known verse of Burns' epistles turning up in Provençal; Tennyson's *In Memoriam* stanza in use by Ben Jonson; the metre of *Christabel* in minor Elizabethan poetry; the peculiar form of Fitzgerald's translation of *Omar Khayyam* followed by so many imitators since, itself to be the actual reflection of the rough metrical scheme of his Persian original. But such a study, though it is profitable and interesting, can never lead to the whole truth. As we saw in the beginning of this book, in the matter of the Renaissance, every age of discovery and re-birth has its double aspect. It is a revolution in style and language, an age of literary experiment and achievement, but its experiments are dictated by the excitement of a new subject-matter, and that subject-matter is so much in the air, so impalpable and universal that it eludes analysis. Only you can be sure that it is this weltering contagion of new ideas, and new thought—the "Zeitgeist," the spirit of the age, or whatever you may call it—that is the essential and controlling force. Literary loans and imports give the forms into which it can be moulded, but without them it would still exist, and they are only the means by which a spirit which is in life itself, and which expresses itself in action, and in concrete human achievement, gets itself into the written word.

The romantic revival numbers Napoleon amongst its leaders as well as Byron, Wellington, Pitt and Wilberforce, as well as Keats and Wordsworth. Only the literary manifestations of the time concern us here, but it is important to remember that the passion for simplification and for a return to nature as a refuge from the artificial complexities of society, which inspired the *Lyrical Ballads*, inspired no less the course of the Revolution in France, and later, the destruction by Napoleon of the smaller feudal states of Germany, which made possible German nationality and a national spirit.

In this romantic revival, however, the revolution in form and style matters more than in most. The classicism of the previous age had been so fixed and immutable; it had been enthroned in high places, enjoyed the esteem of society, arrogated to itself the acceptance which good breeding and good manners demanded. Dryden had been a Court poet, careful to change his allegiance with the changing monarchy. Pope had been the equal and intimate of the great people of his day, and his followers, if they did not enjoy the equality, enjoyed at any rate the patronage of many noble lords. The effect of this was to give the prestige of social usage to the verse in which they wrote and the language they used.

"There was," said Dr. Johnson, "before the time of Dryden no poetical diction, no system of words at once refined from the grossness of domestic use, and free from the harshness of terms appropriated to particular arts. Words too familiar or too remote to defeat the purpose of a poet." This poetic diction, refined from the grossness of domestic use, was the standard poetic speech of the eighteenth century. The heroic couplet in which it was cast was the standard metre. So that the first object of the revolt of the romantics was the purely literary object of getting rid of the vice of an unreal and artificial manner of writing. They desired simplicity of style.

When the *Lyrical Ballads* of Wordsworth and Coleridge were published in 1798, the preface which Wordsworth wrote as their manifesto hardly touched at all on the poetic imagination or the attitude of the poet to life and nature. The only question is that of diction. "The majority of the following poems," he writes, "are to be considered as experiments. They were written chiefly with a view to ascertain how far the language of conversation in the middle and lower classes of society is adapted to the purposes of poetic pleasure." And in the longer preface to the second edition, in which the theories of the new school on the nature and methods of the poetic imagination are set forth at length, he returns to the same point.

"The language too, of these men (that is those in humble and rustic life) has been adopted... because such men hourly communicate with the best objects from which the best part of language is originally derived, and because from their rank in society, and the sameness and narrow circle of their intercourse, being less under the influence of social vanity, they convey their feelings and notions in simple unelaborated expressions." Social vanity—the armour which we wear to conceal our deepest thoughts and feelings—that was what Wordsworth wished to be rid of, and he chose the language of the common people, not because it fitted, as an earlier school of poets who used the common speech had asserted, the utterance of habitual feeling and common sense, but because it is the most sincere expression of the deepest and rarest passion. His object was the object attained by Shakespeare in some of his supremest moments; the bare intolerable force of the speeches after the murder of Macbeth, or of King Lear's

"Do not laugh at me,
For as I am a man, I think this lady
To be my child Cordelia."

Here, then, was one avenue of revolt from the tyranny of artificiality, the getting back of common speech into poetry. But there was another, earlier and more potent in its effect. The eighteenth century, weary of its own good sense and sanity, turned to the Middle Ages for picturesqueness and relief. Romance of course, had not been dead in all these years, when Pope and Addison made wit and good sense the fashionable temper for writing. There was a strong romantic tradition in the eighteenth century, though it does not give its character to the writing of the time.

Dr. Johnson was fond of old romances. When he was in Skye he amused himself by thinking of his Scottish tour as the journey of a knight-errant. "These fictions of the Gothic romances," he said, "are not so remote from credibility as is commonly supposed." It is a mistake to suppose that the passion for mediaevalism began with either Coleridge or Scott. Horace Walpole was as enthusiastic as either of them; good eighteenth century prelates like Hurd and Percy, found in what they called the Gothic an inexhaustible source of delight. As was natural, what attracted them in the Middle Ages was not their resemblances to the time they lived in, but the points in which the two differed. None of them had knowledge enough, or insight enough, to conceive or sympathize with the humanity of the thirteenth century, to shudder at its cruelties and hardnesses and persecutions, or to comprehend the spiritual elevation and insight of its rarest minds.

"It was art," said William Morris, "art in which all men shared, that made life romantic as people called it in those days. That and not robber barons, and inaccessible kings, with their hierarchy of serving nobles, and other rubbish." Morris belonged to a time which knew its middle ages better. To the eighteenth century the robber barons and the "other rubbish" were the essence of romance. For Percy and his followers, medievalism was a collection of what actors call "properties" gargoyles, and odds and ends of armour and castle keeps with secret passages, banners and gay colours, and gay shimmering obsolete words. Mistaking what was on its surface at any rate a subtle and complex civilization, for rudeness and quaintness, they seemed to themselves to pass back into a freer air, where any extravagance was possible, and good breeding and mere circumspection and restraint vanished like the wind.

A similar longing to be rid of the precision and order of everyday life drove them to the mountains, and to the literature of Wales and the Highlands, to Celtic, or pseudo-Celtic romance. To the fashion of the time mountains were still frowning and horrid steeps; in Gray's Journal of his tour in the Lakes, a new understanding and appreciation of nature is only struggling through; and when mountains became fashionable, it was at first and remained in part at least, till the time of Byron, for those very theatrical qualities which had hitherto put them in abhorrence. Wordsworth, in his *Lines written above Tintern Abbey*, in which he sets forth the succeeding stages of his mental development, refers to this love of the mountains for their spectacular qualities, as the first step in the progress of his mind to poetic maturity:

"The sounding cataract
Haunted me like a passion; the tall rock,
The mountain and the deep and gloomy wood,
Their colours and their forms were then to me
An appetite."

This same passion for the "sounding cataract" and the "tall rock," this appetite for the deep and gloomy wood, gave its vogue in Wordsworth's boyhood to Macpherson's *Ossian*, a book which whether it be completely fraudulent or not, was of capital importance in the beginnings of the romantic movement.

The love of mediaeval quaintness and obsolete words, however, led to a more important literary event—the publication of Bishop Percy's edition of the ballads in the Percy folio—the *Reliques of Ancient Poetry*. Percy to his own mind knew the Middle Ages better than they knew themselves, and he took care to dress to advantage the rudeness and plainness of his originals. Perhaps we should not blame him. Sir Walter Scott did the same with better tact and skill in his Border minstrelsy, and how many distinguished editors are there, who have tamed and smoothed down the natural wildness and irregularity of Blake? But it is more important to observe that when Percy's reliques came to have their influence on writing his additions were imitated as much as the poems on which he grafted them. Chatterton's *Rowley Poems,* which in many places seem almost inconceivably banal and artificial to us to-day, caught their accent from the episcopal editor as much as from the ballads themselves. None the less, whatever its fault, Percy's collection gave its impetus to one half of the romantic movement; it was eagerly read in Germany, and when it came to influence Scott and Coleridge it did so not only directly, but through Burger's imitation of it; it began the modern study and love of the ballad which has given us *Sister Helen,* the *White Ship* and the *Lady of Shalott.*

But the romantic revival goes deeper than any change, however momentous of fashion or style. It meant certain fundamental changes in human outlook. In the first place, one notices in the authors of the time an extraordinary development of imaginative sensibility; the mind at its countless points of contact with the sensuous world and the world of thought, seems to become more alive and alert. It is more sensitive to fine impressions, to finely graded shades of difference.

Outward objects and philosophical ideas seem to increase in their content and their meaning, and acquire a new power to enrich the intensest life of the human spirit. Mountains and lakes, the dignity of the peasant, the terror of the supernatural, scenes of history, mediaeval architecture and armour, and mediaeval thought and poetry, the arts and mythology of Greece—all became springs of poetic inspiration and poetic joy. The impressions of all these things were unfamiliar and ministered to a sense of wonder, and by that very fact they were classed as romantic, as modes of escape from a settled way of life. But they were also in a sense familiar too. The mountains made their appeal to a deep implanted feeling in man, to his native sense of his own worth and dignity and splendour as a part of nature, and his recognition of natural scenery as necessary, and in its fullest meaning as sufficient for his spiritual needs.

They called him back from the artificiality and complexity of the cities he had built for himself, and the society he had weaved round him, to the natural world in which Providence had planted him of old, and which was full of significance for his soul. The greatest poets of the romantic revival strove to capture and convey the influence of nature on the mind, and of the mind on nature interpenetrating one another. They were none the less artists because they approached nature in a state of passive receptivity. They believed in the autocracy of the individual imagination none the less because their mission was to divine nature and to understand her, rather than to correct her profusions in the name of art.

In the second place the romantic revival meant a development of the historical sense. Thinkers like Burke and Montesquieu helped students of politics to acquire perspective; to conceive modern institutions not as things separate, and separately created, but as conditioned by, and evolved from, the institutions of an earlier day. Even the revolutionary spirit of the time looked both before and after, and took history as well as the human perfectibility imagined by philosophers into its purview. In France the reformers appealed in the first instance for a States General—a mediaeval institution—as the corrective of their wrongs, and later when they could not, like their neighbours in Belgium, demand reform by way of the restoration of their historical rights, they were driven to go a step further back still, beyond history to what they conceived to be primitive society, and demand the rights of man. This development of the historical sense, which had such a widespread influence on politics, got itself into literature in the creation of the historical novel.

Scott and Chateaubriand revived the old romance in which by a peculiar ingenuity of form, the adventures of a typical hero of fiction are cast in a historical setting and set about with portraits of real personages. The historical sense affected, too, novels dealing with contemporary life. Scott's best work, his novels of Scottish character, catch more than half their excellence from the richness of colour and proportion which the portraiture of the living people acquires when it is aided by historical knowledge and imagination.

Lastly, besides this awakened historical sense, and this quickening of imaginative sensibility to the message of nature, the Romantic revival brought to literature a revival of the sense of the connection between the visible world and another world which is unseen. The supernatural which in all but the crudest of mechanisms had been out of English literature since *Macbeth*, took hold on the imaginations of authors, and brought with it a new subtlety and a new and nameless horror and fascination.

There is nothing in earlier English literature to set beside the strange and terrible indefiniteness of the *Ancient Mariner*, and though much in this kind has been written since, we have not got far beyond the skill and imagination with which Coleridge and Scott worked on the instinctive fears that lie buried in the human mind.

Of all these aspects of the revival, however, the new sensitiveness and accessibility to the influences of external nature was the most pervasive and the most important. Wordsworth speaks for the love that is in homes where poor men lie, the daily teaching that is in

"Woods and rills;
The silence that is in the starry sky,
The peace that is among the lonely hills."

Shelley for the wildness of the west wind, and the ubiquitous spiritual emotion which speaks equally in the song of a skylark or a political revolution. Byron for the swing and roar of the sea. Keats for verdurous glooms and winding mossy ways. Scott and Coleridge, though like Byron they are less with nature than with romance, share the same communion.

This imaginative sensibility of the romantics not only deepened their communion with nature, it brought them into a truer relation with what had before been created in literature and art. The romantic revival is the Golden Age of English criticism; all the poets were critics of one sort or another—either formally in essays and prefaces, or in passing and desultory flashes of illumination in their correspondence. Wordsworth, in his prefaces, in his letter to a friend of Burns which contains such a breadth and clarity of wisdom on things that seem alien to his sympathies, even in some of his poems; Coleridge, in his *Biographia Literaria*, in his notes on Shakespeare, in those rhapsodies at Highgate which were the basis for his recorded table talk; Keats in his letters; Shelley in his *Defence of Poetry*; Byron in his satires and journals; Scott in those lives of the novelists which contain so much truth and insight into the works of fellow craftsmen—they are all to be found turning the new acuteness of impression which was in the air they breathed, to the study of literature, as well as to the study of nature. Alongside of them were two authors, Lamb and Hazlitt, whose bent was rather critical than creative, and the best part of whose intelligence and sympathy was spent on the sensitive and loving divination of our earlier literature. With these two men began the criticism of acting and of pictorial art that have developed since into two of the main kinds of modern critical writing.

Romantic criticism, both in its end and its method, differs widely from that of Dr. Johnson and his school. Wordsworth and Coleridge were concerned with deep-seated qualities and temperamental differences. Their critical work revolved round their conception of the fancy and the imagination, the one dealing with nature on the surface and decorating it with imagery, the other penetrating to its deeper significances. Hazlitt and Lamb applied their analogous conception of wit as a lower quality than humour, in the same fashion. Dr. Johnson looked on the other hand for correctness of form, for the subordination of the parts to the whole, for the self-restraint and good sense which common manners would demand in society, and wisdom in practical life. His school cared more for large general outlines than for truth in detail.

They would not permit the idiosyncrasy of a personal or individual point of view: hence they were incapable of understanding lyricism, and they preferred those forms of writing which set themselves to express the ideas and feelings that most men may be supposed to have in common. Dr. Johnson thought a bombastic and rhetorical passage in Congreve's *Mourning Bride* better than the famous description of Dover cliff in *King Lear*. "The crows, sir," he said of the latter, "impede your fall." Their town breeding, and possibly, as we saw in the case of Dr. Johnson, an actual physical disability, made them distrust any clear and sympathetic rendering of the sense impressions which nature creates. One cannot imagine Dr. Johnson caring much for the minute observations of Tennyson's nature poems, or delighting in the verdurous and mossy alleys of Keats. His test in such a case would be simple; he would not have liked to have been in such places, nor reluctantly compelled to go there would he in all likelihood have had much to say about them beyond that they were damp. For the poetry—such as Shelley's—which worked by means of impalpable and indefinite suggestion, he would, one may conceive, have cared even less. New modes of poetry asked of critics new sympathies and a new way of approach. But it is time to turn to the authors themselves.

(2)

THE ENGLISH POETS STANDING

The case of Wordsworth is peculiar. In his own day he was vilified and misunderstood; poets like Byron, whom most of us would now regard simply as depending from the school he created, sneered at him. Shelley and Keats failed to understand him or his motives; he was suspected of apostasy, and when he became poet laureate he was written off as a turn-coat who had played false to the ideals of his youth. Now common opinion regards him as a poet above all the others of his age, and amongst all the English poets standing beside Milton, but a step below Shakespeare himself—and we know more about him, more about the processes by which his soul moved from doubts to certainties, from troubles to triumph, than we do about any other author we have. This knowledge we have from the poem called, *The Prelude,* which was published after his death. It was designed to be only the opening and explanatory section of a philosophical poem, which was never completed. Had it been published earlier it would have saved Wordsworth from the coldness and neglect he suffered at the hands of younger men like Shelley; it might even have made their work different from what it is. It has made Wordsworth very clear to us now.

Wordsworth is that rarest thing amongst poets, a complete innovator. He looked at things in a new way. He found his subjects in new places; and he put them into a new poetic form. At the turning point of his life, in his early manhood, he made one great discovery, had one great vision. By the light of that vision and to communicate that discovery he wrote his greatest work. By and by the vision faded, the world fell back into the light of common day, his philosophy passed from discovery to acceptance, and all unknown to him his pen fell into a common way of writing.

The faculty of reading which has added fuel to the fire of so many waning inspirations was denied him. He was much too self-centred to lose himself in the works of others. Only the shock of a change of environment—a tour in Scotland, or abroad—shook him into his old thrill of imagination, so that a few fine things fitfully illumine the enormous and dreary bulk of his later work. If we lost all but the *Lyrical Ballads,* the poems of 1804, and the *Prelude,* and the *Excursion,* Wordsworth's position as a poet would be no lower than it is now, and he would be more readily accepted by those who still find themselves uncertain about him.

The determining factor in his career was the French Revolution—that great movement which besides re-making France and Europe, made our very modes of thinking anew. While an undergraduate in Cambridge Wordsworth made several vacation visits to France. The first peaceful phase of the Revolution was at its height; France and the assembly were dominated by the little group of revolutionary orators who took their name from the south-western province from which most of them came, and with this group—the Girondists—Wordsworth threw in his lot.

Had he remained he would probably have gone with them to the guillotine. As it was, the commands of his guardian brought him back to England, and he was forced to contemplate from a distance the struggle in which he burned to take an active part. One is accustomed to think of Wordsworth as a mild old man, but such a picture if it is thrown back as a presentment of the Wordsworth of the nineties is a far way from the truth. This darkly passionate man tortured himself with his longings and his horror. War came and the prayers for victory in churches found him in his heart praying for defeat; then came the execution of the king; then the plot which slew the Gironde. Before all this Wordsworth trembled as Hamlet did when he learned the ghost's story. His faith in the world was shaken. First his own country had taken up arms against what he believed to be the cause of liberty. Then faction had destroyed his friends whom he believed to be its standard bearers. What was in the world, in religion, in morality that such things could be? In the face of this tremendous problem, Wordsworth, unlike Hamlet, was resolute and determined. It was, perhaps, characteristic of him that in his desire to get his feet on firm rock again he fled for a time to the exactest of sciences—to mathematics. But though he got certainties there, they must have been, one judges, certainties too arid for his thirsting mind. Then he made his great discovery—helped to it, perhaps, by his sister Dorothy and his friend Coleridge—he found nature, and in nature, peace.

Not a very wonderful discovery, you will say, but though the cleansing and healing force of natural surroundings on the mind is a familiar enough idea in our own day, that is only because Wordsworth found it. When he gave his message to the world it was a new message. It is worth while remembering that it is still an unaccepted one. Most of his critics still consider it only Wordsworth's fun when he wrote:

"One impulse from the vernal wood
Can teach us more of man,
Of moral evil and of good,
Than all the sages can."

Yet Wordsworth really believed that moral lessons and ideas were to be gathered from trees and stones. It was the main part of his teaching. He claimed that his own morality had been so furnished him, and he wrote his poetry to convince other people that what had been true for him could be true for them too.

For him life was a series of impressions, and the poet's duty was to recapture those impressions, to isolate them and brood over them, till gradually as a result of his contemplation emotion stirred again—an emotion akin to the authentic thrill that had excited him when the impression was first born in experience.

Then poetry is made; this emotion "recollected" as Wordsworth said (we may add, recreated) "in tranquillity" passes into enduring verse. He treasured numberless experiences of this kind in his own life. Some of them are set forth in the *Prelude,* that for instance on which the poem *The Thorn* in the *Lyrical Ballads* is based; they were one or other of them the occasion of most of his poems; the best of them produced his finest work—such a poem for instance as *Resolution and Independence* or *Gipsies,* where some chance sight met with in one of the poet's walks is brooded over till it becomes charged with a tremendous significance for him and for all the world. If we ask how he differentiated his experiences, which had most value for him, we shall find something deficient.

That is to say, things which were unique and precious to him do not always appear so to his readers. He counted as gold much that we regard as dross. But though we may differ from his judgments, the test which he applied to his recollected impressions is clear. He attached most value to those which brought with them the sense of an indwelling spirit, transfusing and interpenetrating all nature, transfiguring with its radiance, rocks and fields and trees and the men and women who lived close enough to them to partake of their strength—the sense, as he calls it in his *Lines above Tintern Abbey* of something "more deeply interfused" by which all nature is made one. Sometimes, as in the hymn to Duty, it is conceived as law. Duty before whom the flowers laugh, is the daughter of the voice of God, through whom the most ancient heavens are fresh and strong. But in most of his poems its ends do not trouble; it is omnipresent; it penetrates everything and transfigures everything; it is God. It was Wordsworth's belief that the perception of this indwelling spirit weakened as age grew. For a few precious and glorious years he had the vision

"When meadow, grove, and stream,
The earth, and every common sight
To me did seem
Apparelled in celestial light,
The glory and the freshness of a dream."

Then as childhood, when "these intimations of immortality," this perception of the infinite are most strong, passed further and further away, the vision faded and he was left gazing in the light of common day. He had his memories and that was all. There is, of course, more in the matter than this, and Wordsworth's beliefs were inextricably entangled with the conception which Coleridge borrowed from German philosophy.

"We receive but what we give"

wrote Coleridge to his friend,

"And in our life alone doth Nature live."

And Wordsworth came to know that the light he had imagined to be bestowed, was a light reflected from his own mind. It is easy to pass from criticism to metaphysics where Coleridge leads, and wise not to follow.

If Wordsworth represents that side of the Romantic Revival which is best described as the return to Nature, Coleridge has justification for the phrase "Renascence of Wonder." He revived the supernatural as a literary force, emancipated it from the crude mechanism which had been applied to it by dilettantes like Horace Walpole and Mrs. Radcliffe, and invested it instead with that air of suggestion and indefiniteness which gives the highest potency to it in its effect on the imagination. But Coleridge is more noteworthy for what he suggested to others than for what he did in himself. His poetry is, even more than Wordsworth's, unequal; he is capable of large tracts of dreariness and flatness; he seldom finished what he began.

he Ancient Mariner, indeed, which was the fruit of his close companionship with Wordsworth, is the only completed thing of the highest quality in the whole of his work. Christabel is a splendid fragment; for years the first part lay uncompleted and when the odd accident of an evening's intoxication led him to commence the second, the inspiration had fled. For the second part, by giving to the fairy atmosphere of the first a local habitation and a name, robbed it of its most precious quality; what it gave in exchange was something the public could get better from Scott. Kubla Khan went unfinished because the call of a friend broke the thread of the reverie in which it was composed. In the end came opium and oceans of talk at Highgate and fouled the springs of poetry. Coleridge never fulfilled the promise of his early days with Wordsworth. "He never spoke out." But it is on the lines laid down by his share in the pioneer work rather than on the lines of Wordsworth's that the second generation of Romantic poets-that of Shelley and Keats-developed.

The work of Wordsworth was conditioned by the French Revolution but it hardly embodied the revolutionary spirit. What he conceived to be its excesses revolted him, and though he sought and sang freedom, he found it rather in the later revolt of the nationalities against the Revolution as manifested in Napoleon himself. The spirit of the revolution, as it was understood in France and in Europe, had to wait for Shelley for its complete expression.

Freedom is the breath of his work-freedom not only from the tyranny of earthly powers, but from the tyranny of religion, expressing itself in republicanism, in atheism, and in complete emancipation from the current moral code both in conduct and in writing. The reaction which had followed the overthrow of Napoleon at Waterloo, sent a wave of absolutism and repression all over Europe, Italy returned under the heel of Austria; the Bourbons were restored in France; in England came the days of Castlereagh and Peterloo. The poetry of Shelley is the expression of what the children of the revolution-men and women who were brought up in and believed the revolutionary gospel-thought about these things.

But it is more than that. Of no poet in English, nor perhaps in any other tongue, could it be said with more surety, that the pursuit of the spirit of beauty dominates all his work. For Shelley it interfused all nature and to possess it was the goal of all endeavour. The visible world and the world of thought mingle themselves inextricably in his contemplation of it. For him there is no boundary-line between the two, the one is as real and actual as the other. In his hands that old trick of the poets, the simile, takes on a new and surprising form.

He does not enforce the creations of his imagination by the analogy of natural appearances; his instinct is just the opposite-to describe and illumine nature by a reference to the creatures of thought. Other poets, Keats for instance, or Tennyson, or the older poets like Dante and Homer, might compare ghosts flying from an enchanter like leaves flying before the wind. They might describe a poet wrapped up in his dreams as being like a bird singing invisible in the brightness of the sky. But Shelley can write of the west wind as

"Before whose unseen presence the leaves, dead,

Are driven like ghosts from an enchanter fleeing,"

and he can describe a skylark in the heavens as

"Like a poet hidden

In the light of thought."

Of all English poets he is the most completely lyrical. Nothing that he wrote but is wrought out of the anguish or joy of his own heart.

"Most wretched souls,"

he writes

"Are cradled into poetry by wrong

They learn in suffering what they teach in song."

Perhaps his work is too impalpable and moves in an air too rarefied. It sometimes lacks strength. It fails to take grip enough of life. Had he lived he might have given it these things; there are signs in his last poems that he would have given it.

But he could hardly have bettered the sheer and triumphant lyricism of *The Skylark,* of some of his choruses, and of the *Ode to Dejection,* and of the *Lines written on the Eugenoen hills.*

If the Romantic sense of the one-ness of nature found its highest exponent in Shelley, the Romantic sensibility to outward impressions reached its climax in Keats.

For him life is a series of sensations, felt with almost febrile acuteness. Records of sight and touch and smell crowd every line of his work; the scenery of a garden in Hampstead becomes like a landscape in the tropics, so extraordinary vivid and detailed is his apprehension and enjoyment of what it has to give him. The luxuriance of his sensations is matched by the luxuriance of his powers of expression.

Adjectives heavily charged with messages for the senses, crowd every line of his work, and in his earlier poems overlay so heavily the thought they are meant to convey that all sense of sequence and structure is apt to be smothered under their weight. Not that consecutive thought claims a place in his conception of his poetry. His ideal was passive contemplation rather than active mental exertion. "O for a life of sensations rather than of thoughts," he exclaims in one of his letters; and in another, "It is more noble to sit like Jove than to fly like Mercury." His work has one message and one only, the lastingness of beauty and its supreme truth. It is stated in *Endymion* in lines that are worn bare with quotation. It is stated again, at the height of his work in his greatest ode,

"Beauty is truth, truth beauty: that is all

We know on earth and all we need to know."

His work has its defects; he died at twenty-six so it would be a miracle if it were not so. He lacks taste and measure; he offends by an over-luxuriousness and sensuousness; he fails when he is concerned with flesh and blood; he is apt, as Mr. Robert Bridges has said, "to class women with roses and sweetmeats." But in his short life he attained with surprising rapidity and completeness to poetic maturity, and perhaps from no other poet could we find things to match his greatest—*Hyperion, Isabella,* the *Eve of St. Agnes* and the *Odes*. There remains a poet over whom opinion is more sharply divided than it is about any other writer in English.

In his day Lord Byron was the idol, not only of his countrymen, but of Europe. Of all the poets of the time he was, if we except Scott, whose vogue he eclipsed, the only one whose work was universally known and popular. Everybody read him; he was admired not only by the multitude and by his equals, but by at least one who was his superior, the German poet Goethe, who did not hesitate to say of him that he was the greatest talent of the century Though this exalted opinion still persists on the Continent, hardly anyone could be found in England to subscribe to it now.

Without insularity, we may claim to be better judges of authors in our own tongue than foreign critics, however distinguished and comprehending. How then shall be explained Lord Byron's instant popularity and the position he won? What were the qualities which gave him the power he enjoyed?

In the first place he appealed by virtue of his subject-matter—the desultory wanderings of *Childe Harold* traversed ground every mile of which was memorable to men who had watched the struggle which had been going on in Europe with scarcely a pause for twenty years.

Descriptive journalism was then and for nearly half a century afterwards unknown, and the poem by its descriptiveness, by its appeal to the curiosity of its readers, made the same kind of success that vividly written special correspondence would to-day, the charm of metre super-added.

Lord Byron gave his readers something more, too, than mere description. He added to it the charm of a personality, and when that personality was enforced by a title, when it proclaimed its sorrows as the age's sorrows, endowed itself with an air of symbolism and set itself up as a kind of scapegoat for the nation's sins, its triumph was complete.

Most men have from time to time to resist the temptation to pose to themselves; many do not even resist it. For all those who chose to believe themselves blighted by pessimism, and for all the others who would have loved to believe it, Byron and his poetry came as an echo of themselves. Shallow called to shallow. Men found in him, as their sons found more reputably in Tennyson, a picture of what they conceived to be the state of their own minds.

But he was not altogether a man of pretence. He really and passionately loved freedom; no one can question his sincerity in that. He could be a fine and scathing satirist; and though he was careless, he had great poetic gifts.

(3)

THE PROSE WRITERS OF THE ROMANTIC MOVEMENT

The age of the Romantic Revival was one of poetry rather than of prose; it was in poetry that the best minds of the time found their means of expression. But it produced prose of rare quality too, and there is delightful reading in the works of its essayists and occasional writers. In its form the periodical essay had changed little since it was first made popular by Addison and Steele. It remained, primarily, a vehicle for the expression of a personality, and it continued to seek the interests of its readers by creating or suggesting an individuality strong enough to carry off any desultory adventure by the mere force of its own attractiveness.

Yet there is all the difference in the world between Hazlitt and Addison, or Lamb and Steele. The *Tatler* and the *Spectator* leave you with a sense of artifice; Hazlitt and Lamb leave you with a grip of a real personality—in the one case very vigorous and combative, in the other set about with a rare plaintiveness and gentleness, but in both absolutely sincere. Addison is gay and witty and delightful but he only plays at being human; Lamb's essays—the translation into print of a heap of idiosyncrasies and oddities, and likes and dislikes, and strange humours—come straight and lovably from a human soul.

The prose writers of the romantic movement brought back two things into writing which had been out of it since the seventeenth century. They brought back egotism and they brought back enthusiasm. They had the confidence that their own tastes and experiences were enough to interest their readers; they mastered the gift of putting themselves on paper. But there is one wide difference between them and their predecessors.

Robert Burton was an egotist but he was an unconscious one; the same is, perhaps, true though much less certainly of Sir Thomas Browne. In Lamb and Hazlitt and De Quincey egotism was deliberate, consciously assumed, the result of a compelling and shaping art. If one reads Lamb's earlier essays and prose pieces one can see the process at work—watch him consciously imitating Fuller, or Burton, or Browne, mirroring their idiosyncrasies, making their quaintnesses and graces his own. By the time he came to write the *Essays of Elia,* he had mastered the personal style so completely that his essays seem simply the overflow of talk. They are so desultory; they move from one subject to another so waywardly—such an essay as a*Chapter on Ears,* for instance, passing with the easy inconsequence of conversation from anatomy through organ music to beer—when they quote, as they do constantly, it is incorrectly, as in the random reminiscences of talk. Here one would say is the cream risen to the surface of a full mind and skimmed at one taking.

How far all this is from the truth we know—know, too, how for months he polished and rewrote these magazine articles, rubbing away roughnesses and corners, taking off the traces of logical sequences and argument, till in the finished work of art he mimicked inconsequence so perfectly that his friends might have been deceived.

And the personality he put on paper was partly an artistic creation, too. In life Lamb was a nervous, easily excitable and emotional man; his years were worn with the memory of a great tragedy and the constantly impending fear of a repetition of it.

One must assume him in his way to have been a good man of business—he was a clerk in the India House, then a throbbing centre of trade, and the largest commercial concern in England, and when he retired his employers gave him a very handsome pension. In the early portrait by Hazlitt there is a dark and gleaming look of fire and decision. But you would never guess it from his books.

There he is the gentle recluse, dreaming over old books, old furniture, old prints, old plays and play-bills; living always in the past, loving in the town secluded byways like the Temple, or the libraries of Oxford Colleges, and in the country quiet and shaded lanes, none of the age's enthusiasm for mountains in his soul. When he turned critic it was not to discern and praise the power and beauty in the works of his contemporaries but to rediscover and interpret the Elizabethan and Jacobean romantic plays.

This quality of egotism Lamb shares with other writers of the time, with De Quincey, for instance, who left buried in work which is extensive and unequal, much that lives by virtue of the singular elaborateness and loftiness of the style which he could on occasion command. For the revival of enthusiasm one must turn to Hazlitt, who brought his passionate and combative disposition to the service of criticism, and produced a series of studies remarkable for their earnestness and their vigour, and for the essential justness which they display despite the prejudice on which each of them was confessedly based.

4

Essayists and Poets in Romantic Period Literature

The Romantic movement, which originated in Germany but quickly spread to England, France, and beyond, reached America around the year 1820, some 20 years after William Wordsworth and Samuel Taylor Coleridge had revolutionized English poetry by publishing *Lyrical Ballads*. In America as in Europe, fresh new vision electrified artistic and intellectual circles. Yet there was an important difference: Romanticism in America coincided with the period of national expansion and the discovery of a distinctive American voice. The solidification of a national identity and the surging idealism and passion of Romanticism nurtured the masterpieces of "the American Renaissance. "

Romantic ideas centered around art as inspiration, the spiritual and aesthetic dimension of nature, and metaphors of organic growth. Art, rather than science, Romantics argued, could best express universal truth. The Romantics underscored the importance of expressive art for the individual and society. In his essay "The Poet" (1844), Ralph Waldo Emerson, perhaps the most influential writer of the Romantic era, asserts:

For all men live by truth, and stand in need of expression. In love, in art, in avarice, in politics, in labour, in games, we study to utter our painful secret. The man is only half himself, the other half is his expression.

The development of the self became a major theme; self-awareness a primary method. If, according to Romantic theory, self and nature were one, self-awareness was not a selfish dead end but a mode of knowledge opening up the universe. If one's self were one with all humanity, then the individual had a moral duty to reform social inequalities and relieve human suffering. The idea of "self" — which suggested selfishness to earlier generations — was redefined. New compound words with positive meanings emerged: "self-realization," "self-expression," "self-reliance. " As the unique, subjective self became important, so did the realm of psychology. Exceptional artistic effects and techniques were developed to evoke heightened psychological states. The "sublime" — an effect of beauty in grandeur (for example, a view from a mountaintop) — produced feelings of awe, reverence, vastness, and a power beyond human comprehension.

Romanticism was affirmative and appropriate for most American poets and creative essayists. America's vast mountains, deserts, and tropics embodied the sublime. The Romantic spirit seemed particularly suited to American democracy: It stressed individualism, affirmed the value of the common person, and looked to the inspired imagination for its aesthetic and ethical values. Certainly the New England Transcendentalists — Ralph Waldo Emerson, Henry David Thoreau, and their associates — were inspired to a new optimistic affirmation by the Romantic movement. In New England, Romanticism fell upon fertile soil.

TRANSCENDENTALISM MOVEMENT IN 18TH CENTURY

The Transcendentalist movement was a reaction against 18th century rationalism and a manifestation of the general humanitarian trend of 19th century thought. The movement was based on a fundamental belief in the unity of the world and God. The soul of each individual was thought to be identical with the world — a microcosm of the world itself. The doctrine of self-reliance and individualism developed through the belief in the identification of the individual soul with God.

Transcendentalism was intimately connected with Concord, a small New England village 32 kilometers west of Boston. Concord was the first inland settlement of the original Massachusetts Bay Colony. Surrounded by forest, it was and remains a peaceful town close enough to Boston's lectures, bookstores, and colleges to be intensely cultivated, but far enough away to be serene. Concord was the site of the first battle of the American Revolution, and Ralph Waldo Emerson's poem commemorating the battle, "Concord Hymn," has one of the most famous opening stanzas in American literature:

By the rude bridge that arched the flood
Their flag to April's breeze unfurled,
Here once the embattled farmers stood
And fired the shot heard round the world.

Concord was the first rural artist's colony, and the first place to offer a spiritual and cultural alternative to American materialism. It was a place of high-minded conversation and simple living (Emerson and Henry David Thoreau both had vegetable gardens). Emerson, who moved to Concord in 1834, and Thoreau are most closely associated with the town, but the locale also attracted the novelist Nathaniel Hawthorne, the feminist writer Margaret Fuller, the educator (and father of novelist Louisa May Alcott) Bronson Alcott, and the poet William Ellery Channing. The Transcendental Club was loosely organized in 1836 and included, at various times, Emerson, Thoreau, Fuller, Channing, Bronson Alcott, Orestes Brownson (a leading minister), Theodore Parker (abolitionist and minister), and others.

The Transcendentalists published a quarterly magazine, *The Dial,* which lasted four years and was first edited by Margaret Fuller and later by Emerson. Reform efforts engaged them as well as literature. A number of Transcendentalists were abolitionists, and some were involved in experimental utopian communities such as nearby Brook Farm (described in Hawthorne's *The Blithedale Romance*) and Fruitlands.

Unlike many European groups, the Transcendentalists never issued a manifesto. They insisted on individual differences— on the unique viewpoint of the individual. American Transcendental Romantics pushed radical individualism to the extreme. American writers often saw themselves as lonely explorers outside society and convention. The American hero— like Herman Melville's Captain Ahab, or Mark Twain's Huck Finn, or Edgar Allan Poe's Arthur Gordon Pym — typically faced risk, or even certain destruction, in the pursuit of metaphysical self-discovery. For the Romantic American writer, nothing was a given. Literary and social conventions, far from being helpful, were dangerous. There was tremendous pressure to discover an authentic literary form, content, and voice — all at the same time. It is clear from the many masterpieces produced in the three decades before the U. S. Civil War (1861) that American writers rose to the challenge.

Ralph Waldo Emerson (1803-1882)

Ralph Waldo Emerson, the towering figure of his era, had a religious sense of mission. Although many accused him of subverting Christianity, he explained that, for him "to be a good minister, it was necessary to leave the church. " The address he delivered in 1838 at his alma mater, the Harvard Divinity School, made him unwelcome at Harvard for 30 years. In it, Emerson accused the church of acting "as if God were dead" and of emphasizing dogma while stifling the spirit.

Emerson's philosophy has been called contradictory, and it is true that he consciously avoided building a logical intellectual system because such a rational system would have negated his Romantic belief in intuition and flexibility. In his essay "Self-Reliance," Emerson remarks: "A foolish consistency is the hobgoblin of little minds. " Yet he is remarkably consistent in his call for the birth of American individualism inspired by nature. Most of his major ideas — the need for a new national vision, the use of personal experience, the notion of the cosmic Over-Soul, and the doctrine of compensation — are suggested in his first publication, *Nature* (1836). This essay opens:

Our age is retrospective. It builds the sepulchres of the fathers. It writes biographies, histories, criticism. The foregoing generations beheld God and nature face to face; we, through their eyes. Why should not we also enjoy an original relation to the universe? Why should not we have a poetry of insight and not of tradition, and a religion by revelation to us, and not the history of theirs. Embosomed for a season in nature, whose floods of life stream around and through us, and invite us by the powers they supply, to action proportioned to nature, why should we grope among the dry bones of the past... ? The sun shines today also. There is more wool and flax in the fields. There are new lands, new men, new thoughts. Let us demand our own works and laws and worship. Emerson loved the aphoristic genius of the 16th-century French essayist Montaigne, and he once told Bronson Alcott that he wanted to write a book like Montaigne's, "full of fun, poetry, business, divinity, philosophy, anecdotes, smut. " He complained that Alcott's abstract style omitted "the light that shines on a man's hat, in a child's spoon. "

Spiritual vision and practical, aphoristic expression make Emerson exhilarating; one of the Concord Transcendentalists aptly compared listening to him with "going to heaven in a swing. " Much of his spiritual insight comes from his readings in Eastern religion, especially Hinduism, Confucianism, and Islamic Sufism. For example, his poem "Brahma" relies on Hindu sources to assert a cosmic order beyond the limited perception of mortals:

If the red slayer think he slay
Or the slain think he is slain,
They know not well the subtle ways
I keep, and pass, and turn again.
Far or forgot to me is near
Shadow and sunlight are the same;
The vanished gods to me appear;
And one to me are shame and fame.
They reckon ill who leave me out;
When me they fly, I am the wings;

I am the doubter and the doubt,
And I the hymn the Brahmin sings
The strong gods pine for my abode,
And pine in vain the sacred Seven,
But thou, meek lover of the good!
Find me, and turn thy back on heaven.

This poem, published in the first number of the *Atlantic Monthly* magazine (1857), confused readers unfamiliar with Brahma, the highest Hindu god, the eternal and infinite soul of the universe. Emerson had this advice for his readers: "Tell them to say Jehovah instead of Brahma."

The British critic Matthew Arnold said the most important writings in English in the 19th century had been Wordsworth's poems and Emerson's essays. A great prose-poet, Emerson influenced a long line of American poets, including Walt Whitman, Emily Dickinson, Edwin Arlington Robinson, Wallace Stevens, Hart Crane, and Robert Frost. He is also credited with influencing the philosophies of John Dewey, George Santayana, Friedrich Nietzsche, and William James.

Henry David Thoreau (1817-1862)

Henry David Thoreau, of French and Scottish descent, was born in Concord and made it his permanent home. From a poor family, like Emerson, he worked his way through Harvard. Throughout his life, he reduced his needs to the simplest level and managed to live on very little money, thus maintaining his independence. In essence, he made living his career. A nonconformist, he attempted to live his life at all times according to his rigorous principles. This attempt was the subject of many of his writings.

Thoreau's masterpiece, *Walden*, or Life in the Woods (1854), is the result of two years, two months, and two days (from 1845 to 1847) he spent living in a cabin he built at Walden Pond on property owned by Emerson. In *Walden*, Thoreau consciously shapes this time into one year, and the book is carefully constructed so the seasons are subtly evoked in order. The book also is organized so that the simplest earthly concerns come first (in the section called "Economy," he describes the expenses of building a cabin); by the ending, the book has progressed to meditations on the stars.

In *Walden*, Thoreau, a lover of travel books and the author of several, gives us an anti-travel book that paradoxically opens the inner frontier of self-discovery as no American book had up to this time. As deceptively modest as Thoreau's ascetic life, it is no less than a guide to living the classical ideal of the good life. Both poetry and philosophy, this long poetic essay challenges the reader to examine his or her life and live it authentically. The building of the cabin, described in great detail, is a concrete metaphor for the careful building of a soul. In his journal for January 30, 1852, Thoreau explains his preference for living rooted in one place: "I am afraid to travel much or to famous places, lest it might completely dissipate the mind." Thoreau's method of retreat and concentration resembles Asian meditation techniques. The resemblance is not accidental: like Emerson and Whitman, he was influenced by Hindu and Buddhist philosophy. His most treasured possession was his library of Asian classics, which he shared with Emerson. His eclectic style draws on Greek and Latin classics and is crystalline, punning, and as richly metaphorical as the English metaphysical writers of the late Renaissance.

In *Walden,* Thoreau not only tests the theories of Transcendentalism, he re-enacts the collective American experience of the 19th century: living on the frontier. Thoreau felt that his contribution would be to renew a sense of the wilderness in language. His journal has an undated entry from 1851: English literature from the days of the minstrels to the Lake Poets, Chaucer and Spenser and Shakespeare and Milton included, breathes no quite fresh and in this sense, wild strain. It is an essentially tame and civilized literature, reflecting Greece and Rome. Her wilderness is a greenwood, her wildman a Robin Hood. There is plenty of genial love of nature in her poets, but not so much of nature herself. Her chronicles inform us when her wild animals, but not the wildman in her, became extinct. There was need of America.

Walden inspired William Butler Yeats, a passionate Irish nationalist, to write "The Lake Isle of Innisfree," while Thoreau's essay "Civil Disobedience," with its theory of passive resistance based on the moral necessity for the just individual to disobey unjust laws, was an inspiration for Mahatma Gandhi's Indian independence movement and Martin Luther King's struggle for black Americans' civil rights in the 20th century.

Thoreau is the most attractive of the Transcendentalists today because of his ecological consciousness, do-it-yourself independence, ethical commitment to abolitionism, and political theory of civil disobedience and peaceful resistance. His ideas are still fresh, and his incisive poetic style and habit of close observation are still modern.

Walt Whitman (1819-1892)

Born on Long Island, New York, Walt Whitman was a part-time carpenter and man of the people, whose brilliant, innovative work expressed the country's democratic spirit. Whitman was largely self-taught; he left school at the age of 11 to go to work, missing the sort of traditional education that made most American authors respectful imitators of the English. *His Leaves of Grass* (1855), which he rewrote and revised throughout his life, contains "Song of Myself," the most stunningly original poem ever written by an American. The enthusiastic praise that Emerson and a few others heaped on this daring volume confirmed Whitman in his poetic vocation, although the book was not a popular success.

A visionary book celebrating all creation, *Leaves of Grass* was inspired largely by Emerson's writings, especially his essay "The Poet," which predicted a robust, open-hearted, universal kind of poet uncannily like Whitman himself. The poem's innovative, unharmed, free-verse form, open celebration of sexuality, vibrant democratic sensibility, and extreme Romantic assertion that the poet's self was one with the poem, the universe, and the reader permanently altered the course of American poetry.

Leaves of Grass is as vast, energetic, and natural as the American continent; it was the epic generations of American critics had been calling for, although they did not recognize it. Movement ripples through "Song of Myself" like restless music:

My ties and ballasts leave me...
I skirt sierras, my palms cover continents
I am afoot with my vision.

The poem bulges with myriad concrete sights and sounds. Whitman's birds are not the conventional "winged spirits" of poetry. His "yellow-crowned heron comes to the edge of the marsh at night and feeds upon small crabs. " Whitman seems to project himself into everything that he sees or imagines. He is mass man, "Voyaging to every port to dicker and adventure,/Hurrying with the modern crowd as eager and fickle as any. " But he is equally the suffering individual, "The mother of old, condemned for a witch, burnt with dry wood, her children gazing on.... I am the hounded slave, I wince at the bite of the dogs.... I am the mashed fireman with breast-bone broken...."

More than any other writer, Whitman invented the myth of democratic America. "The Americans of all nations at any time upon the earth have probably the fullest poetical nature. The United States is essentially the greatest poem. " When Whitman wrote this, he daringly turned upside down the general opinion that America was too brash and new to be poetic. He invented a timeless America of the free imagination, peopled with pioneering spirits of all nations. D. H. Lawrence, the British novelist and poet, accurately called him the poet of the "open road. "

Whitman's greatness is visible in many of his poems, among them "Crossing Brooklyn Ferry," "Out of the Cradle Endlessly Rocking," and "When Lilacs Last in the Dooryard Bloom'd," a moving elegy on the death of Abraham Lincoln. Another important work is his long essay "Democratic Vistas" (1871), written during the unrestrained materialism of industrialism's "Gilded Age. " In this essay, Whitman justly criticizes America for its "mighty, many-threaded wealth and industry" that mask an underlying "dry and flat Sahara" of soul. He calls for a new kind of literature to revive the American population ("Not the book needs so much to be the complete thing, but the reader of the book does"). Yet ultimately, Whitman's main claim to immortality lies in "Song of Myself. " Here he places the Romantic self at the centre of the consciousness of the poem:

I celebrate myself, and sing myself,
And what I assume you shall assume,
For every atom belonging to me as good belongs to you.

Whitman's voice electrifies even modern readers with his proclamation of the unity and vital force of all creation. He was enormously innovative. From him spring the poem as autobiography, the American Everyman as bard, the reader as creator, and the still-contemporary discovery of "experimental," or organic, form.

TWO REFORMERS

New England sparkled with intellectual energy in the years before the Civil War. Some of the stars that shine more brightly today than the famous constellation of Brahmins were dimmed by poverty or accidents of gender or race in their own time. Modern readers increasingly value the work of abolitionist John Greenleaf Whittier and feminist and social reformer Margaret Fuller.

John Greenleaf Whittier (1807-1892)

John Greenleaf Whittier, the most active poet of the era, had a background very similar to Walt Whitman's. He was born and raised on a modest Quaker farm in Massachusetts, had little formal education, and worked as a journalist. For decades before it became popular, he was an ardent abolitionist. Whittier is respected for anti-slavery poems such as "Ichabod," and his poetry is sometimes viewed as an early example of regional realism. Whittier's sharp images, simple constructions, and ballad-like tetrameter couplets have the simple earthy texture of Robert Burns. His best work, the long poem "Snow

Bound," vividly recreates the poet's deceased family members and friends as he remembers them from childhood, huddled cozily around the blazing hearth during one of New England's blustering snowstorms. This simple, religious, intensely personal poem, coming after the long nightmare of the Civil War, is an elegy for the dead and a healing hymn. It affirms the eternity of the spirit, the timeless power of love in the memory, and the undiminished beauty of nature, despite violent outer political storms.

Margaret Fuller (1810-1850)

Margaret Fuller, an outstanding essayist, was born and raised in Cambridge, Massachusetts. From a modest financial background, she was educated at home by her father (women were not allowed to attend Harvard) and became a child prodigy in the classics and modern literatures. Her special passion was German Romantic literature, especially Goethe, whom she translated.

The first professional woman journalist of note in America, Fuller wrote influential book reviews and reports on social issues such as the treatment of women prisoners and the insane. Some of these essays were published in her book *Papers on Literature and Art* (1846). A year earlier, she had her most significant book, *Woman in the Nineteenth Century*. It originally had appeared in the Transcendentalist magazine, *The Dial,* which she edited from 1840 to 1842.

Fuller's *Woman in the Nineteenth Century* is the earliest and most American exploration of women's role in society. Often applying democratic and Transcendental principles, Fuller thoughtfully analyses the numerous subtle causes and evil consequences of sexual discrimination and suggests positive steps to be taken. Many of her ideas are strikingly modern. She stresses the importance of "self-dependence," which women lack because "they are taught to learn their rule from without, not to unfold it from within." Fuller is finally not a feminist so much as an activist and reformer dedicated to the cause of creative human freedom and dignity for all: ... Let us be wise and not impede the soul.... Let us have one creative energy.... Let it take what form it will, and let us not bind it by the past to man or woman, black or white.

Emily Dickinson (1830-1886)

Emily Dickinson is, in a sense, a link between her era and the literary sensitivities of the turn of the century. A radical individualist, she was born and spent her life in Amherst, Massachusetts, a small Calvinist village. She never married, and she led an unconventional life that was outwardly uneventful but was full of inner intensity. She loved nature and found deep inspiration in the birds, animals, plants, and changing seasons of the New England countryside.

Dickinson spent the latter part of her life as a recluse, due to an extremely sensitive psyche and possibly to make time for writing (for stretches of time she wrote about one poem a day). Her day also included homemaking for her attorney father, a prominent figure in Amherst who became a member of Congress.

Dickinson was not widely read, but knew the Bible, the works of William Shakespeare, and works of classical mythology in great depth. These were her true teachers, for Dickinson was certainly the most solitary literary figure of her time. That this shy, withdrawn, village woman, almost unpublished and unknown, created some of the greatest American poetry of the 19th century has fascinated the public since the 1950s, when her poetry was rediscovered.

Dickinson's terse, frequently imagistic style is even more modern and innovative than Whitman's. She never uses two words when one will do, and combines concrete things with abstract ideas in an almost proverbial, compressed style. Her best poems have no fat; many mock current sentimentality, and some are even heretical. She sometimes shows a terrifying existential awareness. Like Poe, she explores the dark and hidden part of the mind, dramatizing death and the grave. Yet she also celebrated simple objects — a flower, a bee. Her poetry exhibits great intelligence and often evokes the agonizing paradox of the limits of the human consciousness trapped in time. She had an excellent sense of humour, and her range of subjects and treatment is amazingly wide. Her poems are generally known by the numbers assigned them in Thomas H. Johnson's standard edition of 1955. They bristle with odd capitalizations and dashes.

A nonconformist, like Thoreau she often reversed meanings of words and phrases and used paradox to great effect. From 435:

Much Madness is divinest sense —

To a discerning Eye —

Much Sense — the starkest Madness —

'Tis the Majority

In this, as All, prevail —

Assent — and you are sane —

Demur — you're straightway dangerous

And handled with a chain —

Her wit shines in the following poem (288), which ridicules ambition and public life:

I'm Nobody! Who are you?
Are you — Nobody — Too?
Then there's a pair of us?
Don't tell! they'd advertise — you know!
How dreary — to be — Somebody!
How public — like a Frog —
To tell one's name — the livelong
June —
To an admiring Bog!

Dickinson's 1,775 poems continue to intrigue critics, who often disagree about them. Some stress her mystical side, some her sensitivity to nature; many note her odd, exotic appeal. One modern critic, R. P. Blackmur, comments that Dickinson's poetry sometimes feels as if "a cat came at us speaking English. " Her clean, clear, chiseled poems are some of the most fascinating and challenging in American literature.

THE BRAHMIN POETS

In their time, the Boston Brahmins (as the patrician, Harvard-educated class came to be called) supplied the most respected and genuinely cultivated literary arbiters of the United States. Their lives fitted a pleasant pattern of wealth and leisure directed by the strong New England work ethic and respect for learning.

In an earlier Puritan age, the Boston Brahmins would have been ministers; in the 19th century, they became professors, often at Harvard. Late in life they sometimes became ambassadors or received honorary degrees from European institutions. Most of them travelled or were educated in Europe: They were familiar with the ideas and books of Britain, Germany, and France, and often Italy and Spain. Upper class in background but democratic in sympathy, the Brahmin poets carried their genteel, European-oriented views to every section of the United States, through public lectures at the 3,000 lyceums (centers for public lectures) and in the pages of two influential Boston magazines, the *North American Review* and the *Atlantic Monthly*.

The writings of the Brahmin poets fused American and European traditions and sought to create a continuity of shared Atlantic experience. These scholar-poets attempted to educate and elevate the general populace by introducing a European dimension to American literature. Ironically, their overall effect was conservative. By insisting on European things and forms, they retarded the growth of a distinctive American consciousness. Well-meaning men, their conservative backgrounds blinded them to the daring innovativeness of Thoreau, Whitman (whom they refused to meet socially), and Edgar Allan Poe (whom even Emerson regarded as the "jingle man"). They were pillars of what was called the "genteel tradition" that three generations of American realists had to battle. Partly because of their benign but bland influence, it was almost 100 years before the distinctive American genius of Whitman, Melville, Thoreau, and Poe was generally recognized in the United States.

James Russell Lowell (1819-1891)

James Russell Lowell, who became professor of modern languages at Harvard after Longfellow retired, is the Matthew Arnold of American literature. He began as a poet but gradually lost his poetic ability, ending as a respected critic and educator. As editor of the *Atlantic* and co-editor of the *North American Review*, Lowell exercised enormous influence. Lowell's *A Fable for Critics* (1848) is a funny and apt appraisal of American writers, as in his comment: "There comes Poe, with his raven, like Barnaby Rudge/Three-fifths of him genius and two-fifths sheer fudge. "

Under his wife's influence, Lowell became a liberal reformer, abolitionist, and supporter of women's suffrage and laws ending child labour. His *Biglow Papers, First Series* (1847-48) creates Hosea Biglow, a shrewd but uneducated village poet who argues for reform in dialect poetry. Benjamin Franklin and Phillip Freneau had used intelligent villagers as mouthpieces for social commentary. Lowell writes in the same vein, linking the colonial "character" tradition with the new realism and regionalism based on dialect that flowered in the 1850s and came to fruition in Mark Twain.

Henry Wadsworth Longfellow (1807-1882)

The most important Boston Brahmin poets were Henry Wadsworth Longfellow, Oliver Wendell Holmes, and James Russell Lowell. Longfellow, professor of modern languages at Harvard, was the best-known American poet of his day. He was responsible for the misty, historical, legendary sense of the past that merged American and European traditions. He wrote three long narrative poems popularizing native legends in European meters "Evangeline" (1847), "The Song of Hiawatha" (1855), and "The Courtship of Miles Standish" (1858).

Longfellow also wrote textbooks on modern languages and a travel book entitled *Outre-Mer*, retelling foreign legends and patterned after Washington

Irving's *Sketch Book*. Although conventionality, sentimentality, and facile handling mar the long poems, haunting short lyrics like "The Jewish Cemetery at Newport" (1854), "My Lost Youth" (1855), and "The Tide Rises, The Tide Falls" (1880) continue to give pleasure.

Oliver Wendell Holmes (1809-1894)

Oliver Wendell Holmes, a celebrated physician and professor of anatomy and physiology at Harvard, is the hardest of the three well-known Brahmins to categorize because his work is marked by a refreshing versatility. It encompasses collections of humorous essays (for example, *The Autocrat of the Breakfast-Table*, 1858), novels (*Elsie Venner*, 1861), biographies (*Ralph Waldo Emerson*, 1885), and verse that could be sprightly ("The Deacon's Masterpiece, or, The Wonderful One-Hoss Shay"), philosophical ("The Chambered Nautilus"), or fervently patriotic ("Old Ironsides").

Born in Cambridge, Massachusetts, the suburb of Boston that is home to Harvard, Holmes was the son of a prominent local minister. His mother was a descendant of the poet Anne Bradstreet. In his time, and more so thereafter, he symbolized wit, intelligence, and charm not as a discoverer or a trailblazer, but rather as an exemplary interpreter of everything from society and language to medicine and human nature.

5

The Post Romantic and Victorian Eras Literature

Self-consciousness was the quality that John Stuart Mill identified, in 1838, as "the daemon of the men of genius of our time." Introspection was inevitable in the literature of an immediately Post-Romantic period, and the age itself was as prone to self-analysis as were its individual authors. Hazlitt's essays in The Spirit of the Age were echoed by Mill's articles of the same title in 1831, by Thomas Carlyle's essays Signs of the Times and Characteristics, and by Richard Henry Horne's New Spirit of the Age in 1844.

This persistent scrutiny was the product of an acute sense of change. Britain had emerged from the long war with France as a great power and as the world's predominant economy. Visiting England in 1847, the American writer Ralph Waldo Emerson observed of the English that "the modern world is theirs. They have made and make it day by day."

This new status as the world's first urban and industrialized society was responsible for the extraordinary wealth, vitality, and self-confidence of the period. Abroad these energies expressed themselves in the growth of the British Empire. At home they were accompanied by rapid social change and fierce intellectual controversy.

The juxtaposition of this new industrial wealth with a new kind of urban poverty is only one of the paradoxes that characterize this long and diverse period. In religion the climax of the Evangelical revival coincided with an unprecedentedly severe set of challenges to faith. The idealism and transcendentalism of Romantic thought were challenged by the growing prestige of empirical science and utilitarian moral philosophy, a process that encouraged more-objective modes in literature.

Realism would be one of the great artistic movements of the era. In politics a widespread commitment to economic and personal freedom was, nonetheless, accompanied by a steady growth in the power of the state. The prudery for which the Victorian Age is notorious in fact went hand in hand with an equally violent immoralism, seen, for example, in Algernon Charles Swinburne's poetry or the writings of the Decadents. Most fundamentally of all, the rapid change that many writers interpreted as progress inspired in others a fierce nostalgia. Enthusiastic rediscoveries of ancient Greece, Elizabethan England, and, especially, the Middle Ages by writers, artists, architects, and designers made this age of change simultaneously an age of active and determined historicism.

John Stuart Mill caught this contradictory quality, with characteristic acuteness, in his essays on Jeremy Bentham and Samuel Taylor Coleridge. Every contemporary thinker, he argued, was indebted to these two "seminal minds." Yet Bentham, as the enduring voice of the Enlightenment, and Coleridge, as the chief English example of the Romantic reaction against it, held diametrically opposed views.

A similar sense of sharp controversy is given by Carlyle in Sartor Resartus. An eccentric philosophical fiction in the tradition of Swift and Sterne, the book argues for a new mode of spirituality in an age that Carlyle himself suggests to be one of mechanism. Carlyle's choice of the novel form and the book's humour, generic flexibility, and political engagement point forward to distinctive characteristics of Victorian literature.

CHARLOTTE BRONTE

Life

Her father was Patrick Brontë, an Anglican clergyman. Irish-born, he had changed his name from the more commonplace Brunty. After serving in several parishes, he moved with his wife, Maria Branwell Brontë, and their six small children to Haworth amid the Yorkshire moors in 1820, having been awarded a rectorship there. Soon after, Mrs. Brontë and the two eldest children died, leaving the father to care for the remaining three girls—Charlotte, Emily, and Anne—and a boy, Patrick Branwell. Their upbringing was aided by an aunt, Elizabeth Branwell, who left her native Cornwall and took up residence with the family at Haworth.

In 1824 Charlotte and Emily, together with their elder sisters before their deaths, attended Clergy Daughters' School at Cowan Bridge, near Kirkby Lonsdale, Lancashire. The fees were low, the food unattractive, and the discipline harsh. Charlotte condemned the school long years afterward in Jane

Eyre, under the thin disguise of Lowood; and the principal, the Rev. William Carus Wilson, has been accepted as the counterpart of Mr. Naomi Brocklehurst in the novel.

Charlotte and Emily returned home in June 1825, and for more than five years the Brontë children learned and played there, writing and telling romantic tales for one another and inventing imaginative games played out at home or on the desolate moors.

In 1831 Charlotte was sent to Miss Wooler's school at Roe Head, near Huddersfield, where she stayed a year and made some lasting friendships; her correspondence with one of her friends, Ellen Nussey, continued until her death, and has provided much of the current knowledge of her life. In 1832 she came home to teach her sisters but in 1835 returned to Roe Head as a teacher. She wished to improve her family's position, and this was the only outlet that was offered to her unsatisfied energies. Branwell, moreover, was to start on his career as an artist, and it became necessary to supplement the family resources. The work, with its inevitable restrictions, was uncongenial to Charlotte. She fell into ill health and melancholia and in the summer of 1838 terminated her engagement.

In 1839 Charlotte declined a proposal from the Rev. Henry Nussey, her friend's brother, and some months later one from another young clergyman. At the same time Charlotte's ambition to make the practical best of her talents and the need to pay Branwell's debts urged her to spend some months as governess with the Whites at Upperwood House, Rawdon. Branwell's talents for writing and painting, his good classical scholarship, and his social charm had engendered high hopes for him; but he was fundamentally unstable, weak willed, and intemperate. He went from job to job and took refuge in alcohol and opium.

Meanwhile his sisters had planned to open a school together, which their aunt had agreed to finance, and in February 1842 Charlotte and Emily went to Brussels as pupils to improve their qualifications in French and acquire some German. The talent displayed by both brought them to the notice of Constantin Héger, a fine teacher and a man of unusual perception. After a brief trip home upon the death of her aunt, Charlotte returned to Brussels as a pupil-teacher. She stayed there during 1843 but was lonely and depressed. Her friends had left Brussels, and Madame Héger appears to have become jealous of her.

The nature of Charlotte's attachment to Héger and the degree to which she understood herself have been much discussed. His was the most interesting mind she had yet met, and he had perceived and evoked her latent talents. His strong and eccentric personality appealed both to her sense of humour and to her affections. She offered him an innocent but ardent devotion, but he tried to repress her emotions. The letters she wrote to him after her return may well be called love letters. When, however, he suggested that they were open to misapprehension, she stopped writing and applied herself, in silence, to disciplining her feelings. However they are interpreted, Charlotte's experiences at Brussels were crucial for her development. She received a strict literary training, became aware of the resources of her own nature, and gathered material that served her, in various shapes, for all her novels.

In 1844 Charlotte attempted to start a school that she had long envisaged in the parsonage itself, as her father's failing sight precluded his being left alone. Prospectuses were issued, but no pupils were attracted to distant Haworth.

In the autumn of 1845 Charlotte came across some poems by Emily, and this led to the publication of a joint volume of Poems by Currer, Ellis and Acton Bell, or Charlotte, Emily, and Anne; the pseudonyms were assumed to preserve secrecy and avoid the special treatment that they believed reviewers accorded to women. The book was issued at their own expense. It received few reviews and only two copies were sold. Nevertheless, a way had opened to them, and they were already trying to place the three novels they had written. Charlotte failed to place The Professor: A Tale but had, however, nearly finished Jane Eyre: An Autobiography, begun in August 1846 in Manchester, where she was staying with her father, who had gone there for an eye operation. When Smith, Elder and Company, declining The Professor, declared themselves willing to consider a three-volume novel with more action and excitement in it, she completed and submitted it at once. Jane Eyre was accepted, published less than eight weeks later, and had an immediate success, far greater than that of the books that her sisters published the same year.

The months that followed were tragic ones. Branwell died in September 1848, Emily in December, and Anne in May 1849. Charlotte completed Shirley: A Tale in the empty parsonage, and it appeared in October. In the following years Charlotte went three times to London as the guest of her publisher; there she met the novelist William Makepeace Thackeray and sat for her portrait by George Richmond. She stayed in 1851 with the writer Harriet Martineau and also visited her future biographer, Mrs. Elizabeth Gaskell, in Manchester and entertained her at Haworth. Villette came out in January 1853. Meanwhile, in 1851, she had declined a third offer of marriage, this time from James

Taylor, a member of Smith, Elder and Company. Her father's curate, Arthur Bell Nicholls, an Irishman, was her fourth suitor.

It took some months to win her father's consent, but they were married on June 29, 1854, in Haworth church. They spent their honeymoon in Ireland and then returned to Haworth, where her husband had pledged himself to continue as curate to her father. He did not share his wife's intellectual life, but she was happy to be loved for herself and to take up her duties as his wife. She began another book, Emma, of which some pages remain. Her pregnancy, however, was accompanied by exhausting sickness, and she died in 1855.

Jane Eyre and other Novels

Charlotte's first novel, The Professor, shows her sobre reaction from the indulgences of her girlhood. Told in the first person by an English tutor in Brussels, it is based on Charlotte's experiences there, with a reversal of sexes and roles. The necessity of her genius, reinforced by reading her sister Emily's Wuthering Heights, modified this restrictive self-discipline; and, though there is plenty of satire and dry, direct phrasing in Jane Eyre, its success was the fiery conviction with which it presented a thinking, feeling woman, craving for love but able to renounce it at the call of impassioned self-respect and moral conviction.

The book's narrator and main character, Jane Eyre, is an orphan and is governess to the ward of Mr. Rochester, the Byronic and enigmatic employer with whom she falls in love. Her love is reciprocated, but on the wedding morning it comes out that Rochester is already married and keeps his mad and depraved wife in the attics of his mansion. Jane leaves him, suffers hardship, and finds work as a village schoolmistress. When Jane learns, however, that Rochester has been maimed and blinded while trying vainly to rescue his wife from the burning house that she herself had set afire, Jane seeks him out and marries him. There are melodramatic naïvetés in the story, and Charlotte's elevated rhetorical passages do not much appeal to modern taste, but she maintains her hold on the reader. The novel is subtitled An Autobiography and is written in the first person; but, except in Jane Eyre's impressions of Lowood, the autobiography is not Charlotte's. Personal experience is fused with suggestions from widely different sources, and the Cinderella theme may well come from Samuel Richardson's Pamela. The action is carefully motivated, and apparently episodic sections, like the return to Gateshead Hall, are seen to be necessary to the full expression of Jane's character and the working out of the threefold moral theme of love, independence, and forgiveness. In her novel Shirley, Charlotte avoided melodrama and coincidences and widened her scope. Setting aside Maria Edgworth and Sir Walter Scott as national novelists, Shirley is the first regional novel in English, full of shrewdly depicted local material—Yorkshire characters, church and chapel, the cloth workers and machine breakers of her father's early manhood, and a sturdy but rather embittered feminism.

In Villette she recurred to the Brussels setting and the first-person narrative, disused in Shirley; the characters and incidents are largely variants of the people and life at the Pension Héger. Against this background she set the ardent heart, deprived of its object, contrasted with the woman happily fulfilled in love. The influence of Charlotte's novels was much more immediate than that of Wuthering Heights. Charlotte's combination of romance and satiric realism had been the mode of nearly all the women novelists for a century. Her fruitful innovations were the presentation of a tale through the sensibility of a child or young woman, her lyricism, and the picture of love from a woman's standpoint.

EMILY BRONTE

Life

Her father, Patrick Brontë, an Irishman, held a number of curacies: Hartshead-cum-Clifton, Yorkshire, was the birthplace of his elder daughters, Maria and Elizabeth, and nearby Thornton that of Emily and her siblings Charlotte, Patrick Branwell, and Anne. In 1820 the father became rector of Haworth, remaining there for the rest of his life.

After the death of their mother in 1821, the children were left very much to themselves in the bleak moorland rectory. The children were educated, during their early life, at home, except for a single year that Charlotte and Emily spent at the Clergy Daughters' School at Cowan Bridge in Lancashire. In 1835, when Charlotte secured a teaching position at Miss Wooler's school at Roe Head, Emily accompanied her as a pupil but suffered from homesickness and remained only three months. In 1838 Emily spent six exhausting months as a teacher in Miss Patchett's school at Law Hill, near Halifax, and then resigned.

To keep the family together at home, Charlotte planned to keep a school for girls at Haworth. In February 1842 she and Emily went to Brussels to learn foreign languages and school management at the Pension Héger. Although Emily pined for home and for the wild moorlands, it seems that in Brussels she was better appreciated than Charlotte. Her passionate nature was more easily understood than Charlotte's decorous temperament. In October, however, when her aunt died, Emily returned permanently to Haworth.

In 1845 Charlotte came across some poems by Emily, and this led to the discovery that all three sisters—Charlotte, Emily, and Anne—had written verse. A year later they published jointly a volume of verse, Poems by Currer, Ellis and Acton Bell, the initials of these pseudonyms being those of the sisters; it contained 21 of Emily's poems, and a consensus of later criticism has accepted the fact that Emily's verse alone reveals true poetic genius. The venture cost the sisters about £50 in all, and only two copies were sold.

By midsummer of 1847 Emily's Wuthering Heights and Anne's Agnes Grey had been accepted for joint publication by J. Cautley Newby of London, but publication of the three volumes was delayed until the appearance of their sister Charlotte's Jane Eyre, which was immediately and hugely successful. Wuthering Heights, when published in December 1847, did not fare well; critics were hostile, calling it too savage, too animal-like, and clumsy in construction. Only later did it come to be considered one of the finest novels in the English language.

Soon after the publication of her novel, Emily's health began to fail rapidly. She had been ill for some time, but now her breathing became difficult, and she suffered great pain. She died of tuberculosis in December 1848.

Wuthering Heights

Emily Brontë's work on Wuthering Heights cannot be dated, and she may well have spent a long time on this intense, solidly imagined novel. It is distinguished from other novels of the period by its dramatic and poetic presentation, its abstention from all comment by the author, and its unusual structure. It recounts in the retrospective narrative of an onlooker, which in turn includes shorter narratives, the impact of the waif Heathcliff on the two families of Earnshaw and Linton in a remote Yorkshire district at the end of the 18th century. Embittered by abuse and by the marriage of Cathy Earnshaw—who shares his stormy nature and whom he loves—to the gentle and prosperous Edgar Linton, Heathcliff plans a revenge on both families, extending into the second generation. Cathy's death in childbirth fails to set him free from his love-hate relationship with her, and the obsessive haunting persists until his death; the marriage of the surviving heirs of Earnshaw and Linton restores peace.

Sharing her sisters' dry humour and Charlotte's violent imagination, Emily diverges from them in making no use of the events of her own life and showing no preoccupation with a spinster's state or a governess's position. Working, like them, within a confined scene and with a small group of characters, she constructs an action, based on profound and primitive energies of love and hate, which proceeds logically and economically, making no use of such coincidences as Charlotte relies on, requiring no rich romantic similes or rhetorical patterns, and confining the superb dialogue to what is immediately relevant to the subject. The sombre power of the book and the elements of brutality in the characters affronted some 19th-century opinion. Its supposed masculine quality was adduced to support the claim, based on the memories of her brother Branwell's friends long after his death, that he was author or part author of it. While it is not possible to clear up all the minor puzzles, neither the external nor the internal evidence offered is substantial enough to weigh against Charlotte's plain statement that Emily was the author.

Early Victorian Verse

Tennyson

Despite the growing prestige and proliferation of fiction, this age of the novel was in fact also an age of great poetry. Alfred Tennyson made his mark very early with Poems, Chiefly Lyrical and Poems, publications that led some critics to hail him as the natural successor to Keats and Shelley. A decade later, in Poems, Tennyson combined in two volumes the best of his early work with a second volume of more-recent writing. The collection established him as the outstanding poet of the era.

In his early work Tennyson brought an exquisite lyric gift to late Romantic subject matter. The result is a poetry that, for all its debt to Keats, anticipates the French Symbolists of the 1880s. The death of his friend and supporter Arthur Hallam in 1833, however, left him vulnerable to accusations from less-sympathetic critics that this highly subjective verse was insufficiently engaged with the public issues of the day. The second volume of the Poems of 1842 contains two remarkable responses to this challenge.

One is the dramatic monologue, a form of poetry in which the speaker is a figure other than the poet. Used occasionally by writers since the time of the Greek poet Theocritus, the technique was developed independently by both Tennyson and his great contemporary Robert Browning in the 1830s, and it became the mode by which many of the greatest achievements of Victorian poetry were expressed. The other is the form that Tennyson called the "English

Idyl," in which he combined brilliant vignettes of contemporary landscape with relaxed debate.

In the major poems of his middle period, Tennyson combined the larger scale required by his new ambitions with his original gift for the brief lyric by building long poems out of short ones. In Memoriam is an elegy for Hallam, formed by 133 individual lyrics. Eloquent, vivid, and ample, it is at the same time an acute pathological study of individual grief and the central Victorian statement of the problems posed by the decline of Christian faith. Maud assembles 27 lyric poems into a single dramatic monologue that disturbingly explores the psychology of violence.

Tennyson became poet laureate in 1850 and wrote some apt and memorable poems on patriotic themes. The chief work of his later period, however, was Idylls of the King. An Arthurian epic constructed as a series of idylls, or "little pictures," it offers a sombre vision of an idealistic community in decay, implicitly articulating Tennyson's anxieties about contemporary society.

G.K. Chesterton described Tennyson as "a suburban Virgil." The elegant Virgilian note was the last thing aimed at by Robert Browning. Browning's work was Germanic rather than Italianate, grotesque rather than idyllic, and colloquial rather than refined. The differences between Browning and Tennyson underline the creative diversity of the period.

THOMAS CARLYLE

Early Life

Carlyle was the second son of James Carlyle, the eldest child of his second marriage. James Carlyle was a mason by trade and, later, a small farmer, a man of profound Calvinist convictions whose character and way of life had a profound and lasting influence on his son. Carlyle was equally devoted to his mother as well as to his eight brothers and sisters, and his strong affection for his family never diminished.

After attending the village school at Ecclefechan, Thomas was sent in 1805 to Annan Academy, where he apparently suffered from bullying, and later to the University of Edinburgh, where he read widely but followed no precise line of study. His father had intended him to enter the ministry, but Thomas became increasingly doubtful of his vocation. He had an aptitude for mathematics, and in 1814 he obtained a mathematical teaching post at Annan. In 1816 he went to another school, at Kirkcaldy, where the Scottish preacher and mystic Edward Irving was teaching. He became one of the few men to whom Carlyle gave complete admiration and affection. "But for Irving," Carlyle commented sometime later, "I had never known what communion of man with man means." Their friendship continued even after Irving moved in 1822 to London, where he became famous as a preacher.

The next years were hard for Carlyle. Teaching did not suit him and he abandoned it. In December 1819 he returned to Edinburgh University to study law, and there he spent three miserable years, lonely, unable to feel certain of any meaning in life, and eventually abandoning the idea of entering the ministry. He did a little coaching and journalism, was poor and isolated, and was conscious of intense spiritual struggles. About 1821 he experienced a kind of conversion, which he described some years later in fictionalized account in Sartor Resartus, whose salient feature was that it was negative—hatred of the devil, not love of God, being the dominating idea.

Though it may be doubted whether everything was really experienced as he described it, this violence is certainly characteristic of Carlyle's tortured and defiant spirit. In those lean years he began his serious study of German, which always remained the literature he most admired and enjoyed. For Goethe, especially, he had the greatest reverence, and he published a translation, Wilhelm Meister's Apprenticeship, in 1824. Meanwhile, he led a nomadic life, holding several brief tutorships at Edinburgh, Dunkeld, and elsewhere.

Marriage

On Oct. 17, 1826, Carlyle married Jane Welsh, an intelligent, attractive, and somewhat temperamental daughter of a well-to-do doctor in Haddington. Welsh had been one of Irving's pupils, and she and Carlyle had known one another for five years. The hesitations and financial worries that beset them are recorded in their letters. It is interesting that Carlyle, usually so imperious, often adopted a weak, pleading tone to his future wife during the time of courtship, though this did not prevent him from being a masterful, difficult, and irritable husband; and, in spite of their strong mutual affection, their marriage was full of quarrels and misunderstandings. Those who knew him best believed Carlyle to be impotent.

In the early years of their marriage the Carlyles lived mostly at Craigenputtock, Dumfriesshire, and Carlyle contributed to the Edinburgh Review and worked on Sartor Resartus. Though this book eventually achieved great popular success, he had at first much difficulty in finding a publisher for it. Written with mingled bitterness and humour, it is a fantastic hodgepodge of autobiography and German philosophy. Its main theme is that the intellectual forms in which men's deepest convictions have been cast are dead and that new ones must be found to fit the time but that the intellectual content of this new religious system is elusive. Its author speaks of "embodying the Divine Spirit of religion in a new Mythus, in a new vehicle and vesture," but he never says very clearly what the new vesture is to be.

London

In 1834, after failing to obtain several posts he had desired, Carlyle moved to London with his wife and settled in Cheyne Row. Though he had not earned anything by his writings for more than a year and was fearful of the day when his savings would be exhausted, he refused to compromise but began an ambitious historical work, The French Revolution. The story of how the partially completed manuscript was lent to J.S. Mill and accidentally burned is well known. After the accident Carlyle wrote to Mill in a generous, almost gay, tone, which is truly remarkable when Carlyle's ambition, his complete dependence upon a successful literary career, his poverty, the months of wasted work, and his habitual melancholy and irritability are considered.

The truth seems to be that he could bear grand and terrible trials more easily than petty annoyances. His habitual, frustrated melancholy arose, in part, from the fact that his misfortunes were not serious enough to match his tragic view of life; and he sought relief in intensive historical research, choosing subjects in which divine drama, lacking in his own life, seemed most evident. His book on the French Revolution is perhaps his greatest achievement. After the loss of the manuscript he worked furiously at rewriting it. It was finished early in 1837 and soon won both serious acclaim and popular success, besides bringing him many invitations to lecture, thus solving his financial difficulties.

True to his idea of history as a "Divine Scripture," Carlyle saw the French Revolution as an inevitable judgment upon the folly and selfishness of the monarchy and nobility. This simple idea was backed with an immense mass of well-documented detail and, at times, a memorable skill in sketching character. The following extract is characteristic of the contorted, fiery, and doom-laden prose, which is alternately colloquial, humorous, and grim:... an august Assembly spread its pavilion; curtained by the dark infinite of discords; founded on the wavering bottomless of the Abyss; and keeps continual hubbub. Time is around it, and Eternity, and the Inane; and it does what it can, what is given it to do.

Though many readers were thrilled by the drama of the narrative, it is not surprising that they were puzzled by Carlyle's prophetic harangues and their relevance to the contemporary situation.

In Chartism he appeared as a bitter opponent of conventional economic theory, but the radical-progressive and the reactionary elements were curiously blurred and mingled. With the publication of On Heroes, Hero-Worship, and the Heroic in History his reverence for strength, particularly when combined with the conviction of a God-given mission, began to emerge. He discussed the hero as divinity, as prophet, as poet, as priest, as man of letters, and as king. It is perhaps in his treatment of poets that Carlyle shows to the best advantage. Perverse though he could be, he was never at the mercy of fashion; and he saw much more, particularly in Dante, than others did. Two years later this idea of the hero was elaborated in Past and Present, which strove "to penetrate... into a somewhat remote century... in hope of perhaps illustrating our own poor century thereby." He contrasts the wise and strong rule of a medieval abbot with the muddled softness and chaos of the 19th century, pronouncing in favour of the former, in spite of the fact that he had rejected dogmatic Christianity and had a special aversion to the Roman Catholic Church.

It was natural that Carlyle should turn to Cromwell as the greatest English example of his ideal man and should produce the bulky Oliver Cromwell's Letters and Speeches. With Elucidations in 1845. His next important work was Latter-Day Pamphlets, in which the savage side of his nature was particularly prominent. In the essay on model prisons, for instance, he tried to persuade the public that the most brutal and useless sections of the population were being coddled in the new prisons of the 19th century. Though incapable of lying, Carlyle was completely unreliable as an observer, since he invariably saw what he had decided in advance that he ought to see.

In 1857 he embarked on a massive study of another of his heroes, Frederick the Great, and The History of Friedrich II of Prussia, Called Frederick the Great appeared between 1858 and 1865. Something of his political attitude at this time can be gathered from a letter written in April 1855 to the exiled Russian revolutionary A.I. Herzen, in which he says "I never had, and have now less than ever, the least hope in 'Universal Suffrage' under any of its modifications" and refers to "the sheer Anarchy which is got by 'Parliamentary eloquence,' Free Press, and counting of heads". Unfortunately, Carlyle was never able to respect ordinary men. Here, perhaps, rather than in any historical doubts about the veracity of the gospels, was the core of his quarrel with Christianity—it set too much value on the weak and sinful. His fierceness of spirit was composed of two elements, a serious Calvinistic desire to denounce evil and a habitual nervous ill temper, for which he often reproached himself but which he never managed to defeat.

Last Years

In 1865 he was offered the rectorship of Edinburgh University. The speech that he delivered at his installation in April 1866 was not very remarkable in itself but its tone of high moral exhortation made it an immediate success. It was published in 1866 under the title On the Choice of Books. Soon after his triumph in Edinburgh, Jane Carlyle died suddenly in London. She was buried in Haddington, and an epitaph by her husband was placed in the church. Carlyle never completely recovered from her death. He lived another 15 years, weary, bored, and a partial recluse. A few public causes gained his support: he was active in the defence of Gov. E.J. Eyre of Jamaica, who was dismissed for his severity in putting down a black uprising in 1865. Carlyle commended him for "saving the West Indies and hanging one incendiary mulatto, well worth gallows, if I can judge." He was excited by the Franco-German War, saying "Germany ought to be President of Europe," but such enthusiastic moments soon faded. In these last years he wrote little. His history The Early Kings of Norway: Also an Essay on the Portraits of John Knox came out in 1875, and Reminiscences was published in 1881. Later he edited his wife's letters, which appeared in 1883 under the title Letters and Memorials of Jane Welsh Carlyle, Prepared for Publication by Thomas Carlyle. Although Westminster Abbey was offered for his burial, he was buried, according to his wish, beside his parents at Ecclefechan.

Algernon Charles Swinburne

English poet and critic, outstanding for prosodic innovations and noteworthy as the symbol of mid-Victorian poetic revolt.The characteristic qualities of his verse are insistent alliteration, unflagging rhythmic energy, sheer melodiousness, great variation of pace and stress, effortless expansion of a given theme, and evocative if rather imprecise use of imagery. His poetic style is highly individual and his command of word-colour and word-music striking. Swinburne's technical gifts and capacity for prosodic invention were extraordinary, but too often his poems' remorseless rhythms have a narcotic effect, and he has been accused of paying more attention to the melody of words than to their meaning. Swinburne was pagan in his sympathies and passionately antitheist.

Swinburne's father was an admiral, and his mother was a daughter of the 3rd Earl of Ashburnham. He attended Eton and Balliol College, Oxford, which he left in 1860 without taking a degree. There he met William Morris, Edward Burne-Jones, and Dante Gabriel Rossetti and was attracted to their Pre-Raphaelite Brotherhood. An allowance from his father enabled him to follow a literary career. In 1861 he met Richard Monckton Milnes, who encouraged his writing and fostered his reputation. In the early 1860s Swinburne apparently suffered from an unhappy love affair about which little is known. Literary success came with the verse drama Atalanta in Calydon, in which he attempted to re-create in English the spirit and form of Greek tragedy; his lyric powers are at their finest in this work. Atalanta was followed by the first series of Poems and Ballads in 1866, which clearly display Swinburne's preoccupation with masochism, flagellation, and paganism.

This volume contains some of his finest poems, among them "Dolores" and "The Garden of Proserpine." The book was vigorously attacked for its "feverish carnality" —Punch referred to the poet as "Mr. Swineborn" —though it was enthusiastically welcomed by the younger generation. In 1867 Swinburne met his idol, Giuseppe Mazzini, and the poetry collection Songs Before Sunrise, which is principally concerned with the theme of political liberty, shows the influence of that Italian patriot. The second series of Poems and Ballads, less hectic and sensual than the first, appeared in 1878. During this time Swinburne's health was being undermined by alcoholism and by the excesses resulting from his abnormal temperament and masochistic tendencies; he experienced periodic fits of intense nervous excitement, from which, however, his remarkable powers of recuperation long enabled him to recover quickly.

In 1879 he collapsed completely and was rescued and restored to health by his friend Theodore Watts-Dunton. The last 30 years of his life were spent at The Pines, Putney, under the guardianship of Watts-Dunton, who maintained a strict regimen and encouraged Swinburne to devote himself to writing. Swinburne eventually became a figure of respectability and adopted reactionary views. He published 23 volumes of poetry, prose, and drama during these years, but, apart from the long poem Tristram of Lyonesse and the verse tragedy Marino Faliero, his most important poetry belongs to the first half of his life.

Swinburne was also an important and prolific English literary critic of the later 19th century. Among his best critical writings are Essays and Studies and his monographs on William Shakespeare, Victor Hugo, and Ben Jonson. His devotion to Shakespeare and his unrivaled knowledge of Elizabethan and Jacobean drama are reflected in his early play Chastelard. The latter work was the first of a trilogy on Mary, queen of Scots, who held a peculiar fascination for him; Bothwell and Mary Stuart followed. He also wrote on William Blake, Percy Bysshe Shelley, and Charles Baudelaire, and his elegy on the latter, Ave Atque Vale, is among his finest works.

ALFRED, LORD TENNYSON

Early Life and Work

Tennyson was the fourth of 12 children, born into an old Lincolnshire family, his father a rector. Alfred, with two of his brothers, Frederick and Charles, was sent in 1815 to Louth grammar school-where he was unhappy. He left in 1820, but, though home conditions were difficult, his father managed to give him a wide literary education. Alfred was precocious, and before his teens he had composed in the styles of Alexander Pope, Sir Walter Scott, and John Milton. To his youth also belongs The Devil and the Lady, which shows an astonishing understanding of Elizabethan dramatic verse. Lord Byron was a dominant influence on the young Tennyson.

At the lonely rectory in Somersby the children were thrown upon their own resources. All writers on Tennyson emphasize the influence of the Lincolnshire countryside on his poetry: the plain, the sea about his home, "the sand-built ridge of heaped hills that mound the sea," and "the waste enormous marsh."

In 1824 the health of Tennyson's father began to break down, and he took refuge in drink. Alfred, though depressed by unhappiness at home, continued to write, collaborating with Frederick and Charles in Poems by Two Brothers. His contributions are mostly in fashionable styles of the day.

In 1827 Alfred and Charles joined Frederick at Trinity College, Cambridge. There Alfred made friends with Arthur Hallam, the gifted son of the historian Henry Hallam. This was the deepest friendship of Tennyson's life. The friends became members of the Apostles, an exclusive undergraduate club of earnest intellectual interests. Tennyson's reputation as a poet increased at Cambridge. In 1829 he won the chancellor's gold medal with a poem called Timbuctoo. In 1830 Poems, Chiefly Lyrical was published; and in the same year Tennyson, Hallam, and other Apostles went to Spain to help in the unsuccessful revolution against Ferdinand VII. In the meantime, Hallam had become attached to Tennyson's sister Emily but was forbidden by her father to correspond with her for a year.

In 1831 Tennyson's father died. Alfred's misery was increased by his grandfather's discovery of his father's debts. He left Cambridge without taking a degree, and his grandfather made financial arrangements for the family. In the same year, Hallam published a eulogistic article on Poems, Chiefly Lyrical in The Englishman's Magazine. He went to Somersby in 1832 as the accepted suitor of Emily.

In 1832 Tennyson published another volume of his poems, including "The Lotos-Eaters," "The Palace of Art," and "The Lady of Shalott." Among them was a satirical epigram on the critic Christopher North, who had attacked Poems, Chiefly Lyrical in Blackwood's Magazine. Tennyson's sally prompted a scathing attack on his new volume in the Quarterly Review. The attacks distressed Tennyson, but he continued to revise his old poems and compose new ones.

In 1833 Hallam's engagement was recognized by his family, but while on a visit to Vienna in September he died suddenly. The shock to Tennyson was severe. It came at a depressing time; three of his brothers, Edward, Charles, and Septimus, were suffering from mental illness, and the bad reception of his own work added to the gloom. Yet it was in this period that he wrote some of his most characteristic work: "The Two Voices", "Ulysses," "St. Simeon Stylites," and, probably, the first draft of "Morte d'Arthur." To this period also belong some of the poems that became constituent parts of In Memoriam, celebrating Hallam's death, and lyrics later worked into Maud.

In May 1836 his brother Charles married Louisa Sellwood of Horncastle, and at the wedding Alfred fell in love with her sister Emily. For some years the lovers corresponded, but Emily's father disapproved of Tennyson because of his bohemianism, addiction to port and tobacco, and liberal religious views; and in 1840 he forbade the correspondence. Meanwhile the Tennysons had left Somersby and were living a rather wandering life nearer London. It was in this period that Tennyson made friends with many famous men, including the politician William Ewart Gladstone, the historian Thomas Carlyle, and the poet Walter Savage Landor.

Assessment

Alfred, Lord Tennyson was the leading poet of the Victorian Age in England and by the mid-19th century had come to occupy a position similar to that of Alexander Pope in the 18th. Tennyson was a consummate poetic artist, consolidating and refining the traditions bequeathed to him by his predecessors in the Romantic movement—especially Wordsworth, Byron, and Keats. His poetry is remarkable for its metrical variety, rich descriptive imagery, and exquisite verbal melodies. But Tennyson was also regarded as the preeminent spokesman for the educated middle-class Englishman, in moral and religious outlook and in political and social consciousness no less than in matters of taste and sentiment.

His poetry dealt often with the doubts and difficulties of an age in which established Christian Faith and traditional assumptions about man's nature and destiny were increasingly called into question by science and modern progress. His poetry dealt with these misgivings, moreover, as the intimate personal problems of a sensitive and troubled individual inclined to melancholy. Yet through his poetic mastery—the spaciousness and nobility of his best verse, its classical aptness of phrase, its distinctive harmony—he conveyed to sympathetic readers a feeling of implicit reassurance, even serenity. Tennyson may be seen as the first great English poet to be fully aware of the new picture of man's place in the universe revealed by modern science. While the contemplation of this unprecedented human situation sometimes evoked his fears and forebodings, it also gave him a larger imaginative range than most of the poets of his time and added a greater depth and resonance to his art.

Tennyson's ascendancy among Victorian poets began to be questioned even during his lifetime, however, when Robert Browning and Algernon Charles Swinburne were serious rivals. And 20th-century criticism, influenced by the rise of a new school of poetry headed by T.S. Eliot, has proposed some drastic devaluations of his work. Undoubtedly much in Tennyson that appealed to his contemporaries has ceased to appeal to many readers today. He can be mawkish and banal, pompous and orotund, offering little more than the mellifluous versifying of shallow or confused thoughts.

The rediscovery of such earlier poets as John Donne or Gerard Manley Hopkins, together with the widespread acceptance of Eliot and W.B. Yeats as the leading modern poets, opened the ears of readers to a very different, and perhaps more varied, poetic music. A more balanced estimate of Tennyson has begun to prevail, however, with the recognition of the enduring greatness of "Ulysses," the unique poignancy of Tennyson's best lyric poems, and, above all, the stature of In Memoriam as the great representative poem of the Victorian Age. It is now also recognized that the realistic and comic aspects of Tennyson's work are more important than they were thought to be during the period of the reaction against him. Finally, the perception of the poet's awed sense of the mystery of life, which lies at the heart of his greatness, as in "Crossing the Bar" or "Flower in the Crannied Wall," unites his admirers in this century with those in the last. Though less of Tennyson's work may survive than appeared likely during his Victorian heyday, what does remain—and it is by no means small in quantity—seems likely to be imperishable.

Arthur Hallam

Hallam was the son of the English historian Henry Hallam. He met Tennyson at Trinity College, Cambridge, where they joined other artistically and politically progressive students in the club called The Apostles. Hallam defended Tennyson's early work, Poems, Chiefly Lyrical, in a review for the Englishman's Magazine and was engaged to Tennyson's sister Emily. Hallam's prizewinning essays and critically acclaimed poems were collected and printed posthumously by his father, the historian Henry Hallam, in Remains, in Verse and Prose, of Arthur Henry Hallam.

Robert Browning and Elizabeth Barrett Browning

Deeply influenced by Shelley, Robert Browning made two false starts. One was as a playwright in the 1830s and '40s. The other was as the late-Romantic poet of the confessional meditation Pauline and the difficult though innovatory narrative poem Sordello.

Browning found his individual and distinctively modern voice in 1842, with the volume Dramatic Lyrics. As the title suggests, it was a collection of dramatic monologues, among them Porphyria's Lover, Johannes Agricola in Meditation, and My Last Duchess. The monologues make clear the radical originality of Browning's new manner: they involve the reader in sympathetic identification with the interior processes of criminal or unconventional minds, requiring active rather than merely passive engagement in the processes of moral judgment and self-discovery. More such monologues and some equally striking lyrics make up Men and Women.

In 1846 Browning married Elizabeth Barrett. Though now remembered chiefly for her love poems Sonnets from the Portuguese and her experiment with the verse novel Aurora Leigh, she was in her own lifetime far better known than her husband. Her Poems established her as a leading poet of the age. Casa Guidi Windows is a subtle reflection on her experience of Italian politics, and A Musical Instrument is one of the century's most memorable expressions of the difficulty of the poet's role. Only with the publication of Dramatis Personae did Robert Browning achieve the sort of fame that Tennyson had enjoyed for more than 20 years. The volume contains, in Rabbi Ben Ezra, the most extreme statement of Browning's celebrated optimism. Hand in hand with this reassuring creed, however, go the skeptical intelligence and the sense of the grotesque displayed in such poems as Caliban upon Setebos and Mr. Sludge, 'The Medium.'

His The Ring and the Book gives the dramatic monologue format unprecedented scope. Published in parts, like a Dickens novel, it tells a sordid murder story in a way that both explores moral issues and suggests the problematic nature of human knowledge. Browning's work after this date, though voluminous, is uneven.

Major Literary Work

In 1842 Tennyson published Poems, in two volumes, one containing a revised selection from the volumes of 1830 and 1832, the other, new poems. The new poems included "Morte d'Arthur," "The Two Voices," "Locksley Hall," and "The Vision of Sin" and other poems that reveal a strange naïveté, such as "The May Queen," "Lady Clara Vere de Vere," and "The Lord of Burleigh." The new volume was not on the whole well received. But the grant to him at this time, by the prime minister, Sir Robert Peel, of a pension of £200 helped to alleviate his financial worries. In 1847 he published his first long poem, The Princess, a singular anti-feminist fantasia.

The year 1850 marked a turning point. Tennyson resumed his correspondence with Emily Sellwood, and their engagement was renewed and followed by marriage. Meanwhile, Edward Moxon offered to publish the elegies on Hallam that Tennyson had been composing over the years. They appeared, at first anonymously, as In Memoriam, which had a great success with both reviewers and the public, won him the friendship of Queen Victoria, and helped bring about, in the same year, his appointment as poet laureate.

In Memoriam is a vast poem of 131 sections of varying length, with a prologue and epilogue. Inspired by the grief Tennyson felt at the untimely death of his friend Hallam, the poem touches on many intellectual issues of the Victorian Age as the author searches for the meaning of life and death and tries to come to terms with his sense of loss.

Most notably, In Memoriam reflects the struggle to reconcile traditional religious faith and belief in immortality with the emerging theories of evolution and modern geology. The verses show the development over three years of the poet's acceptance and understanding of his friend's death and conclude with an epilogue, a happy marriage song on the occasion of the wedding of Tennyson's sister Cecilia.

After his marriage, which was happy, Tennyson's life became more secure and outwardly uneventful. There were two sons: Hallam and Lionel. The times of wandering and unsettlement ended in 1853, when the Tennysons took a house, Farringford, in the Isle of Wight. Tennyson was to spend most of the rest of his life there and at Aldworth.

Tennyson's position as the national poet was confirmed by his Ode on the Death of the Duke of Wellington—though some critics at first thought it disappointing—and the famous poem on the charge of the Light Brigade at Balaklava, published in 1855 in Maud and Other Poems. Maud itself, a strange and turbulent "monodrama," provoked a storm of protest; many of the poet's admirers were shocked by the morbidity, hysteria, and bellicosity of the hero. Yet Maud was Tennyson's favourite among his poems.

A project that Tennyson had long considered at last issued in Idylls of the King, a series of 12 connected poems broadly surveying the legend of King Arthur from his falling in love with Guinevere to the ultimate ruin of his kingdom. The poems concentrate on the introduction of evil to Camelot because of the adulterous love of Lancelot and Queen Guinevere, and on the consequent fading of the hope that had at first infused the Round Table fellowship. Idylls of the King had an immediate success, and Tennyson, who loathed publicity, had now acquired a sometimes embarrassing public fame. The Enoch Arden volume of 1864 perhaps represents the peak of his popularity. New Arthurian Idylls were published in The Holy Grail, and Other Poems in 1869. These were again well received, though some readers were beginning to show discomfort at the "Victorian" moral atmosphere that Tennyson had introduced into his source material from Sir Thomas Malory.

In 1874 Tennyson decided to try his hand at poetic drama. Queen Mary appeared in 1875, and an abridged version was produced at the Lyceum in 1876 with only moderate success. It was followed by Harold, Becket, and the "village tragedy" The Promise of May, which proved a failure at the Globe in November 1882. This play—his only prose work—shows Tennyson's growing despondency and resentment at the religious, moral, and political tendencies of the age. He had already caused some sensation by publishing a poem called "Despair" in The Nineteenth Century. A more positive indication of Tennyson's later beliefs appears in "The Ancient Sage," published in Tiresias and Other Poems. Here the poet records his intimations of a life before and beyond this life.

Tennyson accepted a peerage in 1884. In 1886 he published a new volume containing "Locksley Hall Sixty Years After," consisting mainly of imprecations against modern decadence and liberalism and a retraction of the earlier poem's belief in inevitable human progress. In 1889 Tennyson wrote the famous short poem "Crossing the Bar," during the crossing to the Isle of Wight. In the same year he published Demeter and Other Poems, which contains the charming retrospective "To Mary Boyle," "The Progress of Spring," a fine lyric written much earlier and rediscovered, and "Merlin and the Gleam," an allegorical summing-up of his poetic career. In 1892 his play The Foresters was successfully produced in New York City. Despite ill health, he was able to correct the proofs of his last volume, The Death of Oenone, Akbar's Dream, and Other Poems.

BENJAMIN DISRAELI

Early Life

Disraeli was of Italian-Jewish descent, the eldest son and second child of Isaac D'Israeli and Maria Basevi. The most important event in Disraeli's boyhood was his father's quarrel in 1813 with the synagogue of Bevis Marks, which led to the decision in 1817 to have his children baptized as Christians. Until 1858 Jews by religion were excluded from Parliament; except for the father's decision Disraeli's political career could never have taken the form it did.

Disraeli was educated at small private schools. At the age of 17 he was articled to a firm of solicitors, but he longed to become notable in a more sensational manner. His first efforts were disastrous. In 1824 he speculated recklessly in South American mining shares, and, when he lost all a year later, he was left so badly in debt that he did not recover until well past middle age. Earlier he had persuaded the publisher John Murray, his father's friend, to launch a daily newspaper, the Representative. It was a complete failure. Disraeli, unable to pay his promised share of the capital, quarreled with Murray and others. Moreover, in his novel Vivian Grey, published anonymously, he lampooned Murray while telling the story of the failure. Disraeli was unmasked as the author, and he was widely criticized.

Disraeli suffered what would later be called a nervous breakdown and did little during the next four years. He wrote another extravagant novel, The Young Duke, and in 1830 began 16 months of travel in the Mediterranean countries and the Middle East. These travels not only furnished him with material for Oriental descriptions he used in later novels but also influenced his attitude in foreign relations with India, Egypt, and Turkey in the 1870s.

Back in England, he was active in London social and literary life, where his dandified dress, conceit and affectation, and exotic good looks made him a striking if not always popular figure. He was invited to fashionable parties and met most of the celebrities of the day. His novel Contarini Fleming has considerable autobiographical interest, like many of his novels, as well as echoes of his political thought.

Robert Norman William Blake, Baron Blake

Charles Kingsley

The son of a clergyman, he grew up in Devon, where he developed an interest in nature study and geology. After graduating from Magdalene College,

Cambridge, he was ordained in 1842 as curate of Eversley and two years later became parish priest there. Much influenced by the theologian Frederick Denison Maurice, he became in 1848 a founding member of the Christian Socialist movement, which sought to correct the evils of industrialism through measures based on Christian ethics.

His first novel, Yeast, deals with the relations of the landed gentry to the rural poor. His second, the much superior Alton Locke, is the story of a tailor-poet who rebels against the ignominy of sweated labour and becomes a leader of the Chartist movement. Kingsley advocated adult education, improved sanitation, and the growth of the cooperative movement, rather than political change, for the amelioration of social problems. The strenuous tone of his Broad Church Protestantism is often described as "muscular Christianity." His novels, similarly, are often attributed to the "muscular" school of fiction.

Kingsley soon turned to writing popular historical novels. Hypatia is a luridly erotic story set in early Christian Egypt. Westward Ho! is an imperialist and anti-Roman Catholic adventure set in the Elizabethan period, and Hereward the Wake is about Anglo-Saxon England and the Norman Conquest, also with an anti-Catholic slant. Kingsley's fear of the trend within the church towards Roman Catholicism, growing out of the Oxford Movement, led to a notorious controversy with John Henry Newman. In answer to an attack by Kingsley, Newman wrote his Apologia pro Vita Sua, the history of his religious development.

The didactic children's fantasy The Water-Babies combines Kingsley's concern for sanitary reform with his interest in natural history and the theory of evolution. He was also a very competent poet who wrote some memorable ballads. Kingsley became chaplain to Queen Victoria, professor of modern history at Cambridge, and canon of Westminster. His brother Henry Kingsley was a novelist, and his niece Mary Henrietta Kingsley was a travel writer and adventurer.

The Brontës

In many ways, however, the qualities of Romantic verse could be absorbed, rather than simply superseded, by the Victorian novel. This is suggested clearly by the work of the Brontë sisters. Growing up in a remote but cultivated vicarage in Yorkshire, they, as children, invented the imaginary kingdoms of Angria and Gondal. These inventions supplied the context for many of the poems in their first, and pseudonymous, publication, Poems by Currer, Ellis, and Acton Bell. Their Gothic plots and Byronic passions also informed the novels that began to be published in the following year.

Anne Brontë wrote of the painful reality of disagreeable experience, although both her novels have cheerful romantic endings. Agnes Grey is a stark account of the working life of a governess, and The Tenant of Wildfell Hall paints a grim picture of the heroine's marriage to an abusive husband.

Charlotte Brontë, like her sisters, appears at first sight to have been writing a literal fiction of provincial life. In her first novel, Jane Eyre, for example, the heroine's choice between sexual need and ethical duty belongs very firmly to the mode of moral realism. But her hair's-breadth escape from a bigamous marriage with her employer and the death by fire of his mad first wife derive from the rather different tradition of the Gothic novel. In Shirley Charlotte Brontë strove to be, in her own words, "as unromantic as Monday morning." In Villette the distinctive Gothic elements return to lend this study of the limits of stoicism an unexpected psychological intensity and drama. Emily Brontë united these diverse traditions still more successfully in her only novel, Wuthering Heights. Closely observed regional detail, precisely handled plot, and a sophisticated use of multiple internal narrators are combined with vivid imagery and an extravagantly Gothic theme. The result is a perfectly achieved study of elemental passions and the strongest possible refutation of the assumption that the age of the novel must also be an age of realism.

Anne Brontë

The youngest of six children of Patrick and Marie Brontë, Anne was taught in the family's Haworth home and at Roe Head School. With her sister Emily, she invented the imaginary kingdom of Gondal, about which they wrote verse and prose from the early 1830s until 1845. She took a position as governess briefly in 1839 and then again for four years, 1841–45, with the Robinsons, the family of a clergyman, at Thorpe Green, near York. There her irresponsible brother, Branwell, joined her in 1843, intending to serve as a tutor. Anne returned home in 1845 and was followed shortly by her brother, who had been dismissed, charged with making love to his employer's wife.

In 1846 Anne contributed 21 poems to Poems by Currer, Ellis and Acton Bell, a joint work with her sisters Charlotte and Emily. Her first novel, Agnes Grey, was published together with Emily's Wuthering Heights in three volumes in December 1847. The reception to these volumes, associated in the public mind with the immense popularity of Charlotte's Jane Eyre, led to quick publication of Anne's second novel, The Tenant of Wildfell Hall, published in three volumes in June 1848; it sold well. She fell ill with tuberculosis towards the end of the year and died the following May.

Her novel Agnes Grey, probably begun at Thorpe Green, records with limpidity and some humour the life of a governess. George Moore called it "simple and beautiful as a muslin dress." The Tenant of Wildfell Hall presents an unsoftened picture of the debauchery and degradation of the heroine's first husband and sets against it the Arminian belief, opposed to Calvinist predestination, that no soul shall be ultimately lost. Her outspokenness raised some scandal, and Charlotte deplored the subject as morbid and out of keeping with her sister's nature, but the vigorous writing indicates that Anne found in it not only a moral obligation but also an opportunity of artistic development.

Political Beginnings

By 1831 Disraeli had decided to enter politics and sought a seat in Buckinghamshire, near Wycombe, where his family had settled. As an independent radical, he stood for and lost High Wycombe twice in 1832 and once in 1835. Realizing that he must attach himself to one of the political parties, he made a somewhat eccentric interpretation of Toryism, which some features of his radicalism fitted. In 1835 he unsuccessfully stood for Taunton as the official Conservative candidate. His extravagant behaviour, great debts, and open liaison with Henrietta, wife of Sir Francis Sykes, all gave him a dubious reputation. In 1837, however, he successfully stood for Maidstone in Kent as the Conservative candidate. His maiden speech in the House of Commons was a failure. Elaborate metaphors, affected mannerisms, and foppish dress led to his being shouted down. But he was not silenced. He concluded, defiantly and prophetically, "I will sit down now, but the time will come when you will hear me."

Before long, Disraeli became a speaker who commanded attention. He established his social position by marrying in 1839 Mrs. Wyndham Lewis, a widow with a life interest in a London house and £4,000 a year. She was deeply devoted to Disraeli, and when he teased her in company that he had married for her worldly goods, she would say: "Dizzy married me for my money but if he had the chance again he would marry me for love." Her husband agreed.

Breach with Peel

The Conservative leader, Sir Robert Peel, encouraged Disraeli, but when in 1841 the Conservatives won the election and Peel became prime minister, Disraeli was not given office in the Cabinet. He was mortified at the rebuff, and his attitude towards Peel and his brand of Conservatism became increasingly critical. A group of young Tories, nicknamed Young England, and led by George Smythe, looked to Disraeli for inspiration, and he obliged them, notably in his novel Coningsby; or The New Generation, in which the hero is patterned on Smythe, and the cool, pragmatic, humdrum, middle-class Conservatism that Peel represented is contrasted to Young England's romantic, aristocratic, nostalgic, and escapist attitude.

In 1845, when the combination of the Irish famine and the arguments of Richard Cobden convinced Peel to repeal the protective duties on foreign imported grain known as the Corn Laws, Disraeli found his issue. Young England could rally against Peel not only their own members but the great mass of the country squires who formed the backbone of the Conservative Party.

As lieutenant to Lord George Bentinck, the nominal leader of the rebels, Disraeli consolidated the opposition to Peel in a series of brilliant speeches. His invective greatly embittered the battle and created lasting resentment among Peel's followers. While Disraeli and his fellow protectionists could not stop the repeal of the Corn Laws because the Whigs also backed the bill, the rebels put Peel in the minority on another issue and forced him to resign in 1846.

EARLY VICTORIAN LITERATURE: THE AGE OF THE NOVEL

Several major figures of English Romanticism lived on into this period. Coleridge died in 1834, De Quincey in 1859. Wordsworth succeeded Southey as poet laureate in 1843 and held the post until his own death seven years later. Posthumous publication caused some striking chronological anomalies. Percy Bysshe Shelley's A Defence of Poetry was not published until 1840. Keats's letters appeared in 1848 and Wordsworth's Prelude in 1850. Despite this persistence, critics of the 1830s felt that there had been a break in the English literary tradition, which they identified with the death of Byron in 1824.

The deaths of Austen in 1817 and Scott in 1832 should perhaps have been seen as even more significant, for the new literary era has, with justification, been seen as the age of the novel. More than 60,000 works of prose fiction were published in Victorian Britain by as many as 7,000 novelists. The three-volume format was the standard mode of first publication; it was a form created for sale to and circulation by lending libraries. It was challenged in the 1830s by the advent of serialization in magazines and by the publication of novels in 32-page monthly parts. But only in the 1890s did the three-decker finally yield to the modern single-volume format.

The Victorian Age

(1)

Had it not been that with two exceptions all the poets of the Romantic Revival died early, it might be more difficult to draw a line between their school and that of their successors than it is. As it happened, the only poet who survived and wrote was Wordsworth, the oldest of them all. For long before his death he did nothing that had one touch of the fire and beauty of his earlier work. The respect he began, after a lifetime of neglect, to receive in the years immediately before his death, was paid not to the conservative laureate of 1848, but to the revolutionary in art and politics of fifty years before. He had lived on long after his work was done

"To hear the world applaud the hollow ghost

That blamed the living man."

All the others, Keats, Shelley, Byron were dead before 1830, and the problem which might have confronted us had they lived, of adult work running counter to the tendencies and ideals of youth, does not exist for us. Keats or Shelley might have lived as long as Carlyle, with whom they were almost exactly contemporary; had they done so, the age of the Romantic Revival and the Victorian age would have been united in the lives of authors who were working in both. We should conceive that is, the whole period as one, just as we conceive of the Renaissance in England, from Surrey to Shirley, as one. As it is, we have accustomed ourselves to a strongly marked line of division. A man must be on either one side or the other; Wordsworth, though he wrote on till 1850, is on the further side, Carlyle, though he was born in the same year as Keats, on the hither side. Still the accident of length of days must not blind us to the fact that the Victorian period, though in many respects its ideals and modes of thinking differed from those of the period which preceded it, is essentially an extension of the Romantic Revival and not a fresh start. The coherent inspiration of romanticism disintegrated into separate lines of development, just as in the seventeenth century the single inspiration of the Renaissance broke into different schools.

Along these separate lines represented by such men as Browning, the Pre-Raphaelites, Arnold, and Meredith, literature enriched and elaborated itself into fresh forms. None the less, every author in each of these lines of literary activity invites his readers to understand his direct relations to the romantic movement. Rossetti touches it through his original, Keats; Arnold through Goethe and Byron; Browning first through Shelley and then in item after item of his varied subject-matter.

In one direction the Victorian age achieved a salient and momentous advance. The Romantic Revival had been interested in nature, in the past, and in a lesser degree in art, but it had not been interested in men and women. To Wordsworth the dalesmen of the lakes were part of the scenery they moved in; he saw men as trees walking, and when he writes about them as in such great poems as Resolution and Independence, the Brothers, or Michael, it is as natural objects he treats them, invested with the lonely remoteness that separates them from the complexities and passions of life as it is lived.

They are there, you feel, to teach the same lesson as the landscape teaches in which they are set. The passing of the old Cumberland beggar through villages and past farmsteads, brings to those who see him the same kind of consolation as the impulses from a vernal wood that Wordsworth celebrated in his purely nature poetry. Compare with Wordsworth, Browning, and note the fundamental change in the attitude of the poet that his work reveals. Pippa Passes is a poem on exactly the same scheme as the Old Cumberland Beggar, but in treatment no two things could be further apart. The intervention of Pippa is dramatic, and though her song is in the same key as the wordless message of Wordsworth's beggar she is a world apart from him, because she is something not out of natural history, but out of life. The Victorian age extended the imaginative sensibility which its predecessor had brought to bear on nature and history, to the complexities of human life.

It searched for individuality in character, studied it with a loving minuteness, and built up out of its discoveries amongst men and women a body of literature which in its very mode of conception was more closely related to life, and thus the object of greater interest and excitement to its readers, than anything which had been written in the previous ages. It is the direct result of this extension of romanticism that the novel became the characteristic means of literary expression of the time, and that Browning, the poet who more than all others represents the essential spirit of his age, should have been as it were, a novelist in verse. Only one other literary form, indeed, could have ministered adequately to this awakened interest, but by some luck not easy to understand, the drama, which might have done with greater economy and directness the work the novel had to do, remained outside the main stream of literary activity. To the drama at last it would seem that we are returning, and it may be that in the future the direct representation of the clash of human life which is still mainly in the hands of our novelists, may come back to its own domain.

The Victorian age then added humanity to nature and art as the subject-matter of literature. But it went further than that. For the first time since the

Renaissance, came an era which was conscious of itself as an epoch in the history of mankind, and confident of its mission. The fifteenth and sixteenth centuries revolutionized cosmography, and altered the face of the physical world. The nineteenth century, by the discoveries of its men of science, and by the remarkable and rapid succession of inventions which revolutionized the outward face of life, made hardly less alteration in accepted ways of thinking. The evolutionary theory, which had been in the air since Goethe, and to which Darwin was able to give an incontrovertible basis of scientific fact, profoundly influenced man's attitude to nature and to religion. Physical as apart from natural science made scarcely less advance, and instead of a world created in some fixed moment of time, on which had been placed by some outward agency all the forms and shapes of nature that we know, came the conception of a planet congealing out of a nebula, and of some lower, simpler and primeval form of life multiplying and diversifying itself through succeeding stages of development to form both the animal and the vegetable world. This conception not only enormously excited and stimulated thought, but it gave thinkers a strange sense of confidence and certainty not possessed by the age before. Everything seemed plain to them; they were heirs of all the ages. Their doubts were as certain as their faith.

"There lives more faith in honest doubt
Believe me than in half the creeds."

said Tennyson; "honest doubt," hugged with all the certainty of a revelation, is the creed of most of his philosophical poetry, and what is more to the point was the creed of the masses that were beginning to think for themselves, to whose awakening interest his work so strongly appealed. There were no doubt, literary side-currents. Disraeli survived to show that there were still young men who thought Byronically. Rossetti and his school held themselves proudly aloof from the rationalistic and scientific tendencies of the time, and found in the Middle ages, better understood than they had been either by Coleridge or Scott, a refuge from a time of factories and fact. The Oxford movement ministered to the same tendencies in religion and philosophy; but it is the scientific spirit, and all that the scientific spirit implied, its certain doubt, its care for minuteness, and truth of observation, its growing interest in social processes, and the conditions under which life is lived, that is the central fact in Victorian literature.

Tennyson represents more fully than any other poet this essential spirit of the age. If it be true, as has been often asserted, that the spirit of an age is to be found best in the work of lesser men, his complete identity with the thought of his time is in itself evidence of his inferiority to his contemporary,

Browning. Comparison between the two men seem inevitable; they were made by readers when *In Memoriam* and *Men and Women* came hot from the press, and they have been made ever since.

There could, of course, scarcely be two men more dissimilar, Tennyson elaborating and decorating the obvious; Browning delving into the esoteric and the obscure, and bringing up strange and unfamiliar finds; Tennyson in faultless verse registering current newly accepted ways of thought; Browning in advance thinking afresh for himself, occupied ceaselessly in the arduous labour of creating an audience fit to judge him. The age justified the accuracy with which Tennyson mirrored it, by accepting him and rejecting Browning. It is this very accuracy that almost forces us at this time to minimise and dispraise Tennyson's work. We have passed from Victorian certainties, and so he is apt when he writes in the mood of *Locksley Hall* and the rest, to appear to us a little shallow, a little empty, and a little pretentious.

His earlier poetry, before he took upon himself the burden of the age, is his best work, and it bears strongly marked upon it the influence of Keats. Such a poem for instance as *Oenone* shows an extraordinarily fine sense of language and melody, and the capacity caught from Keats of conveying a rich and highly coloured pictorial effect. No other poet, save Keats, has had a sense of colour so highly developed as Tennyson's. From his boyhood he was an exceedingly close and sympathetic observer of the outward forms of nature, and he makes a splendid use of what his eyes had taught him in these earlier poems. Later his interest in insects and birds and flowers outran the legitimate opportunity he possessed of using it in poetry. It was his habit, his son tells us, to keep notebooks of things he had observed in his garden or in his walks, and to work them up afterwards into similes for the *Princess* and the *Idylls of the King*. Read in the books written by admirers, in which they have been studied and collected (there are several of them) these similes are pleasing enough; in the text where they stand they are apt to have the air of impertinences, beautiful and extravagant impertinences no doubt, but alien to their setting. In one of the *Idylls of the King* the fall of a drunken knight from his horse is compared to the fall of a jutting edge of cliff and with it a lance-like fir-tree, which Tennyson had observed near his home, and one cannot resist the feeling that the comparison is a thought too great for the thing it was meant to illustrate. So, too, in the *Princess* when he describes a handwriting,

"In such a hand as when a field of corn
Bows all its ears before the roaring East."

he is using up a sight noted in his walks and transmuted into poetry on a trivial and frivolous occasion. You do not feel, in fact, that the handwriting visualized spontaneously called up the comparison; you are as good as certain that the simile existed waiting for use before the handwriting was thought of.

The accuracy of his observation of nature, his love of birds and larvae is matched by the carefulness with which he embodies, as soon as ever they were made, the discoveries of natural and physical science. Nowadays, possibly because these things have become commonplace to us, we may find him a little school-boy-like in his pride of knowledge. He knows that

"This world was once a fluid haze of light,
Till towards the centre set the starry tides
And eddied wild suns that wheeling cast
The planets."

just as he knows what the catkins on the willows are like, or the names of the butterflies: but he is capable, on occasion of "dragging it in," as in

"The nebulous star we call the sun,
If that hypothesis of theirs be sound."

from the mere pride in his familiarity with the last new thing. His dealings with science, that is, no more than his dealings with nature, have that inevitableness, that spontaneous appropriateness that we feel we have a right to ask from great poetry.

Had Edgar Allan Poe wanted an example for his theory of the impossibility of writing, in modern times, a long poem, he might have found it in Tennyson. His strength is in his shorter pieces; even where as in *In Memoriam* he has conceived and written something at once extended and beautiful, the beauty lies rather in the separate parts; the thing is more in the nature of a sonnet sequence than a continuous poem.

Of his other larger works, the *Princess,* a scarcely happy blend between burlesque in the manner of the *Rape of the Lock,* and a serious apostleship of the liberation of women, is solely redeemed by these lyrics. Tennyson's innate conservatism hardly squared with the liberalising tendencies he caught from the more advanced thought of his age, in writing it. Something of the same kind is true of *Maud,* which is a novel told in dramatically varied verse. The hero is morbid, his social satire peevish, and a story which could have been completely redeemed by the ending (the death of the hero), which artistic fitness demands, is of value for us now through its three amazing songs, in which the lyric genius of Tennyson reached its finest flower.

It cannot be denied, either, that he failed—though magnificently—in the *Idylls of the King*. The odds were heavily against him in the choice of a subject. Arthur is at once too legendary and too shadowy for an epic hero, and nothing but the treatment that Milton gave to Satan (*i.e.* flat substitution of the legendary person by a newly created character) could fit him for the place. Even if Arthur had been more promising than he is, Tennyson's sympathies were fundamentally alien from the moral and religious atmosphere of Arthurian romance.

His robust Protestantism left no room for mysticism; he could neither appreciate nor render the mystical fervour and exultation which is in the old history of the Holy Grail. Nor could he comprehend the morality of a society where courage, sympathy for the oppressed, loyalty and courtesy were the only essential virtues, and love took the way of freedom and the heart rather than the way of law. In his heart Tennyson's attitude to the ideals of chivalry and the old stories in which they are embodied differed probably very little from that of Roger Ascham, or of any other Protestant Englishman; when he endeavoured to make an epic of them and to fasten to it an allegory in which Arthur should typify the war of soul against sense, what happened was only what might have been expected. The heroic enterprise failed, and left us with a series of mid-Victorian novels in verse in which the knights figure as heroes of the generic mid-Victorian type.

But if he failed in his larger poems, he had a genius little short of perfect in his handling of shorter forms. The Arthurian story which produced only middling moralizing in the *Idylls,* gave us as well the supremely written Homeric episode of the *Morte d'Arthur,* and the sharp and defined beauty of *Sir Galahad* and the *Lady of Shallott*. Tennyson had a touch of the pre-Raphaelite faculty of minute painting in words, and the writing of these poems is as clear and naïve as in the best things of Rossetti. He had also what neither Rossetti nor any of his contemporaries in verse, except Browning, had, a fine gift of understanding humanity.

The peasants of his English idylls are conceived with as much breadth of sympathy and richness of humour, as purely and as surely, as the peasants of Chaucer or Burns. A note of passionate humanity is indeed in all his work. It makes vivid and intense his scholarly handling of Greek myth; always the unchanging human aspect of it attracts him most, in Oenone's grief, in the indomitableness of Ulysses, the weariness and disillusionment in Tithonus.

It has been the cause of the comfort he has brought to sorrow; none of his generation takes such a human attitude to death. Shelley could yearn for the infinite, Browning treat it as the last and greatest adventure, Arnold meet it clear eyed and resigned. To Wordsworth it is the mere return of man the transient to Nature the eternal.

"No motion has she now; no force,
She neither hears nor sees,
Roiled round in earth's diurnal course
With rocks and stones and trees."

To Tennyson it brings the fundamental human home-sickness for familiar things.

"Ah, sad and strange as on dark summer dawns,
The earliest pipe of half-awakened birds
To dying ears when unto dying eyes
The casement slowly grows a glimmering square."

It is an accent which wakes an echo in a thousand hearts.

(2)

While Tennyson, in his own special way and, so to speak, in collaboration with the spirit of the age, was carrying on the work of Romanticism on its normal lines, Browning was finding a new style and a new subject matter. In his youth he had begun as an imitator of Shelley, and Pauline and Paracelsus remain to show what the influence of the "sun-treader" was on his poetry.

But as early as his second publication, Bells and Pomegranates, he had begun to speak for himself, and with Men and Women, a series of poems of amazing variety and brilliance, he placed himself unassailably in the first rank. Like Tennyson's, his genius continued high and undimmed while life was left him. Men and Women was followed by an extraordinary narrative poem, The Ring and the Book, and it by several volumes of scarcely less brilliance, the last of which appeared on the very day of his death.

Of the two classes into which, as we saw when we were studying Burns, creative artists can be divided, Browning belongs to that one which makes everything new for itself, and has in consequence to educate the readers by whom its work can alone be judged. He was an innovator in nearly everything he did; he thought for himself; he wrote for himself, and in his own way. And because he refused to follow ordinary modes of writing, he was and is still widely credited with being tortured and obscure. The charge of obscurity is unfortunate because it tends to shut off from him a large class of readers for whom he has a sane and special and splendid message.

His most important innovation in form was his device of the dramatic lyric. What interested him in life was men and women, and in them, not their actions, but the motives which governed their actions. To lay bare fully the working of motive in a narrative form with himself as narrator was obviously impossible; the strict dramatic form, though he attained some success in it, does not seem to have attracted him, probably because in it the ultimate stress must be on the thing done rather than the thing thought; there remained, therefore, of the ancient forms of poetry, the lyric. The lyric had of course been used before to express emotions imagined and not real to the poet himself; Browning was the first to project it to express imagined emotions of men and women, whether typical or individual, whom he himself had created. Alongside this perversion of the lyric, he created a looser and freer form, the dramatic monologue, in which most of his most famous poems, Cleon, Sludge the Medium, Bishop Blougram's Apology, etc., are cast. In the convention which Browning established in it, all kinds of people are endowed with a miraculous articulation, a new gift of tongues; they explain themselves, their motives, the springs of those motives (for in Browning's view every thought and act of a man's life is part of an interdependent whole), and their author's peculiar and robust philosophy of life. Out of the dramatic monologues he devised the scheme of The Ring and the Book, a narrative poem in which the episodes, and not the plot, are the basis of the structure, and the story of a trifling and sordid crime is set forth as it appeared to the minds of the chief actors in succession. To these new forms he added the originality of an extraordinary realism in style. Few poets have the power by a word, a phrase, a flash of observation in detail to make you see the event as Browning makes you see it.

Many books have been written on the philosophy of Browning's poetry. Stated briefly its message is that of an optimism which depends on a recognition of the strenuousness of life. The base of his creed, as of Carlyle's, is the gospel of labour; he believes in the supreme moral worth of effort. Life is a "training school" for a future existence, and our place in it depends on the courage and strenuousness with which we have laboured here. Evil is in the world only as an instrument in the process of development; by conquering it we exercise our spiritual faculties the more. Only torpor is the supreme sin, even as in The Statue and the Bust where effort would have been to a criminal end.

"The counter our lovers staked was lost

As surely as if it were lawful coin:

And the sin I impute to each frustrate ghost
Was, the unlit lamp and the ungirt loin,
Though the end in sight was a crime, I say."

All the other main ideas of his poetry fit with perfect consistency on to his scheme. Love, the manifestation of a man's or a woman's nature, is the highest and most intimate relationship possible, for it is an opportunity—the highest opportunity—for spiritual growth. It can reach this end though an actual and earthly union is impossible.

"She has lost me, I have gained her;
Her soul's mine and thus grown perfect,
I shall pass my life's remainder.
Life will just hold out the proving
Both our powers, alone and blended:
And then come the next life quickly!
This world's use will have been ended."

It follows that the reward of effort is the promise of immortality, and that for each man, just because his thoughts and motives taken together count, and not one alone, there is infinite hope.

The contemporaries of Tennyson and Browning in poetry divide themselves into three separate schools. Nearest to them in temper is the school of Matthew Arnold and Clough; they have the same quick sensitiveness to the intellectual tendencies of the age, but their foothold in a time of shifting and dissolving creeds is a stoical resignation very different from the buoyant optimism of Browning, or Tennyson's mixture of science and doubt and faith. Very remote from them on the other hand is the backward-gazing mediaevalism of Rossetti and his circle, who revived (Rossetti from Italian sources, Morris from Norman) a Middle age which neither Scott nor Coleridge had more than partially and brokenly understood. The last school, that to which Swinburne and Meredith with all their differences unite in belonging, gave up Christianity with scarcely so much as a regret,

"We have said to the dream that caress'd and the dread that smote us, Good-night and good-bye."

and turned with a new hope and exultation to the worship of our immemorial mother the earth. In both of them, the note of enthusiasm for political liberty which had been lost in Wordsworth after 1815, and was too early extinguished with Shelley, was revived by the Italian Revolution in splendour and fire.

(3)

As one gets nearer one's own time, a certain change comes insensibly over one's literary studies. Literature comes more and more to mean imaginative literature or writing about imaginative literature. The mass of writing comes to be taken not as literature, but as argument or information; we consider it purely from the point of view of its subject matter. A comparison will make this at once clear. When a man reads Bacon, he commonly regards himself as engaged in the study of English literature; when he reads Darwin he is occupied in the study of natural science. A reader of Bacon's time would have looked on him as we look on Darwin now.

The distinction is obviously illogical, but a writer on English literature within brief limits is forced to bow to it if he wishes his book to avoid the dreariness of a summary, and he can plead in extenuation the increased literary output of the later age, and the incompleteness with which time so far has done its work in sifting the memorable from the forgettable, the ephemeral from what is going to last. The main body of imaginative prose literature—the novel—is treated of in the next chapter and here no attempt will be made to deal with any but the admittedly greatest names. Nothing can be said, for instance, of that fluent journalist and biased historian Macaulay, nor of the mellifluousness of Newman, nor of the vigour of Kingsley or Maurice; nor of the writings, admirable in their literary qualities of purity and terseness, of Darwin or Huxley; nor of the culture and apostleship of Matthew Arnold. These authors, one and all, interpose no barrier, so to speak, between their subject-matter and their readers; you are not when you read them conscious of a literary intention, but of some utilitarian one, and as an essay on English literature is by no means a handbook to serious reading they will be no more mentioned here.

In the case of one nineteenth century writer in prose, this method of exclusion cannot apply. Both Carlyle and Ruskin were professional men of letters; both in the voluminous compass of their works touched on a large variety of subjects; both wrote highly individual and peculiar styles; and both without being either professional philosophers or professional preachers, were as every good man of letters, whether he denies it or not, is and must be, lay moralists and prophets. Of the two Ruskin is plain and easily read, and he derives his message; Carlyle, his original, is apt to be tortured and obscure. Inside the body of his work the student of nineteenth century literature is probably in need of some guidance; outside so far as prose is concerned he can fend for himself.

As we saw, Carlyle was the oldest of the Victorians; he was over forty when the Queen came to the throne. Already his years of preparation in Scotland, town and country, were over, and he had settled in that famous little house in Chelsea which for nearly half a century to come was to be one of the central hearths of literary London. More than that, he had already fully formed his mode of thought and his peculiar style. *Sartor Resartus* was written and published serially before the Queen came to the throne; the *French Revolution* came in the year of her accession at the very time that Carlyle's lectures were making him a fashionable sensation; most of his miscellaneous essays had already appeared in the reviews. But with the strict Victorian era, as if to justify the usually arbitrary division of literary history by dynastic periods, there came a new spirit into his work. For the first time he applied his peculiar system of ideas to contemporary politics. *Chartism* appeared in 1839; *Past and Present*, which does the same thing as *Chartism* in an artistic form, three years later. They were followed by one other book—*Latter Day Pamphlets*—addressed particularly to contemporary conditions, and by two remarkable and voluminous historical works. Then came the death of his wife, and for the last fifteen years of his life silence, broken only briefly and at rare intervals.

The reader who comes to Carlyle with preconceived notions based on what he has heard of the subject-matter of his books is certain to be surprised by what he finds. There are histories in the canon of his works and pamphlets on contemporary problems, but they are composed on a plan that no other historian and no other social reformer would own. A reader will find in them no argument, next to no reasoning, and little practical judgment. Carlyle was not a great "thinker" in the strictest sense of that term.

He was under the control, not of his reason, but of his emotions; deep feeling, a volcanic intensity of temperament flaming into the light and heat of prophecy, invective, derision, or a simple splendour of eloquence, is the characteristic of his work. Against cold-blooded argument his passionate nature rose in fierce rebellion; he had no patience with the formalist or the doctrinaire. Nor had he the faculty of analysis; his historical works are a series of pictures or tableaux, splendidly and vividly conceived, and with enormous colour and a fine illusion of reality, but one-sided as regards the truth. In his essays on hero-worship he contents himself with a noisy reiteration of the general predicate of heroism; there is very little except their names and the titles to differentiate one sort of hero from another.

His picture of contemporary conditions is not so much a reasoned indictment as a wild and fantastic orgy of epithets: "dark simmering pit of

Tophet," "bottomless universal hypocrisies," and all the rest. In it all he left no practical scheme. His works are fundamentally not about politics or history or literature, but about himself. They are the exposition of a splendid egotism, fiercely enthusiastic about one or two deeply held convictions; their strength does not lie in their matter of fact.

This is, perhaps, a condemnation of him in the minds of those people who ask of a social reformer an actuarially accurate scheme for the abolition of poverty, or from a prophet a correct forecast of the result of the next general election. Carlyle has little help for these and no message save the disconcerting one of their own futility. His message is at once larger and simpler, for though his form was prose, his soul was a poet's soul, and what he has to say is a poet's word. In a way, it is partly Wordsworth's own. The chief end of life, his message is, is the performance of duty, chiefly the duty of work. "Do thy little stroke of work; this is Nature's voice, and the sum of all the commandments, to each man." All true work is religion, all true work is worship; to labour is to pray. And after work, obedience the best discipline, so he says in *Past and Present,* for governing, and "our universal duty and destiny; wherein whoso will not bend must break." Carlyle asked of every man, action and obedience and to bow to duty; he also required of him sincerity and veracity, the duty of being a real and not a sham, a strenuous warfare against cant. The historical facts with which he had to deal he grouped under these embracing categories, and in the *French Revolution,* which is as much a treasure-house of his philosophy as a history, there is hardly a page on which they do not appear. "Quack-ridden," he says, "in that one word lies all misery whatsoever."

These bare elemental precepts he clothes in a garment of amazing and bizarre richness. There is nothing else in English faintly resembling the astonishing eccentricity and individuality of his style. Gifted with an extraordinarily excitable and vivid imagination; seeing things with sudden and tremendous vividness, as in a searchlight or a lightning flash, he contrived to convey to his readers his impressions full charged with the original emotion that produced them, and thus with the highest poetic effect.

There is nothing in all descriptive writing to match the vividness of some of the scenes in the *French Revolution* or in the narrative part of *Cromwell's Letters and Speeches,* or more than perhaps in any of his books, because in it he was setting down deep-seated impressions of his boyhood rather than those got from brooding over documents, in *Sartor Resartus.* Alongside this unmatched pictorial vividness and a quite amazing richness and rhythm of language, more surprising and original than anything out of Shakespeare, there are of course, striking defects—a wearisome reiteration of emphasis, a clumsiness of construction, a saddening fondness for solecisms and hybrid inventions of his own. The reader who is interested in these (and every one who reads him is forced to become so) will find them faithfully dealt with in John Sterling's remarkable letter (quoted in Carlyle's *Life of Sterling*) on *Sartor Resartus*. But gross as they are, and frequently as they provide matter for serious offence, these eccentricities of language link themselves up in a strange indissoluble way with Carlyle's individuality and his power as an artist. They are not to be imitated, but he would be much less than he is without them, and they act by their very strength and pungency as a preservative of his work. That of all the political pamphlets which the new era of reform occasioned, his, which were the least in sympathy with it and are the furthest off the main stream of our political thinking now, alone continue to be read, must be laid down not only to the prophetic fervour and fire of their inspiration but to the dark and violent magic of their style.

THE VICTORIAN AGE LITERATURE

In 1897 Mark Twain was visiting London during the Diamond Jubilee celebrations honoring the sixtieth anniversary of Queen Victoria's coming to the throne. "British history is two thousand years old," Twain observed, "and yet in a good many ways the world has moved farther ahead since the Queen was born than it moved in all the rest of the two thousand put together." Twain's comment captures the sense of dizzying change that characterized the Victorian period. Perhaps most important was the shift from a way of life based on ownership of land to a modern urban economy based on trade and manufacturing. By the beginning of the Victorian period, the Industrial Revolution, as this shift was called, had created profound economic and social changes, including a mass migration of workers to industrial towns, where they lived in new urban slums. But the changes arising out of the Industrial Revolution were just one subset of the radical changes taking place in mid- and late-nineteenth-century Britain-among others were the democratization resulting from extension of the franchise; challenges to religious faith, in part based on the advances of scientific knowledge, particularly of evolution; and changes in the role of women.

All of these issues, and the controversies attending them, informed Victorian literature. In part because of the expansion of newspapers and the periodical press, debate about political and social issues played an important role in the experience of the reading public. The Victorian novel, with its emphasis on the realistic portrayal of social life, represented many Victorian issues in the stories of its characters. Moreover, debates about political representation involved in expansion both of the franchise and of the rights of women affected literary representation, as writers gave voice to those who had been voiceless.

The section in The Norton Anthology of English Literature entitled "Victorian Issues" contains texts dealing with four controversies that concerned the Victorians: evolution, industrialism, what the Victorians called "The Woman Question", and Great Britain's identity as an imperial power.

The debates on both industrialization and women's roles in society reflected profound social change: the formation of a new class of workers-men, women, and children-who had migrated to cities, particularly in the industrial North, in huge numbers, to take jobs in factories, and the growing demand for expanded liberties for women. The changes were related; the hardships that the Industrial Revolution and all its attendant social developments created put women into roles that challenged traditional ideas about women's nature. Moreover, the rate of change the Victorians experienced, caused to a large degree by advances in manufacturing, created new opportunities and challenges for women. They became writers, teachers, and social reformers, and they claimed an expanded set of rights.

In the debates about industrialism and about the Woman Question, voices came into print that had not been heard before. Not only did women writers play a major role in shaping the terms of the debate about the Woman Question, but also women from the working classes found opportunities to describe the conditions of their lives. Similarly, factory workers described their working and living conditions, in reports to parliamentary commissions, in the encyclopedic set of interviews journalist Henry Mayhew later collected as London Labor and the London Poor, and in letters to the editor that workers themselves wrote. The world of print became more inclusive and democratic. At the same time, novelists and even poets sought ways of representing these new voices. The novelist Elizabeth Gaskell wrote her first novel, Mary Barton, in order to give voice to Manchester's poor, and Elizabeth Barrett Browning tried to find ways in poetry of giving voice to the poor and oppressed.

The third section of this Web site, "The Painterly Image in Victorian Poetry," investigates the rich connection in the Victorian period between visual art and literature. Much Victorian aesthetic theory makes the eye the most authoritative sense and the clearest indicator of truth. Victorian poetry and the Victorian novel both value visual description as a way of portraying their subjects. This emphasis on the visual creates a particularly close connection between poetry and painting. Books of fiction and poetry were illustrated, and the illustrations amplified and intensified the effects of the text. The texts, engravings, and paintings collected here provide insight into the connection between the verbal and the visual so central to Victorian aesthetics.

Britain's identity as an imperial power with considerable global influence is explored more comprehensively in the fourth topic section. For Britain, the Victorian period witnessed a renewed interest in the empire's overseas holdings. British opinions on the methods and justification of imperialist missions overseas varied, with some like author Joseph Conrad throwing into sharp relief the brutal tactics and cold calculations involved in these missions, while others like politician Joseph Chamberlain considered the British to be the "great governing race" with a moral obligation to expand its influence around the globe. Social evolutionists, such as Benjamin Kidd, likewise supported the British dominion through their beliefs about the inherent developmental inferiority of the subject peoples, thus suggesting that Europeans had a greater capacity for ruling-a suggestion that many took as complete justification of British actions overseas. Regardless of dissenting voices, British expansion pushcd forward at an unprecedented rate, ushering in a new era of cultural exchange that irreversibly altered the British worldview.

INDUSTRIALISM: PROGRESS OR DECLINE

The Industrial Revolution-the changes in the making of goods that resulted from substituting machines for hand labor-began with a set of inventions for spinning and weaving developed in England in the eighteenth century. At first this new machinery was operated by workers in their homes, but in the 1780s the introduction of the steam engine to drive the machines led manufacturers to install them in large buildings called at first mills and later factories. Mill towns quickly grew in central and northern England; the population of the city of Manchester, for example, increased by ten times in the years between 1760 and 1830.

By the beginning of the Victorian period, the Industrial Revolution had created profound economic and social changes. Hundreds of thousands of workers had migrated to industrial towns, where they made up a new kind of working class. Wages were extremely low, hours very long-fourteen a day, or even more. Employers often preferred to hire women and children, who worked for even less then men. Families lived in horribly crowded, unsanitary housing. Moved by the terrible suffering resulting from a severe economic depression in the early 1840s, writers and men in government drew increasingly urgent attention to the condition of the working class. In her poem The Cry of the Children, Elizabeth Barrett Browning portrays the suffering of children in mines and factories. In The Condition of the Working Class, Friedrich Engels describes the conclusions he drew during the twenty months he spent observing industrial conditions in Manchester.

His 1845 book prepared the ground for his work with Karl Marx on The Communist Manifesto (1848), which asserts that revolution is the necessary response to the inequity of industrial capitalist society. Elizabeth Gaskell, wife of a Manchester minister, was inspired to begin her writing career with the novel Mary Barton (1848) in order to portray the suffering of the working class. In Hard Times (1854), Charles Dickens created the fictional city of Coketown to depict the harshness of existence in the industrial towns of central and northern England. During the 1830s and 1840s a number of parliamentary committees and commissions introduced testimony about the conditions in mines and factories that led to the beginning of government regulation and inspection, particularly of the working conditions of women and children. Other voices also testified powerfully to the extremities of working-class existence in industrial England. Poverty Knock, a nineteenth-century British folk song, catalogs the hardships of the weaver's job. Correspondent Henry Mayhew's interviews with London's poor portray the miseries of life on the streets. Drawing an analogy from popular travel writings, reformer William Booth's In Darkest England compares the dense and gloomy urban slums to the equatorial forests of Africa. Especially dramatic are the contrasting accounts of C. Duncan Lucas, who writes in 1901 about the pleasant "beehive of activity" that he sees as the typical London factory, and crusader Annie Besant, who passionately analyzes the economic exploitation of workers by wealthy capitalists.

Ada Nield Chew's letter about conditions in a factory in Crewe states strongly the case for improving wages for the tailoresses who "ceaselessly work" six days of the week. These sharply different perspectives define an important argument in the debate over industrialism: Was the machine age a blessing or a curse? Did it make humanity happier or more wretched?

THE WOMAN

Many of the historical changes that characterized the Victorian period motivated discussion and argument about the nature and role of woman-what the Victorians called "The Woman Question." The extension of the franchise by the Reform Bills of 1832 and 1867 stimulated discussion of women's political rights. Although women in England did not get the vote until 1918, petitions to Parliament advocating women's suffrage were introduced as early as the 1840s. Equally important was the agitation to allow married women to own and handle their own property, which culminated in the passing of the Married Women's Property Acts (1870-1908).

The Industrial Revolution resulted in changes for women as well. The explosive growth of the textile industries brought hundreds of thousands of lower-class women into factory jobs with grueling working conditions. The new kinds of labor and poverty that arose with the Industrial Revolution presented a challenge to traditional ideas of woman's place. Middle-class voices also challenged conventional ideas about women. In A Woman's Thoughts About Women, the novelist Dinah Maria Mulock compares the prospects of Tom, Dick, and Harry, who leave school and plunge into life, with those of "the girls," who "likewise finish their education, come home, and stay at home." They have, she laments, "literally nothing to do." Likewise in Cassandra, Florence Nightingale, who later became famous for organizing a contingent of nurses to take care of sick and wounded soldiers during the Crimean War, writes passionately of the costs for women of having no outlet for their heroic aspirations. Popular representations of Florence Nightingale, "The Lady with the Lamp," reflect the paradox of her achievement. While her organization of nurses was an important advance in hospital treatment, the image of her tending the wounded seems to reflect a traditional view of woman's mission. Even Queen Victoria herself represents a similar paradox. Though she was queen of the British Empire, paintings and photographs of her, such as Winterhalter's The Royal Family in 1846, represent her identity in conventional feminine postures and relationships.

Texts in this topic address both the hardships faced by women forced into new kinds of labor and the competing visions of those who exalted domestic life and those who supported women's efforts to move beyond the home. Journalist Henry Mayhew's interviews with a seamstress and a fruit seller vividly portray the difficulties of their lives.

In Of Queen's Gardens John Ruskin celebrates the "true wife," and Elizabeth Eastlake's "Lady Travellers" proposes her as a national ideal, while in The Girl of the Period Eliza Lynn Linton satirizes the modern woman. In contrast, two fictional characters, Charlotte Brontë's Jane Eyre and George Gissing's Miss Barfoot, from The Odd Women, speak passionately of the wish that their existence be "quickened with all of incident, life, fire, and feeling." All of these texts show how complex the debate was on what the Victorians called "The Woman Question."

THE PAINTERLY IMAGE IN POETRY

Nineteenth-century aesthetic theory frequently makes the eye the preeminent means by which we perceive truth.

- In The Hero as Poet (1840), Thomas Carlyle writes, "Poetic creation, what is this but seeing the thing sufficiently? The word that will describe the thing follows of itself from such clear intense sight of the thing."
- In his definition of the pathetic fallacy, which to him characterizes bad poetry, John Ruskin differentiates "between the ordinary, proper, and true appearances of things to us; and the extraordinary, or false appearances, when we are under the influence of emotion."
- In The Function of Criticism at the Present Time, Matthew Arnold defines the ideal in all branches of knowledge as "to see the object as in itself it really is."

This emphasis in nineteenth-century aesthetic theory on seeing the object as it really is has a counterpart in the importance of illustrating literature, particularly novels. Dickens worked most frequently with two great illustrators, George Cruikshank and Phiz (the pseudonym of Hablot Knight Browne). William Makepeace Thackeray drew his own illustrations.

In the works of these authors and others, the juxtaposition of text and picture creates a characteristic nineteenth-century style, which the critic Martin Meisel defines in his book Realizations as a union of pictorialism with narrative, creating richly detailed scenes that at once imply the stories that precede and follow and symbolize their meaning.

At the same time, developments in visual technology made it possible to see more and in new ways. Nineteenth century optical devices, creating illusions of various sorts, were invented near the beginning of the century: the thaumatrope, the phenakistoscope, the zoetrope, the stroboscope, the kaleidoscope, the diorama, and the stereoscope. Other inventions-such as the camera lucida, the graphic telescope, the binocular telescope, the binocular microscope, the stereopticon, and the kinetoscope-projected, recorded, or magnified images. Most important, the photographic camera provided an entirely new way of recording objects and people and transformed many areas of life and work.

The selections in this topic concentrate on one aspect of the Victorian visual imagination: the visual illustration of poetry through the accumulation of visual detail. In Mariana, for example, Tennyson conveys Mariana's despair through the objects that surround her. In a review, Arthur Henry Hallam uses the term "picturesque" to describe Tennyson's first volume of poems. Contrasted with the descriptive, which gives an objective account of appearances, the picturesque presents objects through the medium of emotion. Such poetry lends itself to illustration, and nineteenth-century editions of poetry, such as Moxon's Illustrated Tennyson or Macmillan's 1862 edition of Christina Rossetti's Goblin Market and Other Poems, frequently contained illustrations, much as novels did.

Illustration's importance in nineteenth-century literary theory created a particularly close connection between painting and poetry. Dante Gabriel Rossetti painted portraits to illustrate his poems, such as The Blessed Damozel, and created pairs of poems and paintings such as Lilith, Sibylla Palmifera, and Astarte Syriaca. Poets also frequently took painting as the subject of their poetry, as in Robert Browning's Fra Lippo Lippi or Andrea del Sarto. Similarly, a number of writers created prose descriptions of great paintings that were almost a kind of prose poetry, like John Ruskin's description of J. M. W. Turner's The Slave Ship or Walter Pater's description of Leonardo Da Vinci's La Gioconda. Nineteenth-century artists felt a kinship between picture-making with words and picture-making with images that linked the sister arts of poetry and painting in close relationship.

WILLIAM MAKEPEACE THACKERAY

Life

Thackeray was the only son of Richmond Thackeray, an administrator in the East India Company. His father died in 1815, and in 1816 Thackeray was sent home to England. His mother joined him in 1820, having married an engineering officer with whom she had been in love before she met Richmond Thackeray. After attending several grammar schools Thackeray went in 1822 to Charterhouse, the London public school, where he led a rather lonely and miserable existence.

He was happier while studying at Trinity College, Cambridge. In 1830 he left Cambridge without taking a degree, and during 1831–33 he studied law at the Middle Temple, London. He then considered painting as a profession; his artistic gifts are seen in his letters and many of his early writings, which are amusingly and energetically illustrated. All his efforts at this time have a dilettante air, understandable in a young man who, on coming of age in 1832, had inherited £20,000 from his father. He soon lost his fortune, however, through gambling and unlucky speculations and investments. In 1836, while studying art in Paris, he married a penniless Irish girl, and his stepfather bought a newspaper so that he could remain there as its correspondent. After the paper's failure he took his wife back to Bloomsbury, London, and became a hardworking and prolific professional journalist. Of Thackeray's three daughters, one died in infancy ; and in 1840, after her last confinement, Mrs. Thackeray became insane. She never recovered and long survived her husband, living with friends in the country. Thackeray was, in effect, a widower, relying much on club life and gradually giving more and more attention to his daughters, for whom he established a home in London in 1846. The serial publication in 1847–48 of his novel Vanity Fair brought Thackeray both fame and prosperity, and from then on he was an established author on the English scene.

Thackeray's one serious romantic attachment in his later life, to Jane Brookfield, can be traced in his letters. She was the wife of a friend of his Cambridge days, and during Thackeray's "widowerhood," when his life lacked an emotional centre, he found one in the Brookfield home. Henry Brookfield's insistence in 1851 that his wife's passionate but platonic friendship with Thackeray should end was a grief greater than any the author had known since his wife's descent into insanity.

Thackeray tried to find consolation in travel, lecturing in the United States on The English Humorists of the 18th Century and on The Four Georges. But after 1856 he settled in London. He stood unsuccessfully for Parliament in 1857, quarreled with Dickens, formerly a friendly rival, in the so-called "Garrick Club Affair", and in 1860 founded The Cornhill Magazine, becoming its editor. After he died in 1863, a commemorative bust of him was placed in Westminster Abbey.

Early Writings

The 19th century was the age of the magazine, which had been developed to meet the demand for family reading among the growing middle class. In the late 1830s Thackeray became a notable contributor of articles on varied topics to Fraser's Magazine, The New Monthly Magazine, and, later, to Punch. His work was unsigned or written under such pen names as Mr. Michael Angelo Titmarsh, Fitz-Boodle, The Fat Contributor, or Ikey Solomons. He collected the best of these early writings in Miscellanies, 4 vol.. These include The Yellowplush Correspondence, the memoirs and diary of a young cockney footman written in his own vocabulary and style; Major Gahagan, a fantasy of soldiering in India; Catherine, a burlesque of the popular "Newgate novels" of romanticized crime and low life, and itself a good realistic crime story; The History of Samuel Titmarsh and the Great Hoggarty Diamond, which was an earlier version of the young married life described in Philip; and The Luck of Barry Lyndon, which is a historical novel and his first full-length work.

Barry Lyndon is an excellent, speedy, satirical narrative until the final sadistic scenes and was a trial run for the great historical novels, especially Vanity Fair. The Book of Snobs is a collection of articles that had appeared successfully in Punch. It consists of sketches of London characters and displays Thackeray's virtuosity in quick character-drawing. The Rose and the Ring, Thackeray's Christmas book for 1855, remains excellent entertainment, as do some of his verses; like many good prose writers, he had a facility in writing light verse and ballads.

Mature Writings

With Vanity Fair, the first work published under his own name, Thackeray adopted the system of publishing a novel serially in monthly parts that had been so successfully used by Dickens. Set in the second decade of the 19th century, the period of the Regency, the novel deals mainly with the interwoven fortunes of two contrasting women, Amelia Sedley and Becky Sharp. The latter, an unprincipled adventuress, is the leading personage and is perhaps the most memorable character Thackeray created. Subtitled "A Novel Without a Hero," the novel is deliberately antiheroic: Thackeray states that in this novel his object is to "indicate... that we are for the most part... foolish and selfish people... all eager after vanities."

The wealthy, wellborn, passive Amelia Sedley and the ambitious, energetic, scheming, provocative, and essentially amoral Becky Sharp, daughter of a poor drawing master, are contrasted in their fortunes and reactions to life, but the contrast of their characters is not the simple one between moral good and evil—both are presented with dispassionate sympathy.

Becky is the character around whom all the men play their parts in an upper middle-class and aristocratic background. Amelia marries George Osborne, but George, just before he is killed at the Battle of Waterloo, is ready to desert his young wife for Becky, who has fought her way up through society to marriage with Rawdon Crawley, a young officer of good family. Crawley, disillusioned, finally leaves Becky, and in the end virtue apparently triumphs, Amelia marries her lifelong admirer, Colonel Dobbin, and Becky settles down to genteel living and charitable works.

The rich movement and colour of this panorama of early 19th-century society make Vanity Fair Thackeray's greatest achievement; the narrative skill, subtle characterization, and descriptive power make it one of the outstanding novels of its period. But Vanity Fair is more than a portrayal and imaginative analysis of a particular society. Throughout we are made subtly aware of the ambivalence of human motives, and so are prepared for Thackeray's conclusion: "Ah! Vanitas Vanitatum! Which of us is happy in this world? Which of us has his desire, or having it, is satisfied?" It is its tragic irony that makes Vanity Fair a lasting and insightful evaluation of human ambition and experience.

Successful and famous, Thackeray went on to exploit two lines of development opened up in Vanity Fair: a gift for evoking the London scene and for writing historical novels that demonstrate the connections between past and present. He began with the first, writing The History of Pendennis, which is partly fictionalized autobiography. In it, Thackeray traces the youthful career of Arthur Pendennis—his first love affair, his experiences at "Oxbridge University," his working as a London journalist, and so on—achieving a convincing portrait of a much-tempted young man. Turning to the historical novel, Thackeray chose the reign of Queen Anne for the period of The History of Henry Esmond, Esq., 3 vol.. Some critics had thought that Pendennis was a formless, rambling book. In response, Thackeray constructed Henry Esmond with great care, giving it a much more formal plot structure. The story, narrated by Esmond, begins when he is 12, in 1691, and ends in 1718.

Its complexity of incident is given unity by Beatrix and Esmond, who stand out against a background of London society and the political life of the time. Beatrix dominates the book. Seen first as a charming child, she develops beauty combined with a power that is fatal to the men she loves. One of Thackeray's great creations, she is a heroine of a new type, emotionally complex and compelling, but not a pattern of virtue. Esmond, a sensitive, brave, aristocratic soldier, falls in love with her but is finally disillusioned. Befriended as an orphan by Beatrix' parents, Lord and Lady Castlewood, Henry initially adores Lady Castlewood as a mother and eventually, in his maturity, marries her.

Written in a pastiche of 18th-century prose, the novel is one of the best evocations in English of the atmosphere of a past age. It was not well received, however—Esmond's marriage to Lady Castlewood was criticized. George Eliot called it "the most uncomfortable book you can imagine." But it has come to be accepted as a notable English historical novel.

Thackeray returned to the contemporary scene in his novel The Newcomes. This work is essentially a detailed study of prosperous middle-class society and is centred upon the family of the title. Col. Thomas Newcome returns to London from India to be with his son Clive. The unheroic but attractive Clive falls in love with his cousin Ethel, but the love Clive and Ethel have for each other is fated to be unhappily thwarted for years because of worldly considerations.

Clive marries Rose Mackenzie; the selfish, greedy, cold-hearted Barnes Newcome, Ethel's father and head of the family, intrigues against Clive and the Colonel; and the Colonel invests his fortune imprudently and ends as a pensioner in an almshouse. Rose dies in childbirth, and the narrative ends with the Colonel's death. This deathbed scene, described with deep feeling that avoids sentimentality, is one of the most famous in Victorian fiction. In a short epilogue Thackeray tells us that Clive and Ethel eventually marry—but this, he says, is a fable. The Virginians, Thackeray's next novel, is set partly in America and partly in England in the latter half of the 18th century and is concerned mostly with the vicissitudes in the lives of two brothers, George and Henry Warrington, who are the grandsons of Henry Esmond, the hero of his earlier novel. Thackeray wrote two other serial novels, Lovel the Widower and The Adventures of Philip. He died after having begun writing the novel Denis Duval.

Assessment

In his own time Thackeray was regarded as the only possible rival to Dickens. His pictures of contemporary life were obviously real and were accepted as such by the middle classes. A great professional, he provided novels, stories, essays, and verses for his audience, and he toured as a nationally known lecturer.

He wrote to be read aloud in the long Victorian family evenings, and his prose has the lucidity, spontaneity, and pace of good reading material. Throughout his works, Thackeray analysed and deplored snobbery and frequently gave his opinions on human behaviour and the shortcomings of society, though usually prompted by his narrative to do so.

He examined such subjects as hypocrisy, secret emotions, the sorrows sometimes attendant on love, remembrance of things past, and the vanity of much of life—such moralizing being, in his opinion, an important function of the novelist. He had little time for such favourite devices of Victorian novelists as exaggerated characterization and melodramatic plots, preferring in his own work to be more true to life, subtly depicting various moods and plunging the reader into a stream of entertaining narrative, description, dialogue, and comment.

Thackeray's high reputation as a novelist continued unchallenged to the end of the 19th century but then began to decline. Vanity Fair is still his most interesting and readable work and has retained its place among the great historical novels in the English language.

Elizabeth Gaskell

She was a daughter of a Unitarian minister. When her mother died, she was brought up by a maternal aunt in the Cheshire village of Knutsford in a kindly atmosphere of rural gentility that was already old-fashioned at the time. In 1832 she married William Gaskell, a Unitarian minister, and settled in the overcrowded, problem-ridden industrial city of Manchester, which remained her home for the rest of her life. Domestic life—the Gaskells had six children, of whom four daughters lived to adulthood—and the social and charitable obligations of a minister's wife claimed her time but not all her thoughts. She did not begin her literary career until middle life, when the death of her only son had intensified her sense of community with the poor and her desire to "give utterance" to their "agony."

Her first novel, Mary Barton, reflects the temper of Manchester in the late 1830s. It is the story of a working-class family in which the father, John Barton, lapses into bitter class hatred during a cyclic depression and carries out a retaliatory murder at the behest of his trade union. Its timely appearance in the revolutionary year of 1848 brought the novel immediate success, and it won the praise of Charles Dickens and Thomas Carlyle. Dickens invited her to contribute to his magazine, Household Words, where her next major work, Cranford, appeared. This social history of a gentler era, which describes, without sentimentalizing or satirizing, her girlhood village of Knutsford and the efforts of its shabby-genteel inhabitants to keep up appearances, has remained her most popular work.

The conflict between Mrs. Gaskell's sympathetic understanding and the strictures of Victorian morality resulted in a mixed reception for her next social novel, Ruth. It offered an alternative to the seduced girl's traditional progress to prostitution and an early grave.

Among the many friends attracted by Mrs. Gaskell was Charlotte Brontë, who died in 1855 and whose biography Charlotte's father, Patrick Brontë, urged her to write. The Life of Charlotte Brontë, written with warmhearted admiration, disposed of a mass of firsthand material with unforced narrative skill. It is at once a work of art and a well-documented interpretation of its subject.

Among her later works, Sylvia's Lovers, dealing with the impact of the Napoleonic Wars upon simple people, is notable. Her last and longest work, Wives and Daughters, concerning the interlocking fortunes of two or three country families, is considered by many her finest. It was left unfinished at her death.

Frances Trollope

Frances Trollope was an English novelist and miscellaneous writer who published as Mrs. Trollope or Mrs. Frances Trollope. Her detractors diminished her reputation by making the common name used for her the overly familiar and slightly vulgar diminutive Fanny Trollope. Her third son was Anthony Trollope, the well-known novelist. Her eldest son, Thomas Adolphus Trollope, wrote The Girlhood of Catherine de Medici, History of Florence, What I Remember, Life of Pius IX, and some novels.

She was born at Stapleton, Bristol, and in 1809 married Thomas A. Trollope, a barrister, who fell into financial misfortune. She then in 1827 went with her family to Fanny Wright's utopian community, Nashoba Commune, in America. This community soon failed, and she ended up in Cincinnati, Ohio, where the efforts which she made to support herself were unsuccessful, though she encouraged Hiram Powers to do Dante Alighieri's Commedia in waxworks.

On her return to England, however, she brought herself into notice by publishing Domestic Manners of the Americans, in which she gave an unfavourable and, in the opinions of partisans of America, somewhat exaggerated account of the subject, reflecting the disparaging views of American society allegedly commonplace among English people of the higher social classes at that time; and a novel, The Refugee in America, pursued it on similar lines. Next came The Abbess and Belgium and Western Germany, and other works of the same kind on Paris and the Parisians, and Vienna and the Austrians followed.

Trollope also, however, wrote several strong novels of social protest: Michael Armstrong: Factory Boy began publication in 1840 and was the first industrial novel to be published in Britain. Other socially conscious novels included Jonathan Jefferson Whitlaw about the evils of slavery, and The Vicar of Wrexhill, which took on church corruption. Possibly her greatest work is the Widow Barnaby trilogy, which set a pattern followed by Anthony in the frequent use of sequels in his oeuvre.

In later years she continued to write novels and books on miscellaneous subjects, writing in all over 100 volumes. Though possessed of considerable powers of observation and a sharp and caustic wit, such an output was fatal to permanent literary success, and few of her books are now read. She spent the last 20 years of her life at Florence, where she died in 1863, being buried with four other members of the Trollope household in the English Cemetery of Florence.

ROBERT BROWNING

Life

The son of a clerk in the Bank of England in London, Browning received only a slight formal education, although his father gave him a grounding in Greek and Latin. In 1828 he attended classes at the University of London but left after half a session. Apart from a journey to St. Petersburg in 1834 with George de Benkhausen, the Russian consul general, and two short visits to Italy in 1838 and 1844, he lived with his parents in London until 1846, first at Camberwell and after 1840 at Hatcham. During this period he wrote his early long poems and most of his plays.

Browning's first published work, Pauline: A Fragment of a Confession, although formally a dramatic monologue, embodied many of his own adolescent passions and anxieties. Although it received some favourable comment, it was attacked by John Stuart Mill, who condemned the poet's exposure and exploitation of his own emotions and his "intense and morbid self-consciousness." It was perhaps Mill's critique that determined Browning never to confess his own emotions again in his poetry but to write objectively. In 1835 he published Paracelsus and in 1840 Sordello, both poems dealing with men of great ability striving to reconcile the demands of their own personalities with those of the world. Paracelsus was well received, but Sordello, which made exacting demands on its reader's knowledge, was almost universally declared incomprehensible.

Encouraged by the actor Charles Macready, Browning devoted his main energies for some years to verse drama, a form that he had already adopted for Strafford. Between 1841 and 1846, in a series of pamphlets under the general title of Bells and Pomegranates, he published seven more plays in verse, including Pippa Passes, A Blot in the 'Scutcheon, and Luria. These, and all his earlier works except Strafford, were printed at his family's expense. Although Browning enjoyed writing for the stage, he was not successful in the theatre, since his strength lay in depicting, as he had himself observed of Strafford, "Action in Character, rather than Character in Action."

By 1845 the first phase of Browning's life was near its end. In that year he met Elizabeth Barrett. In her Poems Barrett had included lines praising Browning, who wrote to thank her. In May they met and soon discovered their love for each other. Barrett had, however, been for many years an invalid, confined to her room and thought incurable. Her father, moreover, was a dominant and selfish man, jealously fond of his daughter, who in turn had come to depend on his love. When her doctors ordered her to Italy for her health and her father refused to allow her to go, the lovers, who had been corresponding and meeting regularly, were forced to act. They were married secretly in September 1846; a week later they left for Pisa.

Throughout their married life, although they spent holidays in France and England, their home was in Italy, mainly at Florence, where they had a flat in Casa Guidi. Their income was small, although after the birth of their son, Robert, in 1849 Mrs. Browning's cousin John Kenyon made them an allowance of £100 a year, and on his death in 1856 he left them £11,000.

Browning produced comparatively little poetry during his married life. Apart from a collected edition in 1849 he published only Christmas-Eve and Easter-Day, an examination of different attitudes towards Christianity, perhaps having its immediate origin in the death of his mother in 1849; an introductory essay to some spurious letters of Shelley, Browning's only considerable work in prose and his only piece of critical writing; and Men and Women. This was a collection of 51 poems—dramatic lyrics such as "Memorabilia," "Love Among the Ruins," and "A Toccata of Galuppi's"; the great monologues such as "Fra Lippo Lippi," "How It Strikes a Contemporary," and "Bishop Blougram's Apology"; and a very few poems in which implicitly or explicitly he broke his rule and spoke of himself and of his love for his wife. Men and Women, however, had no great sale, and many of the reviews were unfavourable and unhelpful. Disappointed for the first time by the reception of his work, Browning in the following years wrote little, sketching and modeling in clay by day and enjoying the society of his friends at night. At last Mrs. Browning's health, which had been remarkably restored by her life in Italy, began to fail. On June 29, 1861, she died in her husband's arms. In the autumn he returned slowly to London with his young son.

His first task on his return was to prepare his wife's Last Poems for the press. At first he avoided company, but gradually he accepted invitations more freely and began to move in society. Another collected edition of his poems was called for in 1863, but Pauline was not included. When his next book of poems, Dramatis Personae—including "Abt Vogler," "Rabbi Ben Ezra,"

"Caliban upon Setebos," and "Mr. Sludge, 'The Medium' "—reached two editions, it was clear that Browning had at last won a measure of popular recognition.

In 1868–69 he published his greatest work, The Ring and the Book, based on the proceedings in a murder trial in Rome in 1698. Grand alike in plan and execution, it was at once received with enthusiasm, and Browning was established as one of the most important literary figures of the day. For the rest of his life he was much in demand in London society. He spent his summers with friends in France, Scotland, or Switzerland or, after 1878, in Italy.

The most important works of his last years, when he wrote with great fluency, were the long narrative or dramatic poems, often dealing with contemporary themes, such as Prince Hohenstiel-Schwangau, Fifine at the Fair, Red Cotton Night-Cap Country, The Inn Album, and the two series of Dramatic Idyls. He wrote a number of poems on classical subjects, including Balaustion's Adventure and Aristophanes' Apology. In addition to many collections of shorter poems—Pacchiarotto and How He Worked in Distemper, Jocoseria, Ferishtah's Fancies, and Asolando: Fancies and Facts—Browning published towards the end of his life two books of unusually personal origin—La Saisiaz, at once an elegy for his friend Anne Egerton-Smith and a meditation on mortality, and Parleyings with Certain People of Importance in Their Day, in which he discussed books and ideas that had influenced him since his youth.

While staying in Venice in 1889, Browning caught cold, became seriously ill, and died on December 12. He was buried in Westminster Abbey.

Assessment

Few poets have suffered more than Browning from hostile incomprehension or misplaced admiration, both arising very often from a failure to recognize the predominantly dramatic nature of his work. The bulk of his writing before 1846 was for the theatre; thereafter his major poems showed his increasing mastery of the dramatic monologue. This consists essentially of a narrative spoken by a single character and amplified by his comments on his story and the circumstances in which he is speaking.

From his own knowledge of the historical or other events described, or else by inference from the poem itself, the reader is eventually enabled to assess the intelligence and honesty of the narrator and the value of the views he expresses. This type of dramatic monologue, since it depends on the unconscious provision by the speaker of the evidence by which the reader is to judge him, is eminently suitable for the ironist. Browning's fondness for this form has, however, encouraged the two most common misconceptions of the nature of his poetry—that it is deliberately obscure and that its basic "message" is a facile optimism. Neither of these criticisms is groundless; both are incomplete. Browning is not always difficult. In many poems, especially short lyrics, he achieves effects of obvious felicity. Nevertheless, his superficial difficulties, which prevent an easy understanding of the sense of a passage, are evident enough: his attempts to convey the broken and irregular rhythms of speech make it almost impossible to read the verse quickly; his elliptical syntax sometimes disconcerts and confuses the reader but can be mastered with little effort; certain poems, such as Sordello or "Old Pictures in Florence," require a considerable acquaintance with their subjects in order to be understood; and his fondness for putting his monologues into the mouths of charlatans and sophists, such as Mr. Sludge or Napoleon III, obliges the reader to follow a chain of subtle or paradoxical arguments. All these characteristics stand in the way of easy reading.

But even when individual problems of style and technique have been resolved, the poems' interest is seldom exhausted. First, Browning often chooses an unexpected point of view, especially in his monologues, thus forcing the reader to accept an unfamiliar perspective. Second, he is capable of startling changes of focus within a poem. For example, he chooses subjects in themselves insignificant, as in "Fra Lippo Lippi" and "Master Hugues of Saxe-Gotha," and treats through them the eternal themes of poetry.

This transition from particular observation to transcendental truth presents much the same challenge to the reader as do the metaphysical poets of the 17th century and much the same excitement. Third, because Browning seldom presents a speaker without irony, there is a constant demand on the reader to appreciate exactly the direction of satiric force in the poem. Even in a melodious poem such as "A Toccata of Galuppi's," the valid position must be distinguished from the false at every turn of the argument, while in the major casuistic monologues, such as "Bishop Blougram's Apology," the shifts of sympathy are subtler still.

It has also been objected that Browning uses his poetry as a vehicle for his philosophy, which is not of itself profound or interesting, being limited to an easy optimism. But Browning's dramatic monologues must, as he himself insisted, be recognized as the utterances of fictitious persons drawing their strength from their appropriateness in characterizing the speaker, and not as expressions of Browning's own sentiments. Thus his great gallery of imagined characters is to be regarded as an exhaustive catalog of human motives, not as a series of self-portraits.

Nevertheless, certain fundamental assumptions are made so regularly that they may be taken to represent Browning's personal beliefs, such as his Christian faith. In matters of human conduct his sympathies are with those who show loving hearts, honest natures, and warmth of feeling; certainly these qualities are never satirized. He is in general on the side of those who commit themselves wholeheartedly to an ideal, even if they fail. By itself this might suggest rather a naive system of values, yet he also, sometimes even in the same poem, shows his understanding of those who have been forced to lower their standards and accept a compromise. Thus, although Browning is far from taking a cynical or pessimistic view of man's nature or destiny, his hopes for the world are not simple and unreasoning.

In The Ring and the Book Browning displays all his distinctive qualities. He allows a dramatic monologue to each character he portrays—to the man on trial for murder, to his young wife, whom he has mortally wounded, to her protector, to various Roman citizens, to the opposing lawyers, and to the pope, who ultimately decides the accused's fate. Each monologue deals with substantially the same occurrences, but each, of course, describes and interprets them differently. By permitting the true facts to emerge gradually by inference from these conflicting accounts, Browning reveals with increasing subtlety the true natures of his characters.

As each great monologue illuminates the moral being of the speaker, it becomes clear that nothing less than the whole ethical basis of human actions is in question. For over 20,000 lines Browning explores his theme, employing an unfaltering blank verse, rising often to passages of moving poetry, realizing in extraordinary detail the life of 17th-century Rome, and creating a series of characters as diverse and fully realised as those in any novel. During Browning's lifetime, critical recognition came rapidly after 1864; and, although his books never sold as well as his wife's or Tennyson's, he thereafter acquired a considerable and enthusiastic public. In the 20th century his reputation, along with those of the other great Victorians, declined, and his work did not enjoy a wide reading public, perhaps in part because of increasing skepticism of the values implied in his poetry.

He has, however, influenced many modern poets, such as Robert Frost and Ezra Pound, partly through his development of the dramatic monologue, with its emphasis on the psychology of the individual and his stream of consciousness, but even more through his success in writing about the variety of modern life in language that owed nothing to convention. As long as technical accomplishment, richness of texture, sustained imaginative power, and a warm interest in humanity are counted virtues, Browning will be numbered among the great English poets.

Elizabeth Barrett Browning

Elizabeth was the eldest child of Edward Barrett Moulton. Most of her girlhood was spent at a country house within sight of the Malvern Hills, in Worcestershire, where she was extraordinarily happy. At the age of 15, however, she fell seriously ill, probably as the result of a spinal injury, and her health was permanently affected. In 1832 the family moved to Sidmouth, Devon, and in 1836 they moved to London, where, in 1838, they took up residence at 50 Wimpole Street.

In London she contributed to several periodicals, and her first collection, The Seraphim and Other Poems, appeared in 1838. For reasons of health, she spent the next three years in Torquay, Devon, but after the death by drowning of her brother, Edward, she developed an almost morbid terror of meeting anyone apart from a small circle of intimates.

Her name, however, was well known in literary circles, and in 1844 her second volume of poetry, Poems, by E. Barrett Barrett, was enthusiastically received. In January 1845 she received from the poet Robert Browning a telegram: "I love your verses with all my heart, dear Miss Barrett. I do, as I say, love these books with all my heart-and I love you too." In early summer the two met. Their courtship was kept a close secret from Elizabeth's despotic father, of whom she stood in some fear. Sonnets from the Portuguese records her reluctance to marry, but their wedding had taken place on September 12, 1846. Her father knew nothing of it, and Elizabeth continued to live at home for a week.

The Brownings then left for Pisa. While in Pisa she wrote The Runaway Slave at Pilgrim's Point, a protest against slavery in the United States. The couple then settled in Florence, where their only child, Robert Wiedemann Barrett, was born in 1849. In 1851 and in 1855 the couple visited London; during the second visit, Elizabeth completed her most ambitious work, Aurora Leigh, a long blank-verse poem telling the complicated and melodramatic love story of a young girl and a misguided philanthropist. This work did not impress most critics, though it was a huge popular success.

During the last years of her life, Mrs. Browning developed an interest in spiritualism and the occult, but her energy and attention were chiefly taken up by an obsession, to a degree that alarmed her closest friends, with Italian politics. Casa Guidi Windows had been a deliberate attempt to win sympathy for the Florentines, and she continued to believe in the integrity of Napoleon III. In Poems Before Congress, the poem A Curse for a Nation was mistaken for a denunciation of England, whereas it was aimed at U.S. slavery. In the summer of 1861 Mrs. Browning suffered a severe chill and died.

MATTHEW ARNOLD

Life

Matthew was the eldest son of the renowned Thomas Arnold, who was appointed headmaster of Rugby School in 1828. Matthew entered Rugby and then attended Oxford as a scholar of Balliol College; there he won the Newdigate Prize with his poem Cromwell and was graduated with second-class honours in 1844. For Oxford Arnold retained an impassioned affection. His Oxford was the Oxford of John Henry Newman-of Newman just about to be received into the Roman Catholic Church; and although Arnold's own religious thought, like his father's, was strongly liberal, Oxford and Newman always remained for him joint symbols of spiritual beauty and culture.

In 1847 Arnold became private secretary to Lord Lansdowne, who occupied a high Cabinet post during Lord John Russell's Liberal ministries. And in 1851, in order to secure the income needed for his marriage with Frances Lucy Wightman, he accepted from Lansdowne an appointment as inspector of schools. This was to be his routine occupation until within two years of his death. He engaged in incessant travelling throughout the British provinces and also several times was sent by the government to inquire into the state of education in France, Germany, Holland, and Switzerland. Two of his reports on schools abroad were reprinted as books, and his annual reports on schools at home attracted wide attention, written, as they were, in Arnold's own urbane and civilized prose.

Poetic Achievement

The work that gives Arnold his high place in the history of literature and the history of ideas was all accomplished in the time he could spare from his official duties. His first volume of verse was The Strayed Reveller, and Other Poems. By A. ; this was followed by another under the same initial: Empedocles on Etna, and Other Poems. In 1853 appeared the first volume of poems published under his own name; it consisted partly of poems selected from the earlier volumes and also contained the well-known preface explaining why Empedocles was excluded from the selection: it was a dramatic poem "in which the suffering finds no vent in action," in which there is "everything to be endured, nothing to be done."

This preface foreshadows his later criticism in its insistence upon the classic virtues of unity, impersonality, universality, and architectonic power and upon the value of the classical masterpieces as models for "an age of spiritual discomfort"—an age "wanting in moral grandeur." Other editions followed, and Merope, Arnold's classical tragedy, appeared in 1858, and New Poems in 1867. After that date, though there were further editions, Arnold wrote little additional verse.

Not much of Arnold's verse will stand the test of his own criteria; far from being classically poised, impersonal, serene, and grand, it is often intimate, personal, full of romantic regret, sentimental pessimism, and nostalgia. As a public and social character and as a prose writer, Arnold was sunny, debonair, and sanguine; but beneath ran the current of his buried life, and of this much of his poetry is the echo:

From the soul's subterranean depth upborne
As from an infinitely distant land,
Come airs, and floating echoes, and convey
A melancholy into all our day.

"I am past thirty," he wrote a friend in 1853, "and three parts iced over." The impulse to write poetry came typically when

A bolt is shot back somewhere in the breast,
And a lost pulse of feeling stirs again.

Though he was "never quite benumb'd by the world's sway," these hours of insight became more and more rare, and the stirrings of buried feeling were associated with moods of regret for lost youth, regret for the freshness of the early world, moods of self-pity, moods of longing for

The hills where his life rose
And the sea where it goes.

Yet, though much of Arnold's most characteristic verse is in this vein of soliloquy or intimate confession, he can sometimes rise, as in "Sohrab and Rustum," to epic severity and impersonality; to lofty meditation, as in "Dover Beach"; and to sustained magnificence and richness, as in "The Scholar Gipsy" and "Thyrsis"—where he wields an intricate stanza form without a stumble.

In 1857, assisted by the vote of his godfather John Keble, Arnold was elected to the Oxford chair of poetry, which he held for 10 years. It was characteristic of him that he revolutionized this professorship. The keynote was struck in his inaugural lecture: "On the Modern Element in Literature," "modern" being taken to mean not merely "contemporary", but the spirit that, contemplating the vast and complex spectacle of life, craves for moral and intellectual "deliverance."

Several of the lectures were afterward published as critical essays, but the most substantial fruits of his professorship were the three lectures On Translating Homer—in which he recommended Homer's plainness and nobility as medicine for the modern world, with its "sick hurry and divided aims" and condemned Francis Newman's recent translation as ignoble and eccentric—and the lectures On the Study of Celtic Literature, in which, without much knowledge of his subject or of anthropology, he used the Celtic strain as a symbol of that which rejects the despotism of the commonplace and the utilitarian.

Arnold as Critic

It is said that when the poet in Arnold died, the critic was born; and it is true that from this time onward he turned almost entirely to prose. Some of the leading ideas and phrases were early put into currency in Essays in Criticism and Culture and Anarchy. The first essay in the 1865 volume, "The Function of Criticism at the Present Time," is an overture announcing briefly most of the themes he developed more fully in later work. It is at once evident that he ascribes to "criticism" a scope and importance hitherto undreamed of.

The function of criticism, in his sense, is "a disinterested endeavour to learn and propagate the best that is known and thought in the world, and thus to establish a current of fresh and true ideas." It is in fact a spirit that he is trying to foster, the spirit of an awakened and informed intelligence playing upon not "literature" merely but theology, history, art, science, sociology, and politics, and in every sphere seeking "to see the object as in itself it really is." In this critical effort, thought Arnold, England lagged behind France and Germany, and the English accordingly remained in a backwater of provinciality and complacency. Even the great Romantic poets, with all their creative energy, suffered from the want of it. The English literary critic must know literatures other than his own and be in touch with European standards.

This last line of thought Arnold develops in the second essay, "The Literary Influence of Academies," in which he dwells upon "the note of provinciality" in English literature, caused by remoteness from a "centre" of correct knowledge and correct taste. To realise how much Arnold widened the horizons of criticism requires only a glance at the titles of some of the other essays in Essays in Criticism: "Maurice de Guérin," "Eugénie de Guérin," "Heinrich Heine," "Joubert," "Spinoza," "Marcus Aurelius"; in all these, as increasingly in his later books, he is "applying modern ideas to life" as well as to letters and "bringing all things under the point of view of the 19th century."

The first essay in the 1888 volume, "The Study of Poetry," was originally published as the general introduction to T.H. Ward's anthology, The English Poets. It contains many of the ideas for which Arnold is best remembered. In an age of crumbling creeds, poetry will have to replace religion. More and more, we will "turn to poetry to interpret life for us, to console us, to sustain us." Therefore we must know how to distinguish the best poetry from the inferior, the genuine from the counterfeit; and to do this we must steep ourselves in the work of the acknowledged masters, using as "touchstones" passages exemplifying their "high seriousness," and their superiority of diction and movement.

The remaining essays, with the exception of the last two, all deal with English poets: Milton, Gray, Keats, Wordsworth, Byron, and Shelley. All contain memorable things, and all attempt a serious and responsible assessment of each poet's "criticism of life" and his value as food for the modern spirit. Arnold has been taken to task for some of his judgments and omissions: for his judgment that Dryden and Pope were not "genuine" poets because they composed in their wits instead of "in the soul"; for calling Gray a "minor classic" in an age of prose and spiritual bleakness; for paying too much attention to the man behind the poetry ; for making no mention of Donne; and above all for saying that poetry is "at bottom a criticism of life." On this last point it should be remembered that he added "under the conditions fixed...by the laws of poetic truth and poetic beauty," and that if by "criticism" is understood "evaluation," Arnold's dictum is seen to have wider significance than has been sometimes supposed.

Culture and Anarchy is in some ways Arnold's most central work. It is an expansion of his earlier attacks, in "The Function of Criticism" and "Heinrich Heine," upon the smugness, philistinism, and mammon worship of Victorian England. Culture, as "the study of perfection," is opposed to the prevalent "anarchy" of a new democracy without standards and without a sense of direction. By "turning a stream of fresh thought upon our stock notions and habits," culture seeks to make "reason and the will of God prevail."

Arnold's classification of English society into Barbarians, Philistines, and Populace is well known. Arnold saw in the Philistines the key to the whole position; they were now the most influential section of society; their strength was the nation's strength, their crudeness its crudeness: Educate and humanize the Philistines, therefore. Arnold saw in the idea of "the State," and not in any one class of society, the true organ and repository of the nation's collective "best self." No summary can do justice to this extraordinary book; it can still be read with pure enjoyment, for it is written with an inward poise, a serene detachment, and an infusion of mental laughter, which make it a masterpiece of ridicule as well as a searching analysis of Victorian society. The same is true of its unduly neglected sequel, Friendship's Garland.

Religious Writings

Lastly Arnold turned to religion, the constant preoccupation and true centre of his whole life, and wrote St. Paul and Protestantism, Literature and Dogma, God and the Bible, and Last Essays on Church and Religion. In these books, Arnold really founded Anglican "modernism." Like all religious liberals, he came under fire from two sides: from the orthodox, who accused him of infidelity, of turning God into a "stream of tendency" and of substituting vague emotion for definite belief; and from the infidels, for clinging to the church and retaining certain Christian beliefs of which he had undermined the foundations.

Arnold considered his religious writings to be constructive and conservative. Those who accused him of destructiveness did not realise how far historical and scientific criticism had already riddled the old foundations; and those who accused him of timidity failed to see that he regarded religion as the highest form of culture, the one indispensable without which all secular education is in vain.

His attitude is best summed up in his own words: "At the present moment two things about the Christian religion must surely be clear to anybody with eyes in his head. One is, that men cannot do without it; the other, that they cannot do with it as it is." Convinced that much in popular religion was "touched with the finger of death" and convinced no less of the hopelessness of man without religion, he sought to find for religion a basis of "scientific fact" that even the positive modern spirit must accept. A reading of Arnold's Note Books will convince any reader of the depth of Arnold's spirituality and of the degree to which, in his "buried life," he disciplined himself in constant devotion and self-forgetfulness.

Arnold died suddenly, of heart failure, in the spring of 1888, at Liverpool and was buried at Laleham, with the three sons whose early loss had shadowed his life.

Arthur Hugh Clough

While at Oxford, Clough had intended to become a clergyman, but his increasing religious skepticism caused him to leave the university. He became head of University Hall, London, in 1849, and in 1852, at the invitation of Ralph Waldo Emerson, he spent several months lecturing in Massachusetts. He later worked as a government education official and helped his wife's first cousin, Florence Nightingale, in her philanthropic work. While on a visit to Italy he contracted malaria and died at age 42. Clough's deeply critical and questioning attitude made him as doubtful of his own powers as he was about the spirit of his age, and he gave his contemporaries the impression of promise unfulfilled, especially since he left the bulk of his verse unpublished. Nonetheless, Clough's Poems proved so popular that they were reprinted 16 times within 40 years of his death. His best verse has a flavour that is closer to the taste and temper of the 20th century than to the Victorian age, however. Among his works are Bothie of Tober-na-Vuolich and Amours de Voyage, poems written in classical hexameters and dealing with romantic love, doubt, and social conflict. The long, incomplete poem Dipsychus most fully expresses Clough's doubts about the social and spiritual developments of his era, while his sharpest criticisms of Victorian moral complacency are found in "The Latest Decalogue":

Thou shalt not kill, but need'st not strive

Officiously to keep alive.

The Poems of Arthur Hugh Clough, edited by F.L. Mulhauser, is the standard edition of Clough's work.

THE NOVELISTS OF THE VICTORIAN AGE—CHARLES DICKENS (1812-1870)

When we consider Dickens's life and work, in comparison with that of the two great poets we have been studying, the contrast is startling. While Tennyson and Browning were being educated for the life of literature, and shielded most tenderly from the hardships of the world, Dickens, a poor, obscure, and suffering child, was helping to support a shiftless family by pasting labels on blacking bottles, sleeping under a counter like a homeless cat, and once a week timidly approaching the big prison where his father was confined for debt. In 1836 his Pickwick was published, and life was changed as if a magician had waved his wand over him. While the two great poets were slowly struggling for recognition, Dickens, with plenty of money and too much fame, was the acknowledged literary hero of England, the idol of immense audiences which gathered to applaud him wherever he appeared. And there is also this striking contrast between the novelist and the poets,--that while the whole tendency of the age was toward realism, away from the extremes of the romanticists and from the oddities and absurdities of the early novel writers, it was precisely by emphasizing oddities and absurdities, by making caricatures rather than characters, that Dickens first achieved his popularity.

Charles Dickens first attracted attention with the descriptive essays and tales originally written for newspapers, beginning in 1833, and collected as Sketches by "Boz". On the strength of this volume, Dickens contracted to write a historical novel in the tradition of Scott. By chance his gifts were turned into a more distinctive channel. In February 1836 he agreed to write the text for a series of comic engravings. The unexpected result was The Pickwick Papers, one of the funniest novels in English literature. By July 1837, sales of the monthly installments exceeded 40,000 copies. Dickens's extraordinary popular appeal and the enormous imaginative potential of the Victorian novel were simultaneously established.

The chief technical features of Dickens's fiction were also formed by this success. Serial publication encouraged the use of multiple plot and required that each episode be individually shaped. At the same time it produced an unprecedentedly close relationship between author and reader. Part dramatist, part journalist, part mythmaker, and part wit, Dickens took the picaresque tradition of Smollett and Fielding and gave it a Shakespearean vigour and variety. His early novels have been attacked at times for sentimentality, melodrama, or shapelessness. They are now increasingly appreciated for their comic or macabre zest and their poetic fertility. Dombey and Son marks the beginning of Dickens's later period.

He thenceforth combined his gift for vivid caricature with a stronger sense of personality, designed his plots more carefully, and used symbolism to give his books greater thematic coherence. Of the masterpieces of the next decade, David Copperfield uses the form of a fictional autobiography to explore the great Romantic theme of the growth and comprehension of the self. Bleak House addresses itself to law and litigiousness; Hard Times is a Carlylean defence of art in an age of mechanism; and Little Dorrit dramatizes the idea of imprisonment, both literal and spiritual. Two great novels, both involved with issues of social class and human worth, appeared in the 1860s: Great Expectations and Our Mutual Friend. His final book, The Mystery of Edwin Drood, was left tantalizingly uncompleted at the time of his death.

The defining moment of Dickens's life occurred when he was 12 years old. With his father in debtors' prison, he was withdrawn from school and forced to work in a factory. This deeply affected the sensitive boy. Though he returned to school at 13, his formal education ended at 15. As a young man, he worked as a reporter. His fiction career began with short pieces reprinted as Sketches by "Boz". He exhibited a great ability to spin a story in an entertaining manner and this quality, combined with the serialization of his comic novel The Pickwick Papers, made him the most popular English author of his time.

The serialization of such works as Oliver Twist and The Old Curiosity Shop followed. After a trip to America, he wrote A Christmas Carol in a few weeks. With Dombey and Son, his novels began to express a heightened uneasiness about the evils of Victorian industrial society, which intensified in the semiautobiographical David Copperfield, as well as in Bleak House, Little Dorrit, Great Expectations, and others. A Tale of Two Cities appeared in the period when he achieved great popularity for his public readings. Dickens's works are characterized by an encyclopaedic knowledge of London, pathos, a vein of the macabre, a pervasive spirit of benevolence and geniality, inexhaustible powers of character creation, an acute ear for characteristic speech, and a highly individual and inventive prose style.

Dickens enjoyed a wider popularity than had any previous author during his lifetime. Much in his work could appeal to simple and sophisticated, to the poor and to the Queen, and technological developments as well as the qualities of his work enabled his fame to spread worldwide very quickly. His long career saw fluctuations in the reception and sales of individual novels, but none of them was negligible or uncharacteristic or disregarded, and, though he is now admired for aspects and phases of his work that were given less weight by his contemporaries, his popularity has never ceased and his present critical standing is higher than ever before. The most abundantly comic of English authors, he was much more than a great entertainer. The range, compassion, and intelligence of his apprehension of his society and its shortcomings enriched his novels and made him both one of the great forces in 19th-century literature and an influential spokesman of the conscience of his age.

Early Years

Dickens left Portsmouth in infancy. His happiest childhood years were spent in Chatham, an area to which he often reverts in his fiction. From 1822 he lived in London, until, in 1860, he moved permanently to a country house, Gad's Hill, near Chatham. His origins were middle class, if of a newfound and precarious respectability; one grandfather had been a domestic servant, and the other an embezzler. His father, a clerk in the navy pay office, was well paid, but his extravagance and ineptitude often brought the family to financial embarrassment or disaster.

In 1824 the family reached bottom. Charles, the eldest son, had been withdrawn from school and was now set to manual work in a factory, and his father went to prison for debt. These shocks deeply affected Charles. Though abhorring this brief descent into the working class, he began to gain that sympathetic knowledge of their life and privations that informed his writings. Also, the images of the prison and of the lost, oppressed, or bewildered child recur in many novels. Much else in his character and art stems from this period, including, as the 20th-century novelist Angus Wilson has argued, his later difficulty, as man and author, in understanding women: this may be traced to his bitter resentment against his mother, who had, he felt, failed disastrously at this time to appreciate his sufferings. She had wanted him to stay at work when his father's release from prison and an improvement in the family's fortunes made the boy's return to school possible. Happily the father's view prevailed.

His schooling, interrupted and unimpressive, ended at 15. He became a clerk in a solicitor's office, then a shorthand reporter in the lawcourts, and finally, like other members of his family, a parliamentary and newspaper reporter. These years left him with a lasting affection for journalism and contempt both for the law and for Parliament. His coming to manhood in the reformist 1830s, and particularly his working on the Liberal Benthamite Morning Chronicle, greatly affected his political outlook.

Another influential event now was his rejection as suitor to Maria Beadnell because his family and prospects were unsatisfactory; his hopes of gaining and chagrin at losing her sharpened his determination to succeed. His feelings about Maria then and at her later brief and disillusioning reentry into his life are reflected in David Copperfield's adoration of Dora Spenlow and in the middle-aged Arthur Clennam's discovery that Flora Finching, who had seemed enchanting years ago, was "diffuse and silly," that Flora "whom he had left a lily, had become a peony."

Life

In Dickens's early life we see a stern but unrecognized preparation for the work that he was to do. Never was there a better illustration of the fact that a boy's early hardship and suffering are sometimes only divine messengers disguised, and that circumstances which seem only evil are often the source of a man's strength and of the influence which he is to wield in the world. He was the second of eight poor children, and was born at Landport in 1812. His father, who is supposed to be the original of Mr. Micawber, was a clerk in a navy office. He could never make both ends meet, and after struggling with debts in his native town for many years, moved to London when Dickens was nine years old. The debts still pursued him, and after two years of grandiloquent misfortune he was thrown into the poor-debtors' prison. His wife, the original of Mrs. Micawber, then set up the famous Boarding Establishment for Young Ladies; but, in Dickens's words, no young ladies ever came. The only visitors were creditors, and they were quite ferocious. In the picture of the Micawber family, with its tears and smiles and general shiftlessness, we have a suggestion of Dickens's own family life.

At eleven years of age the boy was taken out of school and went to work in the cellar of a blacking factory. At this time he was, in his own words, a "queer small boy," who suffered as he worked; and we can appreciate the boy and the suffering more when we find both reflected in the character of David Copperfield. It is a heart-rending picture, this sensitive child working from dawn till dark for a few pennies, and associating with toughs and waifs in his brief intervals of labor; but we can see in it the sources of that intimate knowledge of the hearts of the poor and outcast which was soon to be reflected in literature and to startle all England by its appeal for sympathy.

A small legacy ended this wretchedness, bringing the father from the prison and sending the boy to Wellington House Academy,--a worthless and brutal school, evidently, whose head master was, in Dickens's words, a most ignorant fellow and a tyrant. He learned little at this place, being interested chiefly in stories, and in acting out the heroic parts which appealed to his imagination; but again his personal experience was of immense value, and resulted in his famous picture of Dotheboys Hall, in Nicholas Nickleby, which helped largely to mitigate the evils of private schools in England.

Wherever he went, Dickens was a marvelously keen observer, with an active imagination which made stories out of incidents and characters that ordinary men would have hardly noticed. Moreover he was a born actor, and was at one time the leading spirit of a band of amateurs who gave entertainments for charity all over England. These three things, his keen observation, his active imagination, and the actor's spirit which animated him, furnish a key to his life and writings.

When only fifteen years old, he left the school and again went to work, this time as clerk in a lawyer's office. By night he studied shorthand, in order to fit himself to be a reporter,--this in imitation of his father, who was now engaged by a newspaper to report the speeches in Parliament. Everything that Dickens attempted seems to have been done with vigor and intensity, and within two years we find him reporting important speeches, and writing out his notes as the heavy coach lurched and rolled through the mud of country roads on its dark way to London town. It was largely during this period that he gained his extraordinary knowledge of inns and stables and "horsey" persons, which is reflected in his novels. He also grew ambitious, and began to write on his own account. At the age of twenty-one he dropped his first little sketch "stealthily, with fear and trembling, into a dark letter-box, in a dark office up a dark court in Fleet Street."

The name of this first sketch was "Mr. Minns and his Cousin," and it appeared with other stories in his first book, Sketches by Boz, in 1835. One who reads these sketches now, with their intimate knowledge of the hidden life of London, can understand Dickens's first newspaper success perfectly.

His best known work, Pickwick, was published serially in 1836-1837, and Dickens's fame and fortune were made. Never before had a novel appeared so full of vitality and merriment. Though crude in design, a mere jumble of exaggerated characters and incidents, it fairly bubbled over with the kind of humor in which the British public delights, and it still remains, after three quarters of a century, one of our most care-dispelling books.

The remainder of Dickens's life is largely a record of personal triumphs. Pickwick was followed rapidly by Oliver Twist, Nicholas Nickleby, Old Curiosity Shop, and by many other works which seemed to indicate that there was no limit to the new author's invention of odd, grotesque, uproarious, and sentimental characters.

In the intervals of his novel writing he attempted several times to edit a weekly paper; but his power lay in other directions, and with the exception of Household Words, his journalistic ventures were not a marked success. Again the actor came to the surface, and after managing a company of amateur actors successfully, Dickens began to give dramatic readings from his own works. As he was already the most popular writer in the English language, these readings were very successful.

Crowds thronged to hear him, and his journeys became a continuous ovation. Money poured into his pockets from his novels and from his readings, and he bought for himself a home, Gadshill Place, which he had always desired, and which is forever associated with his memory. Though he spent the greater part of his time and strength in travel at this period, nothing is more characteristic of the man than the intense energy with which he turned from his lecturing to his novels, and then, for relaxation, gave himself up to what he called the magic lantern of the London streets.

In 1842, while still a young man, Dickens was invited to visit the United States and Canada, where his works were even better known than in England, and where he was received as the guest of the nation and treated with every mark of honor and appreciation. At this time America was, to most Europeans, a kind of huge fairyland, where money sprang out of the earth, and life was happy as a long holiday. Dickens evidently shared this rosy view, and his romantic expectations were naturally disappointed.

The crude, unfinished look of the big country seems to have roused a strong prejudice in his mind, which was not overcome at the time of his second visit, twenty-five years later, and which brought forth the harsh criticism of his American Notes (1842) and of Martin Chuzzlewit (1843-1844).

These two unkind books struck a false note, and Dickens began to lose something of his great popularity. In addition he had spent money beyond his income. His domestic life, which had been at first very happy, became more and more irritating, until he separated from his wife in 1858. To get inspiration, which seemed for a time to have failed, he journeyed to Italy, but was disappointed.

Then he turned back to the London streets, and in the five years from 1848 to 1853 appeared Dombey and Son, David Copperfield, and Bleak House,--three remarkable novels, which indicate that he had rediscovered his own power and genius. Later he resumed the public readings, with their public triumph and applause, which soon came to be a necessity to one who craved popularity as a hungry man craves bread.

These excitements exhausted Dickens, physically and spiritually, and death was the inevitable result. He died in 1870, over his unfinished Edwin Drood, and was buried in Westminster Abbey.

Dickens's Work in View of His Life

A glance through even this unsatisfactory biography gives us certain illuminating suggestions in regard to all of Dickens's work. First, as a child, poor and lonely, longing for love and for society, he laid the foundation for those heartrending pictures of children, which have moved so many readers to unaccustomed tears.

Second, as clerk in a lawyer's office and in the courts, he gained his knowledge of an entirely different side of human life. Here he learned to understand both the enemies and the victims of society, between whom the harsh laws of that day frequently made no distinction. Third, as a reporter, and afterwards as manager of various newspapers, he learned the trick of racy writing, and of knowing to a nicety what would suit the popular taste. Fourth, as an actor, always an actor in spirit, he seized upon every dramatic possibility, every tense situation, every peculiarity of voice and gesture in the people whom he met, and reproduced these things in his novels, exaggerating them in the way that most pleased his audience.

When we turn from his outward training to his inner disposition we find two strongly marked elements. The first is his excessive imagination, which made good stories out of incidents that ordinarily pass unnoticed, and which described the commonest things--a street, a shop, a fog, a lamp-post, a stagecoach--with a wealth of detail and of romantic suggestion that makes many of his descriptions like lyric poems. The second element is his extreme sensibility, which finds relief only in laughter and tears. Like shadow and sunshine these follow one another closely throughout all his books.

Remembering these two things, his training and disposition, we can easily foresee the kind of novel he must produce. He will be sentimental, especially over children and outcasts; he will excuse the individual in view of the faults of society; he will be dramatic or melodramatic; and his sensibility will keep him always close to the public, studying its tastes and playing with its smiles and tears. If pleasing the public be in itself an art, then Dickens is one of our greatest artists. And it is well to remember that in pleasing his public there was nothing of the hypocrite or demagogue in his make-up. He was essentially a part of the great drifting panoramic crowd that he loved.

His sympathetic soul made all their joys and griefs his own. He fought against injustice; he championed the weak against the strong; he gave courage to the faint, and hope to the weary in heart; and in the love which the public gave him in return he found his best reward. Here is the secret of Dickens's unprecedented popular success, and we may note here a very significant parallel with Shakespeare. The great different in the genius and work of the two men does not change the fact that each won success largely because he studied and pleased his public.

General Plan of Dickens's Novels

An interesting suggestion comes to us from a study of the conditions which led to Dickens's first three novels. Pickwick was written, at the suggestion of an editor, for serial publication. Each chapter was to be accompanied by a cartoon by Seymor (a comic artist of the day), and the object was to amuse the public, and, incidentally, to sell the paper.

The result was a series of characters and scenes and incidents which for vigor and boundless fun have never been equaled in our language. Thereafter, no matter what he wrote, Dickins was lbeled a humorist. Like a certain American writer of our own generation, everything he said, whether for a feast or a funeral, was spposed to contain a laugh. In a word, he was the victim of his own book.

Dickens was keen enough to understand his danger, and his next novel, Oliver Twist, had the serious purpose of mitigating the evils under which the poor were suffering. Its hero was a poor child, the unfortunate victim of society; and, in order to draw attention to the real need, Dickens exaggerated the woeful condition of the poor, and filled his pages with sentiment which easily slipped over into sentimentality.

This also was a popular success, and in his third novel, Nicholas Nickleby, and indeed in most of his remaining works, Dickens combined the principles of his first two books, giving us mirth on the one hand, injustice and suffering on the other; mingling humor and pathos, tears and laughter, as we find them in life itself. And in order to increase the lights and shadows in his scenes, and to give greater dramatic effect to his narrative, he introduced odious and lothsome characters, and made vice more hateful by contrasting it with innocence and virtue.

We find, therefore, in most of Dickens's novels three or four widely different types of character: first, the innocent little child, like Oliver, Joe, Paul, Tiny Tim, and Little Nell, appealing powerfully to the child love in every human heart; scond, the horrible or grotesque foil, like Sqeers, Fagin, Quilp, Uriah Heep, and Bill Sykes; third, the grandiloquent or broadly humorous fellow, the fun maker, like Micawber and Sam Weller; and fourth, a tenderly or powerfully drawn figure, like Lady Deadlock of Bleak House, and Sydney Carton of A Tale of Two Cities, which rise to the dignity of true characters.

We note also that most of Dickens's novels belong decidely to the class of purpose or problem novels. Thus Bleak House attacks "the law's delays"; Little Dorrit, the injustice which persecutes poor debtors; Nicholas Nickleby, the abuses of charity schools and brutal schoolmasters; and Oliver Twist, the unnecessary degradation and suffering of the poor in English workhouses. Dickens's serious purpose was to make the novel the instrument of morality and justice, and whatver we may think of the exaggeration of his characters, it is certain that his stories did more to correct the general selfishness and injustice of society toward the poor than all the works of other literary men of his age combined.

The Limitations of Dickens

Any severe criticism of Dickens as a novelist must seem, at first glance, unkind an unnecessary. In almost every house he is a welcome guest, a personal friend who has beguiled many an hour with his stories, and who has furnished us much good laughter and a few good tears. Moreover, he has always a cheery message. He emphasizes the fact that this is an excellant world; that some errors have crept into it, due largely to thoughtlessness, but that they can be easily remedied by a little human sympathy. That is a most welcome creed to an age overburdened with social problems; and to criticise our cheery companion seems as discourteous as to speak unkindly of a guest who has just left our home. But we must consider Dickens not merely as a friend, but as a novelist, and apply to his work the same standards of art which we apply to other writers; and when we do this we are sometimes a little disappointed.

We must confess that his novels, while they contain many realistic details, seldom give the impression of reality. His characters, though we laugh or weep or shudder at them, are sometimes only caricatures, each one an exaggeration of some peculiarity, which suggest Ben Jonson's Every Man in His Humour. It is Dickens's art to give his heroes sufficient reality to make them suggest certain types of men and women whom we know; but in reading him we find ourselves often in the mental state of a man who is watching through a microscope the swarming life of a water drop.

Here are lively, bustling, extraordinary creatures, some beautiful, some grotesque, but all far apart from the life that we know in daily experience. It is certainly not the reality of these characters, but rather the genius of the author in managing them, which interests us and holds our attention. Notwithstanding this criticism, which we would gladly have omitted, Dickens is excellent reading, and his novels will continue to be popular just so long as men enjoy a wholesome and absorbing story.

Aside from the reforms in schools and prisons and workhouses which Dickens accomplished, he has laid us all, rich and poor alike, under a debt of gratitude. After the year 1843 the one literary work which he never neglected was to furnish a Christmas story for his readers; and it is due in some measure to the help of these stories, brimming over with good cheer, that Christmas has become in all English-speaking countries a season of gladness, of gift giving at home, and of remembering those less fortunate than ourselves, who are still members of a common brotherhood. If we read nothing else of Dickens, once a year, at Christmas time, we should remember him and renew our youth by reading one of his holiday stories,- The Cricket on the Hearth, The Chimes, and above all the unrivaled Christmas Carol. The latter especially will be read and loved as long as men are moved by the spirit of Christmas.

Of the novels, David Copperfield is regarded by many as Dickens's masterpiece. It is well to begin with this novel, not simply for the unusual interest of the story, but also for the glimpse it gives us of the author's own boyhood and family. For pure fun and hilarity Pickwick will always be a favorite; but for artistic finish, and for the portrayal of one great character, Sydney Carton, nothing else that Dickens wrote is comparable to A Tale of Two Cities.

Here is an absorbing story, with a carefully constructed plot, and the action moves swiftly to its thrilling, inevitable conclusion. Usually Dickens introduces several pathetic or grotesque or laughable characters besides the main actors, and records various unnecessary dramatic episodes for their own sake; but in A Tale of Two Cities everything has its place in the development of the main story. There are, as usual, many characters,--Sydney Carton, the outcast, who lays down his life for the happiness of one whom he loves; Charles Darnay, an exiled young French noble; Dr. Manette, who has been "recalled to life" from a frightful imprisonment, and his gentle daughter Lucie, the heroine; Jarvis Lorry, a lovable, old-fashioned clerk in the big banking house; the terrible Madame Defarge, knitting calmly at the door of her wine shop and recording, with the ferocity of a tiger licking its chops, the names of all those who are marked for vengeance; and a dozen others, each well drawn, who play minor parts in the tragedy. The scene is laid in London and Paris, at the time of the French Revolution; and, though careless of historical details, Dickens reproduces the spirit of the Reign of Terror so well that A Tale of Two Cities is an excellent supplement to the history of the period. It is written in Dickens's usual picturesque style, and reveals his usual imaginative outlook on life and his fondness for fine sentiments and dramatic episodes. Indeed, all his qualities are here shown, not brilliantly or garishly, as in other novels, but subdued and softened, like a shaded light, for artistic effect.

Those who are interested in Dickens's growth and methods can hardly do better than to read in succession his first three novels, Pickwick, Oliver Twist, and Nicholas Nickleby, which, as we have indicated, show clearly how he passed from fun to serious purpose, and which furnish in combination the general plan of all his later works. For the rest, we can only indicate those which, in our personal judgment, seem best worth reading,--Bleak House, Dombey and Son, Our Mutual Friend, and Old Curiosity Shop,--but we are not yet far enough away from the first popular success of these works to determine their permanent value and influence.

Beginning of Literary Career

Much drawn to the theatre, Dickens nearly became a professional actor in 1832. In 1833 he began contributing stories and descriptive essays to magazines and newspapers; these attracted attention and were reprinted as Sketches by "Boz". The same month, he was invited to provide a comic serial narrative to accompany engravings by a well-known artist; seven weeks later the first installment of Pickwick Papers appeared.

Within a few months Pickwick was the rage and Dickens the most popular author of the day. During 1836 he also wrote two plays and a pamphlet on a topical issue and, resigning from his newspaper job, undertook to edit a monthly magazine, Bentley's Miscellany, in which he serialized Oliver Twist. Thus, he had two serial installments to write every month. Already the first of his nine surviving children had been born; he had married Catherine, eldest daughter of a respected Scottish journalist and man of letters, George Hogarth.

For several years his life continued at this intensity. Finding serialization congenial and profitable, he repeated the Pickwick pattern of 20 monthly parts in Nicholas Nickleby ; then he experimented with shorter weekly installments for The Old Curiosity Shop and Barnaby Rudge. Exhausted at last, he then took a five-month vacation in America, touring strenuously and receiving quasi-royal honours as a literary celebrity but offending national sensibilities by protesting against the absence of copyright protection. A radical critic of British institutions, he had expected more from "the republic of my imagination," but he found more vulgarity and sharp practice to detest than social arrangements to admire. Some of these feelings appear in American Notes and Martin Chuzzlewit.

First Novels

His writing during these prolific years was remarkably various and, except for his plays, resourceful. Pickwick began as high-spirited farce and contained many conventional comic butts and traditional jokes; like other early works, it was manifestly indebted to the contemporary theatre, the 18th-century English novelists, and a few foreign classics, notably Don Quixote. But, besides giving new life to old stereotypes, Pickwick displayed, if sometimes in embryo, many of the features that were to be blended in varying proportions throughout his fiction: attacks, satirical or denunciatory, on social evils and inadequate institutions; topical references; an encyclopaedic knowledge of London ; pathos; a vein of the macabre; a delight in the demotic joys of Christmas; a pervasive spirit of benevolence and geniality; inexhaustible powers of character creation; a wonderful ear for characteristic speech, often imaginatively heightened; a strong narrative impulse; and a prose style that, if here overdependent on a few comic mannerisms, was highly individual and inventive. Rapidly improvised and written only weeks or days ahead of its serial publication, Pickwick contains weak and jejune passages and is an unsatisfactory whole—partly because Dickens was rapidly developing his craft as a novelist while writing and publishing it. What is remarkable is that a first novel, written in such circumstances, not only established him overnight and created a new tradition of popular literature but also survived, despite its crudities, as one of the best known novels in the world.

Oliver Twist and Others

His self-assurance and artistic ambitiousness had appeared in Oliver Twist, where he rejected the temptation to repeat the successful Pickwick formula. Though containing much comedy still, Oliver Twist is more centrally concerned with social and moral evil ; it culminates in Bill Sikes's murdering Nancy and Fagin's last night in the condemned cell at Newgate. The latter episode was memorably depicted in George Cruikshank's engraving; the imaginative potency of Dickens' characters and settings owes much, indeed, to his original illustrators.

The currency of his fiction owed much, too, to its being so easy to adapt into effective stage versions. Sometimes 20 London theatres simultaneously were producing adaptations of his latest story; so even nonreaders became acquainted with simplified versions of his works. The theatre was often a subject of his fiction, too, as in the Crummles troupe in Nicholas Nickleby. This novel reverted to the Pickwick shape and atmosphere, though the indictment of the brutal Yorkshire schools continued the important innovation in English fiction seen in Oliver Twist—the spectacle of the lost or oppressed child as an occasion for pathos and social criticism. This was amplified in The Old Curiosity Shop, where the death of Little Nell was found overwhelmingly powerful at the time, though a few decades later it became a byword for "Victorian sentimentality." In Barnaby Rudge he attempted another genre, the historical novel. Like his later attempt in this kind, A Tale of Two Cities, it was set in the late 18th century and presented with great vigour and understanding the spectacle of large-scale mob violence.

To create an artistic unity out of the wide range of moods and materials included in every novel, with often several complicated plots involving scores of characters, was made even more difficult by Dickens' writing and publishing them serially. In Martin Chuzzlewit he tried "to resist the temptation of the current Monthly Number, and to keep a steadier eye upon the general purpose and design". Its American episodes had, however, been unpremeditated. A concentration on "the general purpose and design" was more effective in the next novel, Dombey and Son, though the experience of writing the shorter, and unserialized, Christmas books had helped him obtain greater coherence.

Christmas Books

A Christmas Carol, suddenly conceived and written in a few weeks, was the first of these Christmas books. Tossed off while he was amply engaged in writing Chuzzlewit, it was an extraordinary achievement—the one great Christmas myth of modern literature. His view of life was later to be described or dismissed as "Christmas philosophy," and he himself spoke of "Carol philosophy" as the basis of a projected work. His "philosophy," never very elaborated, involved more than wanting the Christmas spirit to prevail throughout the year, but his great attachment to Christmas is indeed significant and has contributed to his popularity. "Dickens dead?" exclaimed a London costermonger's girl in 1870. "Then will Father Christmas die too?"—a tribute both to his association with Christmas and to the mythological status of the man as well as of his work. The Carol immediately entered the general consciousness; Thackeray, in a review, called it "a national benefit, and to every man and woman who reads it a personal kindness." Further Christmas books, essays, and stories followed annually through 1867. None equalled the Carol in potency, though some achieved great immediate popularity. Cumulatively they represent a celebration of Christmas attempted by no other great author.

Modern Criticism

Modern Dickens criticism dates from 1940–41, with the very different impulses given by George Orwell, Edmund Wilson, and Humphry House. In the 1950s, a substantial reassessment and re-editing of the works began, his finest artistry and greatest depth now being discovered in the later novels—Bleak House, Little Dorrit, and Great Expectations—and in Hard Times and Our Mutual Friend.

Scholars have explored his working methods, his relations with his public, and the ways in which he was simultaneously an eminently Victorian figure and an author "not of an age but for all time." Biographically, little had been added to Forster's massive and intelligent Life, except the Ellen Ternan story, until Edgar Johnson's in 1952. Since then, no radically new view has emerged, though several works—including those by Joseph Gold and Fred Kaplan—have given particular phases or aspects fuller attention. The centenary in 1970 demonstrated a critical consensus about his standing second only to William Shakespeare in English literature, which would have seemed incredible 40 or even 20 years earlier.

Thackeray, Gaskell, and Others

Unlike Dickens, William Makepeace Thackeray came from a wealthy and educated background. The loss of his fortune at age 22, however, meant that he too learned his trade in the field of sketch writing and occasional journalism. His early fictions were published as serials in Fraser's Magazine or as contributions to the great Victorian comic magazine Punch. For his masterpiece, Vanity Fair, however, he adopted Dickens's procedure of publication in monthly parts. Thackeray's satirical acerbity is here combined with a broad narrative sweep, a sophisticated self-consciousness about the conventions of fiction, and an ambitious historical survey of the transformation of English life in the years between the Regency and the mid-Victorian period. His later novels never match this sharpness. Vanity Fair was subtitled "A Novel Without a Hero." Subsequently, it has been suggested, a more sentimental Thackeray wrote novels without villains.

6

Romantic Period Writers

JOHN KEATS

John Keats (31 October 1795 – 23 February 1821) was an English Romantic poet. He was one of the main figures of the second generation of Romantic poets, along with Lord Byron and Percy Bysshe Shelley, despite his works having been in publication for only four years before his death at age 25 in the year 1821.

Although his poems were not generally well received by critics during his lifetime, his reputation grew after his death, and by the end of the 19th century, he had become one of the most beloved of all English poets. He had a significant influence on a diverse range of poets and writers. Jorge Luis Borges stated that his first encounter with Keats's work was the most significant literary experience of his life.

The poetry of Keats is characterized by sensual imagery, most notably in the series of odes. This is typical of romantic poets, as they aimed to accentuate extreme emotion through the emphasis of natural imagery. Today his poems and letters are some of the most popular and most analysed in English literature. Some of the most acclaimed works of Keats are "I Stood Tip-toe Upon a Little Hill", "Sleep and Poetry", and the famous sonnet "On First Looking into Chapman's Homer".

Early life

John Keats, who died at the age of twenty-five, had perhaps the most remarkable career of any English poet. English Romantic poet John Keats was born on October 31, 1795, in London. The oldest of four children, he lost both his parents at a young age. His father, a livery-stable keeper, died when Keats was eight; his mother died of tuberculosis six years later. After his mother's death, Keats's maternal grandmother appointed two London merchants, Richard Abbey and John Rowland Sandell, as guardians. Abbey, a prosperous tea broker, assumed the bulk of this responsibility, while Sandell played only a minor role. When Keats was fifteen, Abbey withdrew him from the Clarke School, Enfield, to apprentice with an apothecary-surgeon and study medicine in a London hospital. In 1816 Keats became a licensed apothecary, but he never practiced his profession, deciding instead to write poetry.

Keats give up poetry

We know little of Keats's life during these years 1811-1814, other than that Keats assisted Hammond and began the study of anatomy and physiology. Surgery would have been a respectable and reasonable profession for one of Keats's means: unlike the profession of medicine, the job of surgeon in Keats's day did not require a university degree. A surgeon, licensed by examination, was a general practitioner, setting bones, dressing wounds, giving vaccinations. Keats always maintained he was "ambitious of doing the world some good." It is likely that he began his career with enthusiasm, but living in the small rooms over the surgery, Keats grew restless and lonely; he began to wander the woods and walk the four miles to Enfield to see the Clarkes. He completed his translation of the Aeneid, and, according to Cowden Clarke, he "devoured rather than read" books he borrowed: Ovid's Metamorphosis , John Milton's Paradise Lost, Virgil's Eclogues, and dozens of others. But the book that decisively awakened his love of poetry, indeed shocked him suddenly into self-awareness of his own powers of imagination, was Edmund Spenser's Faerie Queene.

His friend Charles Brown believed Keats first read Spenser when he was eighteen, in 1813 or 1814: "From his earliest boyhood he had an acute sense of beauty, whether in a flower, a tree, the sky, or the animal world; how was it that his sense of beauty did not naturally seek in his mind for images by which he could best express his feelings? It was the `Fairy Queen' that awakened his genius. In Spenser's fairy land he was enchanted, breathed in a new world, and became another being. . . ." Soon, wrote Brown, he "was entirely absorbed in poetry." (Brown subsequently struck out the word entirely.) Clarke recalled Keats's exuberant joy, "he ramped through the scenes of that purely poetical romance, like a young horse into a Spring meadow." Some time in 1814 Keats wrote his first poem, "In Imitation of Spenser." What is remarkable about this first poem is its vitality, its appropriation of the Spenserian rhyme scheme and richly compressed imagery to evoke a romantically voluptuous dream world. It is a youthful piece. But the poetic ear is acute, the natural description delights in itself, and even when clumsy the verse dares with naive persistence to draw attention to the power of poetic image to set a dreamy scene ("Ah! could I tell the wonders of an isle / That in that fairest lake had been / I could e'en Dido of her grief beguile." And of course he does attempt to tell).

if these elements in Hunt's poetry seemed declassé to his and Keats's critics, today one cannot say that Hunt's influence on Keats was in any simple sense bad. For one thing Hunt was not Keats's only model. Spenser was a more serious and enduring influence, as were Browne, Drayton, Milton, Wordsworth, and later, Shakespeare. Most twenty-year-old poets need a model of some sort, and there were certainly more banal models in his day from which to choose. On the other hand (as Walter Jackson Bate suggests), to attempt to have written like a greater and more popular poet, like Byron, would not have had the energizing effect on Keats's verse that Hunt had. Hunt enabled Keats to write and, eventually, to surpass him.

For a young middle-class liberal with no university training, a healthy dislike of Pope and an enthusiasm for Hunt and Wordsworth provided an enabling sense of identity. Finally, Keats was by no means, even in 1815-1816, a slavish imitator. His works have a troubled sense of self-consciousness completely absent from Hunt's. Keats's are also poems of escape to nature, and in these tropes we can sense as much Keats's very shrewd (and early) understanding of Wordsworth's poetic project as of Hunt's. In poems such as the fine sonnet "How many bards gild the lapses of time!" or the "Ode to Apollo," or the lovely (summer 1816) sonnet "Oh! how I love, on a fair summer's eve," one finds an important Keatsian trope: the poem about the poet's own sense of himself as a modern, preparing to write from his experience a new poetry to match that of England's great writers.

As he would so often, Keats wrote the "Homer" sonnet in response to the power and imaginative vision of another poet. And again, that power is perceived as an absence, a gap between Keats's small voice—or the concrete experience of any individual—and the sublime limitlessness of a great and distant imagination (this tension reappears in the more complex relation of the poet to the Grecian urn and the nightingale). Unlike his first sonnets, inspired by the natural charm of Hunt's sonnets, this sonnet is based on a structural principle that he would later bring to perhaps its greatest fulfillment in English poetry in his odes, the expression of the irresolvable contrarieties of experience in the interplay of verse elements—quatrain, octave and sestet, rhymes, words, and even sounds. In this sonnet, the energy and excitement of literary discovery—Keats, in reading Homer, feels not bookish pleasure but the awe of a conquistador reaching the edge of an uncharted sea—is presented as direct emotion, not, as it had been in the epistles, a disabling and self-conscious pose. The emotion is, for the first time, sustained and controlled throughout the verse, with a sureness of diction, and even sound, that never falters: for example, the sense of openness to a vast sea of wonder is suggested by long vowels ("wild," "surmise," "silent"), tapering off to hushed awe in the weak syllables of the final word, "Silent, upon a peak in Darien." As published (with line 7 altered, in The Examiner , 1 December 1816), the sonnet takes its place with Wordsworth's and some of Keats's own, as among the finest of the nineteenth century.

Keats's first volume, Poems, appeared on 3 March 1817, with its dedicatory sonnet to Leigh Hunt. It begins with "I stood tip-toe," ends with another long poem, "Sleep and Poetry," and includes youthful poems as well as some recent, good work, "Keen, fitful gusts"; the poem to Wordsworth, Hunt, and Haydon, "Addressed to the Same Haydon"; and the three long verse epistles, to Mathew, George Keats, and Clarke.

Endymion is in many ways a response to Shelley's Alastor (1816), where a young poet dreams of an ideal mate, in fruitless pursuit of whom he quests across the world, only to die alone and unloved. Keats's poem begins with a mortal, Endymion, discovered restless and unhappy with the pastoral delights of his kingdom, for he has become enraptured with a dream vision, the moon goddess Cynthia. After a series of adventures, he abandons his restless quest, which by book 4 has come to seem illusory, in favour of an earthly Indian maid, who is eventually revealed to have been Cynthia all along. Although the actual narrative will hardly bear much scrutiny, the themes evoked here would haunt Keats all his life. Only through a love for the earthly is the ideal reached, the real and the ideal becoming one through an intense, sensuous love that leads to a "fellowship with essence." The theme of a mortal's love for an ideal figure that proves either illusory or redemptive would be a continuing source of philosophical exploration and ironic play for Keats, as would the paradox of redemption or transcendence evolving from a fuller engagement with human suffering and finitude.

The poetry of Endymion varies widely from some thoughtful speeches and lovely description to some of the most awful and self-indulgent verse ever written by a mature major English poet. The story is tedious and the point often obscure. The critical reaction to Endymion was infamous for its ferocity. The poem appeared in late April 1818; there was a supportive notice by Bailey in the Oxford University and City Herald (30 May and 6 June 1818) and an extremely perceptive review (by Reynolds or perhaps John Scott) in the

Champion (7 and 14 June 1818): "Mr. Keats goes out of himself into a world of abstraction:—his passions, feelings, are all as much imaginative as his situations when he writes of passion, it seems to have possessed him. This, however, is what Shakespeare did."

Poetically, as Endymion was finished and a new poem, Isabella, begun, it was a time of intense introspection and transition marking Keats's emergence as a poet whose most authentic subject would be the difficulties of writing romance itself, the genre paradigmatic for Keats of the transforming power of art, of the simple wonder of storytelling. Romance also implies a quest for closure, for a realized (or at least clearly envisioned) dream, and Keats questioned whether modern poetry can embody such belief. The romance he wrote in March 1818, Isabella, based on a tale of Boccaccio, is an uneven poem, and though some of his contemporaries (including Lamb) admired it, Keats came to dislike it. It is best thought of as an experiment in tone, teetering uneasily between poignant, romantic tragedy and a dry, uneasy, narrational pose.

Throughout the autumn of 1818 he began composing his most brilliant work yet, a poem even his critics saw as a major achievement, Hyperion. Keats's biographer Walter Jackson Bate has observed that the year that began with the fragment epic Hyperion "may be soberly described as the most productive in the life of any poet of the past three centuries." One senses, too, in this annus mirabilis, an unprecedented engagement with three centuries of literary convention, a stretching out and probing of the limits of epic, ode, pastoral, and romance that realigns these forms with Keats's modern sense of an uncanny reciprocity between myth and history, fantasy and experience, noble aspiration and tragic disillusionment. This is the stuff of Hyperion, and its interest is its fresh engagement with these issues, as they cluster around a traditional Western icon: the fall into suffering of the mighty or good and the hope for compensatory redemption. Hyperion tells the story of the fall of the Titans and their replacement by the Gods, more beautiful than the Titans by virtue of their superior knowledge, and, so, by implication, their insight into the suffering of humanity.

It is impossible to say how much has been lost by Keats's early death. His reputation grew steadily throughout the 19th century, though as late as the 1840s the Pre-Raphaelite painter William Holman could refer to him as "this little-known poet." His influence is found everywhere in the decorative Romantic verse of the Victorian Age, from the early work of Alfred Tennyson onward. His general emotional temper and the minute delicacy of his natural observation were greatly admired by the Pre-Raphaelites, who both echoed his poetry in their own and illustrated it in their paintings. Keats's 19th-century followers on the whole valued the more superficial aspects of his work; and it was largely left for the 20th century to realize the full range of his technical and intellectual achievement

Wentworth Place

John Keats moved to the newly built Wentworth Place, owned by his friend Charles Armitage Brown. It was on the edge of Hampstead Heath, ten minutes' walk south of his old home in Well Walk. The winter of 1818–19, though a difficult period for the poet, marked the beginning of his annus mirabilis in which he wrote his most mature work. He had been inspired by a series of recent lectures by Hazlitt on English poets and poetic identity and had also met Wordsworth. Keats may have seemed to his friends to be living on comfortable means, but in reality he was borrowing regularly from Abbey and his friends.

He composed five of his six great odes at Wentworth Place in April and May and, although it is debated in which order they were written, "Ode to Psyche" opened the published series. According to Brown, "Ode to a Nightingale" was composed under a plum tree in the garden. Brown wrote, "In the spring of 1819 a nightingale had built her nest near my house. Keats felt a tranquil and continual joy in her song; and one morning he took his chair from the breakfast-table to the grass-plot under a plum-tree, where he sat for two or three hours. When he came into the house, I perceived he had some scraps of paper in his hand, and these he was quietly thrusting behind the books. On inquiry, I found those scraps, four or five in number, contained his poetic feelings on the song of our nightingale." Dilke, co-owner of the house, strenuously denied the story, printed in Richard Monckton Milnes' 1848 biography of Keats, dismissing it as 'pure delusion'.

"My heart aches, and a drowsy numbness pains
My sense, as though of hemlock I had drunk,
Or emptied some dull opiate to the drains
One minute past, and Lethe-wards had sunk:
Tis not through envy of thy happy lot,
But being too happy in thine happiness,—
That thou, light-winged Dryad of the trees,
In some melodious plot

Of beechen green, and shadows numberless,
Singest of summer in full-throated ease".

–First stanza of "Ode to a Nightingale",
May 1819

"Ode on a Grecian Urn" and "Ode on Melancholy" were inspired by sonnet forms and probably written after "Ode to a Nightingale". Keats's new and progressive publishers Taylor and Hessey issued Endymion, which Keats dedicated to Thomas Chatterton, a work that he termed "a trial of my Powers of Imagination". It was damned by the critics, giving rise to Byron's quip that Keats was ultimately "snuffed out by an article", suggesting that he never truly got over it.

A particularly harsh review by John Wilson Crokerappeared in the April 1818 edition of The Quarterly Review. John Gibson Lockhart writing in Blackwood's Magazine, described Endymion as "imperturbable drivelling idiocy".

With biting sarcasm, Lockhart advised, "It is a better and a wiser thing to be a starved apothecary than a starved poet; so back to the shop Mr John, back to plasters, pills, and ointment boxes". It was Lockhart at Blackwoods who coined the defamatory term "the Cockney School" for Hunt and his circle, which included both Hazlitt and Keats. The dismissal was as much political as literary, aimed at upstart young writers deemed uncouth for their lack of education, non-formal rhyming and "low diction". They had not attended Eton, Harrow or Oxbridge and they were not from the upper classes.

In 1819, Keats wrote "The Eve of St. Agnes", "La Belle Dame sans Merci", "Hyperion", "Lamia" and a play, Otho the Great (critically damned and not performed until 1950).[46] The poems "Fancy" and "Bards of passion and of mirth" were inspired by the garden of Wentworth Place. In September, very short of money and in despair considering taking up journalism or a post as a ship's surgeon, he approached his publishers with a new book of poems. They were unimpressed with the collection, finding the presented versions of "Lamia" confusing, and describing "St Agnes" as having a "sense of pettish disgust" and "a 'Don Juan' style of mingling up sentiment and sneering" concluding it was "a poem unfit for ladies". The final volume Keats lived to see, Lamia, Isabella, The Eve of St. Agnes, and Other Poems, was eventually published in July 1820. It received greater acclaim than had Endymion or Poems, finding favourable notices in both The Examiner and Edinburgh Review. It would come to be recognised as one of the most important poetic works ever published. Wentworth Place now houses the Keats House museum.

Isabella Jones and Fanny Brawne

Keats befriended Isabella Jones in May 1817, while on holiday in the village of Bo Peep, near Hastings. She is described as beautiful, talented and widely read, not of the top flight of society yet financially secure, an enigmatic figure who would become a part of Keats's circle. Throughout their friendship Keats never hesitates to own his sexual attraction to her, although they seem to enjoy circling each other rather than offering commitment. He writes that he "frequented her rooms" in the winter of 1818–19, and in his letters to George says that he "warmed with her" and "kissed her". The trysts may have been a sexual initiation for Keats according to Bate and Gittings. Jones inspired and was a steward of Keats's writing. The themes of "The Eve of St. Agnes" and "The Eve of St Mark" may well have been suggested by her, the lyric Hush, Hush! "o sweet Isabel" was about her, and that the first version of "Bright Star" may have originally been for her. In 1821, Jones was one of the first in England to be notified of Keats's death.

Letters and drafts of poems suggest that Keats first met Frances (Fanny) Brawne between September and November 1818. It is likely that the 18-year-old Brawne visited the Dilke family at Wentworth Place before she lived there. She was born in the hamlet of West End (now in the district of West Hampstead), on 9 August 1800. Like Keats's grandfather, her grandfather kept a London inn, and both lost several family members to tuberculosis. She shared her first name with both Keats's sister and mother, and had a talent for dress-making and languages as well as a natural theatrical bent. During November 1818 she developed an intimacy with Keats, but it was shadowed by the illness of Tom Keats, whom John was nursing through this period.

On 3 April 1819, Brawne and her widowed mother moved into the other half of Dilke's Wentworth Place, and Keats and Brawne were able to see each other every day. Keats began to lend Brawne books, such as Dante's Inferno, and they would read together. He gave her the love sonnet "Bright Star" (perhaps revised for her) as a declaration. It was a work in progress which he continued at until the last months of his life, and the poem came to be associated with their relationship. "All his desires were concentrated on Fanny". From this point there is no further documented mention of Isabella Jones. Sometime before the end of June, he arrived at some sort of understanding with Brawne, far from a formal engagement as he still had too little to offer, with no prospects and financial stricture. Keats endured great conflict knowing his expectations as a struggling poet in increasingly hard straits would preclude marriage to Brawne. Their love remained unconsummated; jealousy for his 'star' began to gnaw at him. Darkness, disease and depression surrounded him, reflected in poems such as "The Eve of St. Agnes" and "La Belle Dame sans Merci" where love and death both stalk. "I have two luxuries to brood over in my walks;" he wrote to her, "...your loveliness, and the hour of my death".

In one of his many hundreds of notes and letters, Keats wrote to Brawne on 13 October 1819: "My love has made me selfish. I cannot exist without you – I am forgetful of every thing but seeing you again – my Life seems to stop there – I see no further. You have absorb'd me. I have a sensation at the present moment as though I was dissolving – I should be exquisitely miserable without the hope of soon seeing you ... I have been astonished that Men could die Martyrs for religion – I have shudder'd at it – I shudder no more – I could be martyr'd for my Religion – Love is my religion – I could die for that – I could die for you."

Tuberculosis took hold and he was advised by his doctors to move to a warmer climate. In September 1820 Keats left for Rome knowing he would probably never see Brawne again. After leaving he felt unable to write to her or read her letters, although he did correspond with her mother. He died there five months later. None of Brawne's letters to Keats survive.

It took a month for the news of his death to reach London, after which Brawne stayed in mourning for six years. In 1833, more than 12 years after his death, she married and went on to have three children; she outlived Keats by more than 40 years.

His Work

Keats met Leigh Hunt, an influential editor of the Examiner, who published his sonnets "On First Looking into Chapman's Homer" and "O Solitude." Hunt also introduced Keats to a circle of literary men, including the poets Percy Bysshe Shelley and William Wordsworth. The group's influence enabled Keats to see his first volume, Poems by John Keats, published in 1817. Shelley, who was fond of Keats, had advised him to develop a more substantial body of work before publishing it. Keats, who was not as fond of Shelley, did not follow his advice. Endymion, a four-thousand-line erotic/allegorical romance based on the Greek myth of the same name, appeared the following year. Two of the most influential critical magazines of the time, the Quarterly Review and Blackwood's Magazine, attacked the collection. Calling the romantic verse of Hunt's literary circle "the Cockney school of poetry," Blackwood's declared Endymion to be nonsense and recommended that

From 1814, Keats had two bequests, held in trust for him until his 21st birthday: £800 willed by his grandfather John Jennings (about £50,000 in today's money) and a portion of his mother's legacy, £8000 (about £500,000 today), to be equally divided between her living children. It seems he was not told of either, since he never applied for any of the money. Historically, blame has often been laid on Abbey as legal guardian, but he may also have been unaware. William Walton, solicitor for Keats's mother and grandmother, definitely did know and had a duty of care to relay the information to Keats. It seems he did not. The money would have made a critical difference to the poet's expectations. Money was always a great concern and difficulty for him, as he struggled to stay out of debt and make his way in the world independently.

Having finished his apprenticeship with Hammond, Keats registered as a medical student at Guy's Hospital (now part of King's College London) and began studying there in October 1815. Within a month of starting, he was accepted as a dresser at the hospital, assisting surgeons during operations, the equivalent of a junior house surgeon today. It was a significant promotion, that marked a distinct aptitude for medicine; it brought greater responsibility and a heavier workload. Keats's long and expensive medical training with Hammond and at Guy's Hospital led his family to assume he would pursue a lifelong career in medicine, assuring financial security, and it seems that at this point Keats had a genuine desire to become a doctor. He lodged near the hospital, at 28 St Thomas's Street in Southwark, with other medical students, including Henry Stephens who became a famous inventor and ink magnate.

However, Keats's training took up increasing amounts of his writing time, and he was increasingly ambivalent about his medical career. He felt that he faced a stark choice. He had written his first extant poem, "An Imitation of Spenser," in 1814, when he was 19. Now, strongly drawn by ambition, inspired by fellow poets such as Leigh Hunt and Lord Byron, and beleaguered by family financial crises, he suffered periods of depression. His brother George wrote that John "feared that he should never be a poet, & if he was not he would destroy himself". In 1816, Keats received his apothecary's licence, which made him eligible to practise as an apothecary, physician, and surgeon, but before the end of the year he announced to his guardian that he was resolved to be a poet, not a surgeon.

Although he continued his work and training at Guy's, Keats devoted more and more time to the study of literature, experimenting with verse forms, particularly the sonnet. In May 1816, Leigh Hunt agreed to publish the sonnet "O Solitude" in his magazine, The Examiner, a leading liberal magazine of the day. It was the first appearance in print of Keats's poetry, and Charles Cowden Clarke described it as his friend's red letter day, the first proof that Keats's ambitions were valid. Among his poems of 1816 was To My Brothers. In the summer of that year, Keats went with Clarke to the seaside town of Margate to write. There he began "Calidore" and initiated the era of his great letter writing. On his return to London, he took lodgings at 8 Dean Street, Southwark, and braced himself for further study in order to become a member of the Royal College of Surgeons.

In October 1816, Clarke introduced Keats to the influential Leigh Hunt, a close friend of Byron and Shelley. Five months later came the publication of Poems, the first volume of Keats's verse, which included "I stood tiptoe" and "Sleep and Poetry," both strongly influenced by Hunt. The book was a critical failure, arousing little interest, although Reynolds reviewed it favourably in The Champion. Clarke commented that the book "might have emerged in Timbuctoo." Keats's publishers, Charles and James Ollier, felt ashamed of the book. Keats immediately changed publishers to Taylor and Hessey on Fleet Street. Unlike the Olliers, Keats's new publishers were enthusiastic about his work. Within a month of the publication of Poems they were planning a new Keats volume and had paid him an advance. Hessey became a steady friend to Keats and made the company's rooms available for young writers to meet. Their publishing lists eventually included Coleridge, Hazlitt, Clare, Hogg, Carlyle and Lamb.

Through Taylor and Hessey, Keats met their Eton-educated lawyer, Richard Woodhouse, who advised them on literary as well as legal matters and was deeply impressed by Poems. Although he noted that Keats could be "wayward, trembling, easily daunted," Woodhouse was convinced of Keats's genius, a poet to support as he became one of England's greatest writers. Soon after they met, the two became close friends, and Woodhouse started to collect Keatsiana, documenting as much as he could about Keats's poetry. This archive survives as one of the main sources of information on Keats's work. Andrew Motion represents him as Boswell to Keats' Johnson, ceaselessly promoting the writer's work, fighting his corner, and spurring his poetry to greater heights. In later years, Woodhouse was one of the few people to accompany Keats to Gravesend to embark on his final trip to Rome.

In spite of the bad reviews of Poems, Hunt published the essay "Three Young Poets" (Shelley, Keats, and Reynolds) and the sonnet "On First Looking into Chapman's Homer," foreseeing great things to come. He introduced Keats to many prominent men in his circle, including the editor of The Times,

Thomas Barnes; the writer Charles Lamb; the conductor Vincent Novello; and the poet John Hamilton Reynolds, who would become a close friend. He was also regularly meeting William Hazlitt, a powerful literary figure of the day. It was a decisive turning point for Keats, establishing him in the public eye as a figure in what Hunt termed "a new school of poetry." At this time Keats wrote to his friend Bailey: "I am certain of nothing but the holiness of the Heart's affections and the truth of the imagination. What imagination seizes as Beauty must be truth." This passage would eventually be transmuted into the concluding lines of "Ode on a Grecian Urn": "'Beauty is truth, truth beauty' – that is all / Ye know on earth, and all ye need to know". In early December 1816, under the heady influence of his artistic friends, Keats told Abbey that he had decided to give up medicine in favour of poetry, to Abbey's fury. Keats had spent a great deal on his medical training and, despite his state of financial hardship and indebtedness, had made large loans to friends such as painter Benjamin Haydon. Keats would go on to lend £700 to his brother George. By lending so much, Keats could no longer cover the interest of his own debts.

Having left his training at the hospital, suffering from a succession of colds, and unhappy with living in damp rooms in London, Keats moved with his brothers into rooms at 1 Well Walk in the village of Hampstead in April 1817. Both John and George nursed their brother Tom, who was suffering from tuberculosis. The house was close to Hunt and others from his circle in Hampstead, as well as to Coleridge, respected elder of the first wave of Romantic poets, at that time living in Highgate. On 11 April 1818, Keats reported that he and Coleridge had a long walk together on Hampstead Heath. In a letter to his brother George, Keats wrote that they talked about "a thousand things,... nightingales, poetry, poetical sensation, metaphysics." Around this time he was introduced to Charles Wentworth Dilke and James Rice.

In June 1818, Keats began a walking tour of Scotland, Ireland, and the Lake District with his friend Charles Armitage Brown. Keats' brother George and his wife Georgina accompanied them as far as Lancaster and then continued to Liverpool, from where the couple emigrated to America. They lived in Ohio and Louisville, Kentucky, until 1841, when George's investments failed. Like Keats' other brother, they both died penniless and racked by tuberculosis, for which there was no effective treatment until the next century. In July, while on the Isle of Mull, Keats caught a bad cold and "was too thin and fevered to proceed on the journey." After his return south in August, Keats continued to nurse Tom, exposing himself to infection. Some biographers suggest that this is when tuberculosis, his "family disease," first took hold. "Consumption" was not identified as a disease with a single infectious origin until 1820, and there was considerable stigma attached to the condition, as it was often associated with weakness, repressed sexual passion, or masturbation. Keats "refuses to give it a name" in his letters. Tom Keats died on 1 December 1818.

Last months: Rome

During 1820 Keats displayed increasingly serious symptoms of tuberculosis, suffering two lung haemorrhages in the first few days of February. He lost large amounts of blood and was bled further by the attending physician. Hunt nursed him in London for much of the following summer. At the suggestion of his doctors, he agreed to move to Italy with his friend Joseph Severn. On 13 September, they left for Gravesend and four days later boarded the sailing brig Maria Crowther, where he made the final revisions of "Bright Star". The journey was a minor catastrophe: storms broke out followed by a dead calm that slowed the ship's progress. When they finally docked in Naples, the ship was held in quarantine for ten days due to a suspected outbreak of cholera in Britain. Keats reached Rome on 14 November, by which time any hope of the warmer climate he sought had disappeared.

Keats wrote his last letter on 30 November 1820 to Charles Armitage Brown; "Tis the most difficult thing in the world to me to write a letter. My stomach continues so bad, that I feel it worse on opening any book – yet I am much better than I was in Quarantine. Then I am afraid to encounter the proing and conning of any thing interesting to me in England. I have an habitual feeling of my real life having past, and that I am leading a posthumous existence".

On arrival in Italy, he moved into a villa on the Spanish Steps in Rome, today the Keats–Shelley Memorial House museum. Despite care from Severn and Dr. James Clark, his health rapidly deteriorated. The medical attention Keats received may have hastened his death. In November 1820, Clark declared that the source of his illness was "mental exertion" and that the source was largely situated in his stomach. Clark eventually diagnosed consumption (tuberculosis) and placed Keats on a starvation diet of an anchovy and a piece of bread a day intended to reduce the blood flow to his stomach. He also bled the poet: a standard treatment of the day, but also likely a significant contributor to Keats's weakness. Severn's biographer Sue Brown writes: "They could have used opium in small doses, and Keats had asked Severn to buy a bottle of opium when they were setting off on their voyage. What Severn didn't realise was that Keats saw it as a possible resource if he wanted to commit suicide.

He tried to get the bottle from Severn on the voyage but Severn wouldn't let him have it. Then in Rome he tried again... Severn was in such a quandary he didn't know what to do, so in the end he went to the doctor who took it away. As a result Keats went through dreadful agonies with nothing to ease the pain at all." Keats was angry with both Severn and Clark when they would not give him laudanum (opium). He repeatedly demanded "how long is this posthumous existence of mine to go on?"

Death

The first months of 1821 marked a slow and steady decline into the final stage of tuberculosis. Keats was coughing up blood and covered in sweat. On first coughing up blood, he said "I know the colour of that blood! It is arterial blood. I cannot be deceived in that colour. That drop of blood is my death warrant. I must die." Severn nursed him devotedly and observed in a letter how Keats would sometimes cry upon waking to find himself still alive. Severn writes, Keats raves till I am in a complete tremble for him...about four, the approaches of death came on. Keats said "Severn—I—lift me up—I am dying—I shall die easy; don't be frightened—be firm, and thank God it has come." I lifted him up in my arms. The phlegm seem'd boiling in his throat, and increased until eleven, when he gradually sank into death, so quiet, that I still thought he slept.

John Keats died in Rome on 23 February 1821 and was buried in the Protestant Cemetery, Rome. His last request was to be placed under a tombstone bearing no name or date, only the words, "Here lies One whose Name was writ in Water." Severn and Brown erected the stone, which under a relief of a lyrewith broken strings, includes the epitaph:

This Grave / contains all that was Mortal / of a / Young English Poet / Who / on his Death Bed, in the Bitterness of his Heart / at the Malicious Power of his Enemies / Desired / these Words to be / engraven on his Tomb Stone: / Here lies One / Whose Name was writ in Water. 24 February 1821

The text bears an echo from Catullus LXX

Sed mulier cupido quod dicit amanti / in vento et rapida scribere oportet aqua (What a woman says to a passionate lover / should be written in the wind and the running water).

There is a discrepancy of one day between the official date of death and that on the gravestone. Severn and Brown added their lines to the stone in protest at the critical reception of Keats's work. Hunt blamed his death on the Quarterly Review's scathing attack of "Endymion". As Byron quipped in his narrative poem Don Juan;

'Tis strange the mind, that very fiery particle Should let itself be snuffed out by an article. (canto 11, stanza 60)

Seven weeks after the funeral Shelley memorialised Keats in his poem Adonaïs. Clark saw to the planting of daisies on the grave, saying that Keats would have wished it. For public health reasons, the Italian health authorities burned the furniture in Keats's room, scraped the walls, made new windows, doors and flooring. The ashes of Shelley, one of Keats's most fervent champions, are buried in the cemetery and Joseph Severn is buried next to Keats. Describing the site today, Marsh wrote, "In the old part of the graveyard, barely a field when Keats was buried here, there are now umbrella pines, myrtle shrubs, roses, and carpets of wild violets".

Letters

Keats' letters were first published in 1848 and 1878. During the 19th century, critics deemed them unworthy of attention, distractions from his poetic works. During the 20th century they became almost as admired and studied as his poetry, and are highly regarded within the canon of English literary correspondence.

T. S. Eliot described them as "certainly the most notable and most important ever written by any English poet." Keats spent a great deal of time considering poetry itself, its constructs and impacts, displaying a deep interest unusual amongst his milieu who were more easily distracted by metaphysics or politics, fashions or science. Eliot wrote of Keats's conclusions; "There is hardly one statement of Keats' about poetry which ... will not be found to be true, and what is more, true for greater and more mature poetry than anything Keats ever wrote."

Few of Keats's letters are extant from the period before he joined his literary circle. From spring 1817, however, there is a rich record of his prolific and impressive skills as letter writer. Keats and his friends, poets, critics, novelists, and editors wrote to each other daily, and Keats' ideas are bound up in the ordinary, his day-to-day missives sharing news, parody and social commentary. They glitter with humour and critical intelligence. Born of an "unself-conscious stream of consciousness," they are impulsive, full of awareness of his own nature and his weak spots. When his brother George went to America, Keats wrote to him in great detail, the body of letters becoming "the real diary" and self-revelation of Keats's life, as well as containing an exposition of his philosophy, and the first drafts of poems containing some of Keats's finest writing and thought. Gittings describes them as akin to a "spiritual journal" not written for a specific other, so much as for synthesis.

Keats also reflected on the background and composition of his poetry, and specific letters often coincide with or anticipate the poems they describe. In February to May 1819 he produced many of his finest letters". Writing to his brother George, Keats explored the idea of the world as "the vale of Soul-making", anticipating the great odes that he would write some months later. In the letters, Keats coined ideas such as the Mansion of Many Apartments and the Chameleon Poet, concepts that came to gain common currency and capture the public imagination, despite only making single appearances as phrases in his correspondence. The poetical mind, Keats argued:

has no self – it is every thing and nothing – It has no character – it enjoys light and shade;... What shocks the virtuous philosopher, delights the camelion [chameleon] Poet. It does no harm from its relish of the dark side of things any more than from its taste for the bright one; because they both end in speculation. A Poet is the most unpoetical of any thing in existence; because he has no Identity – he is continually in for – and filling some other Body – The Sun, the Moon, the Sea and Men and Women who are creatures of impulse are poetical and have about them an unchangeable attribute – the poet has none; no identity – he is certainly the most unpoetical of all God's Creatures.

He used the term negative capability to discuss the state in which we are "capable of being in uncertainties, Mysteries, doubts without any irritable reaching after fact & reason ...[Being] content with half knowledge" where one trusts in the heart's perceptions. He wrote later: "I am certain of nothing but the holiness of the Heart's affections and the truth of Imagination – What the imagination seizes as Beauty must be truth – whether it existed before or not – for I have the same Idea of all our Passions as of Love they are all in their sublime, creative of essential Beauty" again and again turning to the question of what it means to be a poet. "My Imagination is a Monastery and I am its Monk", Keats notes to Shelley. In September 1819, Keats wrote to Reynolds "How beautiful the season is now – How fine the air. A temperate sharpness about it ... I never lik'd the stubbled fields as much as now – Aye, better than the chilly green of spring. Somehow the stubble plain looks warm – in the same way as some pictures look warm – this struck me so much in my Sunday's walk that I composed upon it". The final stanza of his last great ode: "To Autumn" runs:

Where are the songs of Spring? Ay, where are they? Think not of them, thou hast thy music too,- While barred clouds bloom the soft-dying day, And touch the stubble-plains with rosy hue;

Later, To Autumn became one of the most highly regarded poems in the English language.

There are areas of his life and daily routine that Keats does not describe. He mentions little about his childhood or his financial straits and is seemingly embarrassed to discuss them. There is a total absence of any reference to his parents. In his last year, as his health deteriorated, his concerns often gave way to despair and morbid obsessions. The publications of letters to Fanny Brawne in 1870 focused on this period and emphasised this tragic aspect, giving rise to widespread criticism at the time.

Works

- Keats's Poetry and Prose. Ed. Jeffrey N. Cox. New York: W.W. Norton Co., 2008. ISBN 978-0393924916
- John Keats. Ed. Susan Wolfson. Longman, 2007.
- Selected Letters of John Keats. Ed. Grant F. Scott. Harvard University Press, 2002.
- John Keats: Poetry Manuscripts at Harvard, a Facsimile Edition.Ed. Jack Stillinger. Harvard University Press, 1990. ISBN 0-674-47775-8
- Complete Poems. Ed. Jack Stillinger. Harvard University Press, 1982.
- The Poems of John Keats. Ed. Jack Stillinger. Harvard University Press, 1978.
- The Letters of John Keats 1814–1821 Volumes 1 and 2 Ed. Hyder Edward Rollins. Harvard University Press, 1958.
- The Complete Poetical Works of John Keats. Ed. H. Buxton Forman. Oxford: Oxford University Press, 1907.
- The Complete Poetical Works and Letters of John Keats. ed. Horace Elisha Scudder. Boston: Riverside Press, 1899.

LORD BYRON

Lord Byron, in full George Gordon Byron, 6th Baron Byron (born January 22, 1788, London, England—died April 19, 1824, Missolonghi, Greece), British Romantic poet and satirist whose poetry and personality captured the imagination of Europe. Renowned as the "gloomy egoist" of his autobiographical poem Childe Harold's Pilgrimage (1812–18) in the 19th century, he is now more generally esteemed for the satiric realism of Don Juan (1819–24).

The most flamboyant and notorious of the major Romantics, George Gordon, Lord Byron, was likewise the most fashionable poet of the day. He created an immensely popular Romantic hero—defiant, melancholy, haunted by secret guilt—for which, to many, he seemed the model. He is also a Romantic paradox: a leader of the era's poetic revolution, he named Alexander Pope as his master; a worshiper of the ideal, he never lost touch with reality; a deist and freethinker, he retained from his youth a Calvinist sense of original sin; a peer of the realm, he championed liberty in his works and deeds, giving money, time, energy, and finally his life to the Greek war of independence. His faceted personality found expression in satire, verse narrative, ode, lyric, speculative drama, historical tragedy, confessional poetry, dramatic monologue, seriocomic epic, and voluminous correspondence, written in Spenserian stanzas, heroic couplets, blank verse, terza rima, ottava rima, and vigorous prose. In his dynamism, sexuality, self-revelation, and demands for freedom for oppressed people everywhere, Byron captivated the Western mind and heart as few writers have, stamping upon nineteenth-century letters, arts, politics, even clothing styles, his image and name as the embodiment of Romanticism.

Early in 1804 he began an intimate correspondence with his half sister, Augusta, five years his senior. He asked that she consider him "not only as a Brother" but as her "warmest and most affectionate Friend." As he grew apart from his coarse, often violent, mother, he drew closer to Augusta.

Byron attended Trinity College, Cambridge, intermittently from October 1805 until July 1808, when he received an M.A. degree. During "the most romantic period of [his] life," he experienced a "violent, though pure, love and passion" for John Edleston, a choirboy at Trinity two years younger than he. Intellectual pursuits interested him less than such London diversions as fencing and boxing lessons, the theater, demimondes, and gambling. Living extravagantly, he began to amass the debts that would bedevil him for years. In Southwell, where his mother had moved in 1803, he prepared his verses for publication.

Education and early loves

Byron received his early formal education at Aberdeen Grammar School, and in August 1799 entered the school of Dr. William Glennie, in Dulwich. Placed under the care of a Dr. Bailey, he was encouraged to exercise in moderation but could not restrain himself from "violent" bouts in an attempt to overcompensate for his deformed foot. His mother interfered with his studies, often withdrawing him from school, with the result that he lacked discipline and his classical studies were neglected.

In 1801, he was sent to Harrow, where he remained until July 1805. An undistinguished student and an unskilled cricketer, he did represent the school during the very first Eton Harrow cricket match at Lord's in 1805. His lack of moderation was not restricted to physical exercise. Byron fell in love with Mary Chaworth, whom he met while at school, and she was the reason he refused to return to Harrow in September 1803. His mother wrote, "He has no indisposition that I know of but love, desperate love, the worst of all maladies in my opinion. In short, the boy is distractedly in love with Miss Chaworth." In Byron's later memoirs, "Mary Chaworth is portrayed as the first object of his adult sexual feelings."

Byron finally returned in January 1804, to a more settled period which saw the formation of a circle of emotional involvements with other Harrow boys, which he recalled with great vividness: "My school friendships were with me passions (for I was always violent)." The most enduring of those was with John FitzGibbon, 2nd Earl of Clare — four years Byron's junior — whom he was to meet unexpectedly many years later in Italy (1821). His nostalgic poems about his Harrow friendships, Childish Recollections (1806), express a prescient "consciousness of sexual differences that may in the end make England untenable to him". Letters to Byron in the John Murray archive contain evidence of a previously unremarked if short-lived romantic relationship with a younger boy at Harrow, John Thomas Claridge.

Ah! Sure some stronger impulse vibrates here, Which whispers friendship will be doubly dear

To one, who thus for kindred hearts must roam, And seek abroad, the love denied at home.

The following autumn, he went up to Trinity College, Cambridge, where he met and formed a close friendship with the younger John Edleston. About his "protégé" he wrote, "He has been my almost constant associate since October, 1805, when I entered Trinity College. His voice first attracted my attention, his countenance fixed it, and his manners attached me to him for ever." In his memory Byron composed Thyrza, a series of elegies. He spent three years at Trinity College, engaging in sexual escapades, boxing, horse riding and gambling. By 1807, he formed a friendship with John Cam Hobhouse who initiated him into the Cambridge Whig Club, which endorsed liberal politics.

In later years, he described the affair as "a violent, though pure love and passion". This statement, however, needs to be read in the context of hardening public attitudes toward homosexuality in England, and the severe sanctions (including public hanging) against convicted or even suspected offenders. The liaison, on the other hand, may well have been "pure" out of respect for

Edleston's innocence, in contrast to the (probably) more sexually overt relations experienced at Harrow School. Also while at Cambridge he formed lifelong friendships with men such as John Cam Hobhouse and Francis Hodgson, a Fellow at King's College, with whom he corresponded on literary and other matters until the end of his life.

The work

In 1806 Byron self-published his first book of poetry, Fugitive Pieces. His mentor, the Reverend John Thomas Becher, raised objections to some of the more erotic lines of verse, so Byron suppressed the book. He republished many of the poems—now heavily edited—along with new verse in his 1807 Poems on Various Occasions, followed later by an expanded edition titled Hours of Idleness, this last edition being the first published work bearing his name. Hours Of Idleness appeared. The new poems in this first public volume of his poetry are little more than schoolboy translations from the classics and imitations of such pre-Romantics as Thomas Gray, Thomas Chatterton, Robert Burns, and James Macpherson's Ossian, and of contemporaries including Walter Scott and Thomas Moore. Missing were the original flashes of eroticism and satire that had enlivened poems in the private editions that were omitted from *Hours of Idleness*. The work has value for what it reveals about the youthful poet's influences, interests, talent, and direction. It received bad reviews. The poet answered his critics with the satire English Bards And Scotch Reviewersin 1808.

In obviously autobiographical poems Byron experiments with personae, compounded of his true self and of fictive elements, which both disclose and disguise him. Groups of verses on a single subject show his understanding of the effectiveness of multiple points of view. He continued to refine these techniques in works from Childe Harold's Pilgrimage and the Oriental tales through the dramas to Don Juan.

Shortly thereafter, Byron's first major poetic work, English Bards, and Scotch Reviewers. A Satire, was published anonymously in an edition of one thousand copies. Inspired by the Dunciad (1728, 1742) of his idol, Pope, and modeled largely on William Gifford's Baviad (1791) and Maeviad (1795), the poem, in heroic couplets, takes indiscriminate aim at most of the poets and playwrights of the moment, notably Walter Scott, Robert Southey, William Wordsworth, and Samuel Taylor Coleridge, sparing only Gifford, Samuel Rogers, and Thomas Campbell, who deferred to Pope, along with dramatists George Colman the Younger, Richard Cumberland, and Richard Brinsley Sheridan. His main target is the critics. From these "harpies that must be fed" he singles out for condemnation "immortal" Francis Jeffrey, whom he mistakenly assumed had written the offending comments on Hours of Idleness in the Edinburgh Review. The satire created a stir and found general favour with the reviewers. The Gentleman's Magazine (March 1809) praised the poem as "unquestionably an original work," replete with a "mingled genius, good sense, and spirited animadversion" unseen in many years.

Byron most sympathized with neoclassicism, with its order, discipline, and clarity. The importance of English Bards, and Scotch Reviewers lies not only in its vigor and vitality but in Byron's lively advocacy of the neoclassical virtues found in such seventeenth- and eighteenth-century poets as Dryden and Pope, and, from his own day, in Gifford. His admiration for Pope never wavered, nor did he ever totally abandon the heroic couplet and Augustan role of censor and moralist, as seen in Hints from Horace (written 1811), The Curse of Minerva (written 1811), and The Age of Bronze (written 1822-1823).

Byron began an autobiographical poem in Jannina on 31 October 1809, wherein he recorded the adventures and reflections of Childe Burun (a combination of the archaic title for a youth of noble birth and an ancient form of his own surname); he subsequently renamed the hero Harold. The Spenserian stanza in which he cast his impressions no doubt derived from his readings in Edmund Spenser's Faerie Queene (1590, 1596) reprinted in an anthology he had carried to Albania. Byron completed the first canto in Athens at the end of the year.

On 28 March 1810, in Smyrna, he completed the second canto of Childe Harold, incorporating his adventures in Albania and his thoughts on Greece. In February and March 1811, he wrote two poems in heroic couplets. Hints from Horace, an inferior sequel to English Bards, and Scotch Reviewers, satirizes contemporary poetry and drama, while praising Dryden, Pope, Swift, and Butler. The Curse of Minerva, in its attack on Lord Elgin for pillaging Greece's heritage, records for the first time the full extent of Byron's sympathy for classical Greek culture as well as for modern Greece and her people. In January 1812 took his seat in the House of Lords, and set out on his grand tour, visiting Spain, Malta, Albania, Greece, and the Aegean. Real poetic success came in 1812 when Byron published the first two cantos of Childe Harold's Pilgrimage (1812-1818). He became an adored character of London society; he spoke in the House of Lords effectively on liberal themes, and had a hectic love-affair with Lady Caroline Lamb. Byron's The Corsair (1814), sold 10,000 copies on the first day of publication. He married Anne Isabella Milbanke in 1815, and their daughter Ada was born in the same year. The marriage was unhappy, and they obtained legal separation next year.

Arriving in Lisbon at the height of the English-French conflict, Byron remained mostly oblivious to the political climate of the world around him, so focused was he on enjoying himself. It was from this journey that Byron produced the work that would make him famous: Childe Harold's Pilgrimage. The first two cantos, written during his European travels, were published in 1812. The print run sold out in three days, making Byron suddenly famous. Soon Byron was a sought-after attendee at salons throughout England, where he also met a number of influential and impassioned women. From 1813 to 1816, Byron published several works, most of them inspired by his travels in Turkey and Greece: The Giaour in June of 1813, followed by The Bride of Abydos later that year; then The Corsair in February 1814 and Lara in August; finally The Siege of Corinth and Parisina in February of 1816. All the while, Byron continued revising and adding to Childe Harold's Pilgrimage. Byron's travels with Shelley inspired him to write *The Prisoner of Chillon,* published in 1817. Byron proclaimed in Don Juan, Canto XV. The outstanding elements of his poetry both support his self-analysis and insure his enduring reputation. As a major political and social satirist, he starts, in the Classical and Augustan manner, with a fixed standard of judgment, then, in either seriocomic or savage tones, repeatedly denounces war, tyranny, and hypocrisy. As an untiring champion of liberty, he firmly believed that "Revolution / Alone can save the earth from hell's pollution""(Don Juan, Canto VIII), a tenet he defended with his life.

The last word properly belongs to Byron, who perceptively captured his essence in Canto IV of Childe Harold:

But I have lived, and have not lived in vain:
My mind may lose its force, my blood its fire,
And my frame perish even in conquering pain,
But there is that within me which shall tire
Torture and Time, and breathe when I expire .

Career

Early Career

While not at school or college, Byron lived with his mother in Southwell, Nottinghamshire, in some antagonism. While there, he cultivated friendships with Elizabeth Pigot and her brother, John, with whom he staged two plays for the entertainment of the community. During this time, with the help of

Elizabeth Pigot, who copied many of his rough drafts, he was encouraged to write his first volumes of poetry. Fugitive Pieces was printed by Ridge of Newark, which contained poems written when Byron was only 17. However, it was promptly recalled and burned on the advice of his friend, the Reverend J. T. Becher, on account of its more amorous verses, particularly the poem To Mary.

Hours of Idleness, which collected many of the previous poems, along with more recent compositions, was the culminating book. The savage, anonymous criticism this received (now known to be the work of Henry Peter Brougham) in the Edinburgh Review prompted his first major satire, English Bards and Scotch Reviewers (1809). It was put into the hands of his relation, R. C. Dallas, requesting him to "...get it published without his name". Alexander Dallas gives a large series of changes and alterations, as well as the reasoning for some of them. He also states that Byron had originally intended to prefix an argument to this poem, and Dallas quotes it. Although the work was published anonymously, by April, R. C. Dallas is writing that "you are already pretty generally known to be the author". The work so upset some of his critics they challenged Byron to a duel; over time, in subsequent editions, it became a mark of prestige to be the target of Byron's pen.

After his return from his travels, he again entrusted R. C. Dallas as his literary agent to publish his poem Childe Harold's Pilgrimage, which Byron thought of little account. The first two cantos of Childe Harold's Pilgrimage were published in 1812, and were received with acclaim. In his own words, "I awoke one morning and found myself famous". He followed up his success with the poem's last two cantos, as well as four equally celebrated "Oriental Tales": The Giaour, The Bride of Abydos, The Corsair and Lara. About the same time, he began his intimacy with his future biographer, Thomas Moore.

First Travels to the East

Byron racked up numerous debts as a young man, owing to what his mother termed a "reckless disregard for money". She lived at Newstead during this time, in fear of her son's creditors. He had planned to spend early 1808 cruising with his cousin, George Bettesworth, who was captain of the 32-gun frigate HMS Tartar. Bettesworth's unfortunate death at the Battle of Alvøen in May 1808 made that impossible.

From 1809 to 1811, Byron went on the Grand Tour, then customary for a young nobleman. He travelled with Hobhouse for the first year and his entourage of servants included the trusty butt of the young men's humour, William Fletcher, Byron's valet. The Napoleonic Wars forced him to avoid most of Europe, and he instead turned to the Mediterranean. The journey provided the opportunity to flee creditors, as well as a former love, Mary Chaworth (the subject of his poem from this time, "To a Lady: On Being Asked My Reason for Quitting England in the Spring"). Letters to Byron from his friend Charles Skinner Matthews reveal that a key motive was also the hope of homosexual experience.

Attraction to the Levant was probably also a reason; he had read about the Ottoman and Persian lands as a child, was attracted to Islam (especially Sufi mysticism), and later wrote, "With these countries, and events connected with them, all my really poetical feelings begin and end." He travelled from England over Portugal, Spain and the Mediterranean to Albania and spent time at the court of Ali Pasha of Ioannina, and in Athens. For most of the trip, he had a travelling companion in his friend John Cam Hobhouse. Many of these letters are referred to with details in Recollections of the Life of Lord Byron.

Byron began his trip in Portugal from where he wrote a letter to his friend Mr. Hodgson in which he describes his mastery of the Portuguese language, consisting mainly of swearing and insults. Byron particularly enjoyed his stay in Sintra that is described in Childe Harold's Pilgrimage as "glorious Eden". From Lisbon he travelled overland to Seville, Jerez de la Frontera, Cádiz, Gibraltar and from there by sea on to Malta and Greece.

While in Athens, Byron met 14-year-old Nicolo Giraud, who became quite close and taught him Italian. It has been suggested that the two had an intimate relationship involving a sexual affair. Byron sent Giraud to school at a monastery in Malta and bequeathed him a sizeable sum of seven thousand pounds sterling. The will, however, was later cancelled. "I am tired of pl & opt Cs, the last thing I could be tired of", Byron wrote to Hobhouse from Athens (an abbreviation of "coitum plenum et optabilem" – complete intercourse to one's heart's desire, from Petronius's Satyricon), which, as an earlier letter establishes, was their shared code for homosexual experience. In 1810 in Athens Byron wrote Maid of Athens, ere we part for a 12-year-old girl, Teresa Makri (1798–1875), and reportedly offered £500 for her. The offer was not accepted.

Byron made his way to Smyrna, where he and Hobhouse cadged a ride to Constantinople on HMS Salsette. While Salsette was anchored awaiting Ottoman permission to dock at the city, on 3 May 1810 Byron and Lieutenant Ekenhead, of Salsette's Marines, swam the Hellespont. Byron commemorated this feat in the second canto of Don Juan. He returned to England from Malta in July 1811 aboard HMS Volage.

England 1811–1816

Byron became a celebrity with the publication of the first two cantos of "Childe Harold's Pilgrimage" (1812). "He rapidly became the most brilliant star in the dazzling world of Regency London. He was sought after at every society venue, elected to several exclusive clubs, and frequented the most fashionable London drawing-rooms." During this period in England he produced many works including The Giaour, The Bride of Abydos (1813), Parisina and The Siege of Corinth (1815). Involved at first in an affair with Lady Caroline Lamb (who called him "mad, bad and dangerous to know") and with other lovers and also pressed by debt, he began to seek a suitable marriage, considering – amongst others – Annabella Millbanke. However, in 1813 he met for the first time in four years his half-sister, Augusta Leigh. Rumours of incest surrounded the pair; Augusta's daughter Medora (b. 1814) was suspected to have been Byron's. To escape from growing debts and rumours, Byron pressed his determination to marry Annabella, who was said to be the likely heiress of a rich uncle. They married on 2 January 1815, and their daughter, Ada, was born in December of that year. However Byron's continuing obsession with Augusta (and his continuing sexual escapades with actresses and others) made their marital life a misery. Annabella considered Byron insane, and in January 1816 she left him, taking their daughter, and began proceedings for a legal separation. Their separation was made legal in a private settlement in March 1816. The scandal of the separation, the rumours about Augusta, and ever-increasing debts forced him to leave England in April 1816, never to return.

SAMUEL TAYLOR COLERIDGE

Samuel Taylor Coleridge (21 October 1772 – 25 July 1834) was an English poet, literary critic, philosopher and theologian who, with his friend William Wordsworth, was a founder of the Romantic Movement in England and a member of the Lake Poets. He wrote the poems The Rime of the Ancient Mariner and Kubla Khan, as well as the major prose work Biographia Literaria. His critical work, especially on William Shakespeare, was highly influential, and he helped introduce German idealist philosophy to English-speaking culture. Coleridge coined many familiar words and phrases, including suspension of disbelief. He was a major influence on Ralph Waldo Emerson and American transcendentalism.

Throughout his adult life Coleridge had crippling bouts of anxiety and depression; it has been speculated that he had bipolar disorder, which had not been defined during his lifetime. He was physically unhealthy, which may have stemmed from a bout of rheumatic fever and other childhood illnesses. He was treated for these conditions with laudanum, which fostered a lifelong opium addiction.

Early life

A leader of the British Romantic movement, was born on October 21, 1772, in Devonshire, England. Samuel Taylor Coleridge is the premier poet-critic of modern English tradition, distinguished for the scope and influence of his thinking about literature as much as for his innovative verse. Active in the wake of the French Revolution as a dissenting pamphleteer and lay preacher, he inspired a brilliant generation of writers and attracted the patronage of progressive men of the rising middle class.

Coleridge's father was vicar of Ottery and headmaster of the local grammar school. As a child Coleridge was already a prodigious reader, and he immersed himself to the point of morbid fascination in romances and Eastern tales such as The Arabian Nights' Entertainments. In 1781 his father died suddenly, and in the following year Coleridge entered Christ's Hospital in London, where he completed his secondary education. In 1791 he entered Jesus College, Cambridge. At both school and university he continued to read voraciously, particularly in works of imagination and visionary philosophy, and he was remembered by his schoolmates for his eloquence and prodigious memory. In his third year at Cambridge, oppressed by financial difficulties, he went to London and enlisted as a dragoon under the assumed name of Silas Tomkyn Comberbache. Despite his unfitness for the life, he remained until discovered by his friends; he was then bought out by his brothers and restored to Cambridge.

On his return, he was restless. The intellectual and political turmoil surrounding the French Revolution had set in motion intense and urgent discussion concerning the nature of society. Coleridge now conceived the design of circumventing the disastrous violence that had destroyed the idealism of the French Revolution by establishing a small society that should organize itself and educate its children according to better principles than those obtaining in the society around them. A chance meeting with the poet Robert Southey led the two men to plan such a "pantisocracy" and to set up a community by the Susquehanna River in Pennsylvania. To this end Coleridge left Cambridge for good and set up with Southey as a public lecturer in Bristol. In October 1795 he married Sara Fricker, daughter of a local schoolmistress. Shortly afterward, Southey defected from the pantisocratic scheme, leaving

Coleridge married to a woman whom he did not really love. In a sense his career never fully recovered from this blow: if there is a makeshift quality about many of its later events, one explanation can be found in his constant need to reconcile his intellectual aspirations with the financial needs of his family. During this period, however, Coleridge's intellect flowered in an extraordinary manner, as he embarked on an investigation of the nature of the human mind, joined by William Wordsworth, with whom he had become acquainted in 1795. Together they entered upon one of the most influential creative periods of English literature. Coleridge's intellectual ebullience and his belief in the existence of a powerful "life consciousness" in all individuals rescued Wordsworth from the depression into which recent events had cast him and made possible the new approach to nature that characterized his contributions to Lyrical Ballads (which was to be published in 1798).

Later life and increasing drug use

Travel and the Friend

In 1804, he travelled to Sicily and Malta, working for a time as Acting Public Secretary of Malta under the Civil Commissioner, Alexander Ball, a task he performed quite successfully. He lived in San Anton Palace in the village of Attard. However, he gave this up and returned to England in 1806. Dorothy Wordsworth was shocked at his condition upon his return. From 1807 to 1808, Coleridge returned to Malta and then travelled in Sicily and Italy, in the hope that leaving Britain's damp climate would improve his health and thus enable him to reduce his consumption of opium. Thomas De Quincey alleges in his Recollections of the Lakes and the Lake Poets that it was during this period that Coleridge became a full-blown opium addict, using the drug as a substitute for the lost vigour and creativity of his youth. It has been suggested, however, that this reflects de Quincey's own experiences more than Coleridge's.

His opium addiction (he was using as much as two quarts of laudanum a week) now began to take over his life: he separated from his wife Sara in 1808, quarrelled with Wordsworth in 1810, lost part of his annuity in 1811, and put himself under the care of Dr. Daniel in 1814. His addiction caused severe constipation, which required regular and humiliating enemas.

In 1809, Coleridge made his second attempt to become a newspaper publisher with the publication of the journal entitled The Friend. It was a weekly publication that, in Coleridge's typically ambitious style, was written, edited, and published almost entirely single-handedly. Given that Coleridge tended to be highly disorganised and had no head for business, the publication was probably doomed from the start. Coleridge financed the journal by selling over five hundred subscriptions, over two dozen of which were sold to members of Parliament, but in late 1809, publication was crippled by a financial crisis and Coleridge was obliged to approach "Conversation Sharp", Tom Poole and one or two other wealthy friends for an emergency loan to continue. The Friend was an eclectic publication that drew upon every corner of Coleridge's remarkably diverse knowledge of law, philosophy, morals, politics, history, and literary criticism. Although it was often turgid, rambling, and inaccessible to most readers, it ran for 25 issues and was republished in book form a number of times. Years after its initial publication, The Friend became a highly influential work and its effect was felt on writers and philosophers from John Stuart Mill to Ralph Waldo Emerson.

The Work

He was an English poet, literary critic, philosopher and theologian who, with his friend William Wordsworth, was a founder of the Romantic Movement in England and a member of the Lake Poets. Coleridge was a founder of the English Romantic Movement. His best known poems are "The Rime of the Ancient Mariner" and "Kubla Khan," the latter of which was reportedly written under the influence of opium. His critical work, especially on William Shakespeare, was highly influential, and he helped introduce German idealist philosophy to English-speaking culture. Coleridge coined many familiar words and phrases, including suspension of disbelief. He was a major influence on Ralph Waldo Emerson and American transcendentalism. In the context of literary history, Samuel Taylor Coleridge is often seen as "the most intellectual of the English Romantics" due to his extensive forays into critical writing, especially his Biographia Literaria (1817) and lectures on Shakespeare. This is not to say that Coleridge's creative side received short shrift; friends and colleagues knew him as an unrelentingly passionate poet.

In October 1795 he wrote "The Eolian Harp," a meditative poem different in every way from "Religious Musings" and the real inauguration of his mature voice. In its primitive form, as the effusion of 1796, it reflects the conflict between natural response—"the sense of beauty in forms and sounds," as he put it in the Biographia Literaria—and higher responsibility. Nature as an animated, omnipresent life force, a benevolent companion, is memorably characterized through the image of the wind harp, which is identified with the poet's "indolent and passive brain." Poetic imagination is simply an instrument of this Nature, one "organic harp" among others in its universal symphony. In the exemplary setting of the new life he was undertaking, the claims of enlightenment thinking succumbed to faith.

"The Eolian Harp"establishes the terms of this important conflict, which was not simply intellectual but broadly social in implication. For pantheism was associated with the progressive scientific culture for which the empirical world of nature was simply reality itself. A personal God had no empirical reality. Unitarians and various sorts of deists adhered to a divinity which was known through sensation: a Nature god of sorts. This was Coleridge's intellectual milieu, and he tried out its ideas in his Bristol period. Yet his enduring commitments showed through. The community espoused in the conclusion of "The Eolian Harp" is not the egalitarian utopia of scientific aspiration, but "the family of Christ." The ideals of Pantisocracy triumph over the temptations of the new science. In his extensive correspondence of the period Coleridge proclaimed himself a Necessitarian for whom everything had a place in the divine scheme. "The Eolian Harp" shows how the lure of an alternative vision of human experience dominated by sensation could provoke an equal and opposite reaffirmation of first principles to the contrary. A traditional faith was confirmed through temptation.

It was in "This Lime-Tree Bower My Prison," which describes a walk some of them took one day in Coleridge's absence. The jealous Sara had spilled a pan of boiling milk on his foot, excluding him from the company of Dorothy (In the late 1790s, Coleridge began his famous friendship with William Wordsworth and his sister, Dorothy.) and William Wordsworth, as well as Charles Lamb, on a jaunt in the surrounding spur of low hills—combes, in local parlance—the Quantocks. From his confinement in the garden, he celebrates the pleasures of the natural world as seen from within this harmonious community of like-minded individuals. The detailed evocation of their itinerary marks the apogee of his response to landscape. In the end, the poet's imagination triumphs over his separation: his bower reveals pleasures of its own; Nature is hospitable to human response. Sensation proves adequate to human need; Nature is a providential resource against isolation. The poem's conclusion dwells on the joy of companionship in such a world. Their intellectual and artistic exchanges culminated in Lyrical Ballads 1798, in which "The Rime of the Ancient Mariner" was first published. The collection was a major landmark in the Romantic Movement; in it, the two writers exemplified the examination of the mundane, natural, and intensely subjective. Many of the poems were also written in everyday language, avoiding the ornamented styles of speech and elaborate rhyme schemes favored by poets of earlier periods.

"The Rime of the Ancient Mariner" is one exception to this trend, as in it Coleridge used both a rhyme scheme and words derived from Middle English. Soon after the publication of Lyrical Ballads, Coleridge fell in love with Sara Hutchinson, the sister of Wordsworth's future wife. Since he was already married, he was forced to channel his love for Sara Hutchinson into his poetry, where he referred to her by an anagram of her name, "Asra." Coleridge published the second version of "The Rime of the Ancient Mariner" in 1817 in the volume Sibylline Leaves. In it he removed much of the original poem's deliberate archaism and added marginal glosses. Coleridge was enabled to explore the same range of themes less egotistically in "The Rime of the Ancient Mariner," composed during the autumn and winter of 1797–98. For this, his most famous poem, he drew upon the ballad form. The main narrative tells how a sailor who has committed a crime against the life principle by slaying an albatross suffers from torments, physical and mental, in which the nature of his crime is made known to him. The underlying life power against which he has transgressed is envisaged as a power corresponding to the influx of the sun's energy into all living creatures, thereby binding them together in a joyful communion. By killing the bird that hovered near the ship, the mariner has destroyed one of the links in this process. His own consciousness is consequently affected: the sun, previously glorious, is seen as a bloody sun, and the energies of the deep are seen as corrupt.

All in a hot and copper sky,
The bloody Sun, at noon,
Right up above the mast did stand,
No bigger than the Moon.
The very deep did rot; O Christ!
That ever this should be!
Yea, slimy things did crawl with legs
Upon the slimy sea.

Only at night do these energies display a sinister beauty.

About, about, in reel and rout
Thedeath-fires danced at night;
The water, like a witch's oils,
Burnt green, and blue and white.

After the death of his shipmates, alone and becalmed, devoid of a sense of movement or even of time passing, the mariner is in a hell created by the absence of any link with life. Eventually, however, a chance sight of water snakes flashing like golden fire in the darkness, answered by an outpouring of love from his heart, reinitiates the creative process: he is given a brief vision of the inner unity of the universe, in which all living things hymn their source in an interchange of harmonies. Restored to his native land, he remains haunted by what he has experienced but is at least delivered from nightmare, able to see the ordinary processes of human life with a new sense of their wonder and mercifulness. These last qualities are reflected in the poem's attractive combination of vividness and sensitivity. The placing of it at the beginning of Lyrical Ballads was evidently intended to provide a context for the sense of wonder in common life that marks many of Wordsworth's contributions. While this volume was going through the press, Coleridge began a complementary poem, a Gothic ballad entitled "Christabel," in which he aimed to show how naked energy might be redeemed through contact with a spirit of innocent love.

Most extraordinary of all, in the eyes of later readers, is "Kubla Khan," an opium-induced, orientalizing fantasia of the unconscious. It is important to recognize that Coleridge himself claimed nothing for this production's "supposed poetic merits." He did not publish it until 1816, under financial pressure as usual and at the urging of Lord Byron, and only as an appendage to the more substantial "Christabel," which Wordsworth had excluded from the second edition of Lyrical Ballads (1800). The poem was not liked even then. As a "psychological curiosity" it was interesting to its author mainly as evidence of a state of extreme imaginative excitement. "Kubla Khan" had nothing to do with the reflective idiom to which Coleridge was committed. It might be verse, but it was not good poetry.

In the summer of the year 1797, the Author, then in ill health, had retired to a lonely farm house between Porlock and Linton, on the Exmoor confines of Somerset and Devonshire. In consequence of a slight indisposition, an anodyne had been prescribed, from the effects of which he fell asleep in his chair at the moment that he was reading the following sentence, or words of the same substance, in 'Purchas's Pilgrimes:' 'Here the Khan Kubla commanded a palace to be built, and a stately garden thereunto: and thus ten miles of fertile ground were inclosed with a wall.'

Coleridge continued for about three hours in a profound sleep, at least of the external senses, during which time he has the most vivid confidence, that he could not have composed less than from two to three hundred lines; if that indeed can be called composition in which all the images rose up before him as things, with a parallel production of the correspondent expressions, without any sensation or consciousness of effort. On awakening he appeared to himself to have a distinct recollection of the whole, and taking his pen, ink, and paper, instantly and eagerly wrote down the lines that are here preserved. At this moment he was unfortunately called out by a person on business from Porlock, and detained by him above an hour, and on his return to his room, found, to his no small surprise and mortification, that though he still retained some vague and dim recollection of the general purport of the vision, yet, with the exception of some eight or ten scattered lines and images, all the rest had passed away like the images on the surface of a stream into which a stone had been cast, but, alas! without the after restoration of the latter:

Then all the charm
Is broken—all that phantom-world so fair
Vanishes, and a thousand circlets spread,
And each mis-shape the other. Stay awhile,
Poor youth! who scarcely dar'st lift up thine eyes—
The stream will soon renew its smoothness, soon
The visions will return! And lo! he stays,
And soon the fragments dim of lovely forms
Come trembling back, unite, and now once more
The pool becomes a mirror.

Yet from the still surviving recollections in his mind, Coleridge has frequently purposed to finish for himself what had been originally, as it were, given to him. but the to-morrow is yet to come. As a contrast to this vision, we have annexed a fragment of a very different character, describing with equal fidelity the dream of pain and disease.

Coleridge died in 1834 after years of personal discomfort and disappointment. A legend in his time, he came to be seen by friends and contemporaries as the genius who failed. The failure was largely relative to early expectations, however, and to hopes defeated by disease and drugs. Despite everything, Coleridge can still be regarded as a groundbreaking and, at his best, a powerful poet of lasting influence. His idea of poetry remains the standard by which others in the English sphere are tried. As a political thinker, and as a Christian apologist, Coleridge proved an inspiration to the important generation after his own. Recent publication of his private notebooks has provided further evidence of the constant ferment and vitality of his inquiring spirit.

Coleridge's achievement has been given more widely varying assessments than that of any other English literary artist, though there is broad agreement that his enormous potential was never fully realized in his works. His stature as a poet has never been in doubt; in "Kubla Khan" and "The Rime of the Ancient Mariner" he wrote two of the greatest poems in English literature and perfected a mode of sensuous lyricism that is often echoed by later poets. But he also has a reputation as one of the most important of all English literary critics, largely on the basis of his Biographia Literaria. In Coleridge's view, the essential element of literature was a union of emotion and thought that he described as imagination. He especially stressed poetry's capacity for integrating the universal and the particular, the objective and the subjective, the generic and the individual. The function of criticism for Coleridge was to discern these elements and to lift them into conscious awareness, rather than merely to prescribe or to describe rules or forms.

In all his roles, as poet, social critic, literary critic, theologian, and psychologist, Coleridge expressed a profound concern with elucidating an underlying creative principle that is fundamental to both human beings and the universe as a whole. To Coleridge, imagination is the archetype of this unifying force because it represents the means by which the twin human capacities for intuitive, non-rational understanding and for organizing and discriminating thought concerning the material world are reconciled. It was by means of this sort of reconciliation of opposites that Coleridge attempted, with considerable success, to combine a sense of the universal and ideal with an acute observation of the particular and sensory in his own poetry and in his criticism.

Literary Criticism

Biographia Literaria

In addition to his poetry, Coleridge also wrote influential pieces of literary criticism including Biographia Literaria, a collection of his thoughts and opinions on literature which he published in 1817. The work delivered both biographical explanations of the author's life as well as his impressions on literature. The collection also contained an analysis of a broad range of philosophical principles of literature ranging from Aristotle to Immanuel Kant and Schelling and applied them to the poetry of peers such as William Wordsworth. Coleridge's explanation of metaphysical principles were popular topics of discourse in academic communities throughout the 19th and 20th centuries, and T.S. Eliot stated that he believed that Coleridge was "perhaps the greatest of English critics, and in a sense the last." Eliot suggests that Coleridge displayed "natural abilities" far greater than his contemporaries, dissecting literature and applying philosophical principles of metaphysics in a way that brought the subject of his criticisms away from the text and into a world of logical analysis that mixed logical analysis and emotion. However, Eliot also criticises Coleridge for allowing his emotion to play a role in the metaphysical process, believing that critics should not have emotions that are not provoked by the work being studied. Hugh Kenner in Historical Fictions, discusses Norman Fruman's Coleridge, the Damaged Archangel and suggests that the term "criticism" is too often applied to Biographia Literaria, which both he and Fruman describe as having failed to explain or help the reader understand works of art. To Kenner, Coleridge's attempt to discuss complex philosophical concepts without describing the rational process behind them displays a lack of critical thinking that makes the volume more of a biography than a work of criticism.

In Biographia Literaria and his poetry, symbols are not merely "objective correlatives" to Coleridge, but instruments for making the universe and personal experience intelligible and spiritually covalent. To Coleridge, the "cinque spotted spider," making its way upstream "by fits and starts," [Biographia Literaria] is not merely a comment on the intermittent nature of creativity, imagination, or spiritual progress, but the journey and destination of his life. The spider's five legs represent the central problem that Coleridge lived to resolve, the conflict between Aristotelian logic and Christian philosophy. Two legs of the spider represent the "me-not me" of thesis and antithesis, the idea that a thing cannot be itself and its opposite simultaneously, the basis of the clockwork Newtonian world view that Coleridge rejected. The remaining three legs—exothesis, mesothesis and synthesis or the Holy trinity—represent the idea that things can diverge without being contradictory. Taken together, the five legs—with synthesis in the center, form the Holy Cross of Ramist logic. The cinque-spotted spider is Coleridge's emblem of holism, the quest and substance of Coleridge's thought and spiritual life.

Coleridge and the Influence of the Gothic

Coleridge wrote reviews of Ann Radcliffe's books and The Mad Monk, among others. He comments in his reviews: "Situations of torment, and images of naked horror, are easily conceived; and a writer in whose works they abound, deserves our gratitude almost equally with him who should drag us by way of sport through a military hospital, or force us to sit at the dissecting-table of a natural philosopher. To trace the nice boundaries, beyond which terror and sympathy are deserted by the pleasurable emotions, – to reach those limits, yet never to pass them, hic labour, hic opus est." and "The horrible and the preternatural have usually seized on the popular taste, at the rise and decline of literature. Most powerful stimulants, they can never be required except by the torpor of an unawakened, or the languor of an exhausted, appetite... We trust, however, that satiety will banish what good sense should have prevented; and that, wearied with fiends, incomprehensible characters, with shrieks, murders, and subterraneous dungeons, the public will learn, by the multitude of the manufacturers, with how little expense of thought or imagination this species of composition is manufactured."

However, Coleridge used these elements in poems such as The Rime of the Ancient Mariner (1798), Christabel and Kubla Khan (published in 1816, but known in manuscript form before then) and certainly influenced other poets and writers of the time. Poems like these both drew inspiration from and helped to inflame the craze for Gothic romance. Coleridge also made considerable use of Gothic elements in his commercially successful play Remorse.

Mary Shelley, who knew Coleridge well, mentions The Rime of the Ancient Mariner twice directly in Frankenstein, and some of the descriptions in the novel echo it indirectly. Although William Godwin, her father, disagreed with Coleridge on some important issues, he respected his opinions and Coleridge often visited the Godwins. Mary Shelley later recalled hiding behind the sofa and hearing his voice chanting The Rime of the Ancient Mariner.

Theological Legacy

Despite being mostly remembered today for his poetry and literary criticism, Coleridge was also (perhaps in his own eyes primarily) a theologian. His writings include discussions of the status of Scripture, the doctrines of the Fall, justification and sanctification, and the personality and infinity of God. A key figure in the Anglican theology of his day, his writings are still regularly referred to by contemporary Anglican theologians, and key figures such as F.D. Maurice, F.J.A. Hort, F.W. Robertson, B.F. Westcott, John Oman and Thomas Erskine (once called the 'Scottish Coleridge') were all influenced by him.

Collected Works

A current standard edition is The Collected Works of Samuel Taylor Coleridge, edited by Kathleen Coburn and many other editors (1969–2002), which appeared (from Princeton University Press and Routledge and Kegan

Paul) in Bollingen Series 75, in 16 volumes, broken down as follows into further volumes and parts, to a total of 34 separate printed volumes:

- Lectures 1795 on Politics and Religion (1971);
- The Watchman (1970);
- Essays on his Times in the Morning Post and the Courier(1978) in 3 vols;
- The Friend (1969) in 2 vols;
- Lectures, 1808–1819, on Literature (1987) in 2 vols;
- Lay Sermons (1972);
- Biographia Literaria (1983) in 2 vols;
- Lectures 1818–1819 on the History of Philosophy (2000) in 2 vols;
- Aids to Reflection (1993);
- On the Constitution of the Church and State (1976);
- Shorter Works and Fragments (1995) in 2 vols;
- Marginalia (1980 and following) in 6 vols;
- Logic (1981);
- Table Talk (1990) in 2 vols;
- Opus Maximum (2002);
- Poetical Works (2001) in 6 vols (part1 Reading Edition in 2 vols; part 2 Variorum Text in 2 vols; part 3 Plays in 2 vols).

London: Final Years and Death

Between 1810 and 1820, Coleridge gave a series of lectures in London and Bristol – those on Shakespeare renewed interest in the playwright as a model for contemporary writers. Much of Coleridge's reputation as a literary critic is founded on the lectures that he undertook in the winter of 1810–11, which were sponsored by the Philosophical Institution and given at Scot's Corporation Hall off Fetter Lane, Fleet Street. These lectures were heralded in the prospectus as "A Course of Lectures on Shakespeare and Milton, in Illustration of the Principles of Poetry." Coleridge's ill-health, opium-addiction problems, and somewhat unstable personality meant that all his lectures were plagued with problems of delays and a general irregularity of quality from one lecture to the next. As a result of these factors, Coleridge often failed to prepare anything but the loosest set of notes for his lectures and regularly entered into extremely long digressions which his audiences found difficult to follow. However, it was the lecture on Hamlet given on 2 January 1812 that was considered the best and has influenced Hamlet studies ever since. Before Coleridge, Hamlet was often denigrated and belittled by critics from Voltaire to Dr. Johnson. Coleridge rescued the play's reputation, and his thoughts on it are often still published as supplements to the text.

In August 1814, Coleridge was approached by Lord Byron's publisher, John Murray, about the possibility of translating Goethe's classic Faust (1808). Coleridge was regarded by many as the greatest living writer on the demonic and he accepted the commission, only to abandon work on it after six weeks. Until recently, scholars were in agreement that Coleridge never returned to the project, despite Goethe's own belief in the 1820s that he had in fact completed a long translation of the work. In September 2007, Oxford University Press sparked a heated scholarly controversy by publishing an English translation of Goethe's work that purported to be Coleridge's long-lost masterpiece (the text in question first appeared anonymously in 1821).

Between 1814 and 1816, Coleridge lived in Calne, Wiltshire and seemed able to focus on his work and manage his addiction, drafting Biographia Literaria. He rented rooms from local surgeon, Mr Page, on Church Street, just opposite the entrance to the churchyard. A blue plaque marks the property today.

In April 1816, Coleridge, with his addiction worsening, his spirits depressed, and his family alienated, took residence in the Highgatehomes, then just north of London, of the physician James Gillman, first at South Grove and later at the nearby 3 The Grove. It is unclear whether his growing use of opium (and the brandy in which it was dissolved) was a symptom or a cause of his growing depression. Gillman was partially successful in controlling the poet's addiction. Coleridge remained in Highgate for the rest of his life, and the house became a place of literary pilgrimage for writers including Carlyle and Emerson.

In Gillman's home, Coleridge finished his major prose work, the Biographia Literaria (mostly drafted in 1815, and finished in 1817), a volume composed of 23 chapters of autobiographical notes and dissertations on various subjects, including some incisive literary theory and criticism. He composed a considerable amount of poetry, of variable quality. He published other writings while he was living at the Gillman homes, notably the Lay Sermons of 1816 and 1817, Sibylline Leaves (1817), Hush (1820), Aids to Reflection (1825), and On the Constitution of the Church and State (1830).[31] He also produced essays published shortly after his death, such as Essay on Faith (1838) and Confessions Of An Inquiring Spirit (1840). A number of his followers were central to the Oxford Movement, and his religious writings profoundly shaped Anglicanism in the mid-nineteenth century.

Coleridge also worked extensively on the various manuscripts which form his "Opus Maximum", a work which was in part intended as a post-Kantian work of philosophical synthesis. The work was never published in his lifetime, and has frequently been seen as evidence for his tendency to conceive grand projects which he then had difficulty in carrying through to completion. But while he frequently berated himself for his "indolence", the long list of his published works calls this myth into some question. Critics are divided on whether the "Opus Maximum", first published in 2002, successfully resolved the philosophical issues he had been exploring for most of his adult life.

Coleridge died in Highgate, London on 25 July 1834 as a result of heart failure compounded by an unknown lung disorder, possibly linked to his use of opium. Coleridge had spent 18 years under the roof of the Gillman family, who built an addition onto their home to accommodate the poet.

Faith may be defined as fidelity to our own being, so far as such being is not and cannot become an object of the senses; and hence, by clear inference or implication to being generally, as far as the same is not the object of the senses; and again to whatever is affirmed or understood as the condition, or concomitant, or consequence of the same. This will be best explained by an instance or example. That I am conscious of something within me peremptorily commanding me to do unto others as I would they should do unto me; in other words a categorical (that is, primary and unconditional) imperative; that the maxim (regula maxima, or supreme rule) of my actions, both inward and outward, should be such as I could, without any contradiction arising therefrom, will to be the law of all moral and rational beings. Essay On Faith

Carlyle described him at Highgate: "Coleridge sat on the brow of Highgate Hill, in those years, looking down on London and its smoke-tumult, like a sage escaped from the inanity of life's battle ... The practical intellects of the world did not much heed him, or carelessly reckoned him a metaphysical dreamer: but to the rising spirits of the young generation he had this dusky sublime character; and sat there as a kind of Magus, girt in mystery and enigma; his Dodona oak-grove (Mr. Gilman's house at Highgate) whispering strange things, uncertain whether oracles or jargon."

Coleridge is buried in the aisle of St. Michael's Parish Church, Highgate, London, England. He was originally buried at Old Highgate Chapel but was re-interred in St. Michael's Church in 1961.

WILLIAM WORDSWORTH

William Wordsworth, (born April 7, 1770, Cockermouth, Cumberland, England—died April 23, 1850, Rydal Mount, Westmorland), English poet whose Lyrical Ballads (1798), written with Samuel Taylor Coleridge, helped launch the English Romantic movement.

Early Life and Education

Wordsworth was born in the Lake District of northern England, the second of five children of a modestly prosperous estate manager. He lost his mother when he was 7 and his father when he was 13, upon which the orphan boys were sent off by guardian uncles to a grammar school at Hawkshead, a village in the heart of the Lake District. At Hawkshead Wordsworth received an excellent education in classics, literature, and mathematics, but the chief advantage to him there was the chance to indulge in the boyhood pleasures of living and playing in the outdoors. The natural scenery of the English lakes could terrify as well as nurture, as Wordsworth would later testify in the line "I grew up fostered alike by beauty and by fear," but its generally benign aspect gave the growing boy the confidence he articulated in one of his first important poems, "Lines Composed a Few Miles Above Tintern Abbey...," namely, "that Nature never did betray the heart that loved her."

Wordsworth moved on in 1787 to St. John's College, Cambridge. Repelled by the competitive pressures there, he elected to idle his way through the university, persuaded that he "was not for that hour, nor for that place." The most important thing he did in his college years was to devote his summer vacation in 1790 to a long walking tour through revolutionary France. There he was caught up in the passionate enthusiasm that followed the fall of the Bastille, and became an ardent republican sympathizer. Upon taking his Cambridge degree—an undistinguished "pass"—he returned in 1791 to France, where he formed a passionate attachment to a Frenchwoman, Annette Vallon. But before their child was born in December 1792, Wordsworth had to return to England and was cut off there by the outbreak of war between England and France. He was not to see his daughter Caroline until she was nine.

The three or four years that followed his return to England were the darkest of Wordsworth's life. Unprepared for any profession, rootless, virtually penniless, bitterly hostile to his own country's opposition to the French, he lived in London in the company of radicals like William Godwin and learned to feel a profound sympathy for the abandoned mothers, beggars, children, vagrants, and victims of England's wars who began to march through the sombre poems he began writing at this time. This dark period ended in 1795, when a friend's legacy made possible Wordsworth's reunion with his beloved sister Dorothy—the two were never again to live apart—and their move in 1797 to Alfoxden House, near Bristol. While living with Dorothy at Alfoxden House, Wordsworth became friends with a fellow poet, Samuel Taylor Coleridge. They formed a partnership that would change both poets' lives and alter the course of English poetry.

Marriage and children

In 1802 Lowther's heir, William Lowther, 1st Earl of Lonsdale, paid the 4,000 pounds owed to Wordsworth's father through Lowther's failure to pay his aide. It was this repayment that afforded Wordsworth the financial means to marry. On 4 October, following his visit with Dorothy to France to arrange matters with Annette, Wordsworth married his childhood friend Mary Hutchinson. Dorothy continued to live with the couple and grew close to Mary. The following year Mary gave birth to the first of five children, three of whom predeceased her and William:

- John Wordsworth (18 June 1803 – 1875). Married four times:
  - Isabella Curwen (d. 1848) had six children: Jane, Henry, William, John, Charles and Edward.
  - Helen Ross (d. 1854). No children
  - Mary Ann Dolan (d. after 1858) had one daughter Dora (b. 1858).
  - Mary Gamble. No children
- Dora Wordsworth (16 August 1804 – 9 July 1847). Married Edward Quillinan in 1841.
- Thomas Wordsworth (15 June 1806 – 1 December 1812).
- Catherine Wordsworth (6 September 1808 – 4 June 1812).
- William "Willy" Wordsworth (12 May 1810 – 1883). Married Fanny Graham and had four children: Mary Louisa, William, Reginald, Gordon

Autobiographical work and Poems in Two Volumes

Wordsworth had for years been making plans to write a long philosophical poem in three parts, which he intended to call The Recluse. In 1798–99 he started an autobiographical poem, which he referred to as the "poem to Coleridge" and which he planned would serve as an appendix to a larger work called The Recluse. In 1804 he began expanding this autobiographical work, having decided to make it a prologue rather than an appendix. He completed this work, now generally referred to as the first version of The

Prelude, in 1805, but refused to publish such a personal work until he had completed the whole of The Recluse. The death of his brother John, also in 1805, affected him strongly and may have influenced his decisions about these works.

Wordsworth's philosophical allegiances as articulated in The Preludeand in such shorter works as "Lines written a few miles above Tintern Abbey" have been a source of critical debate. It was long supposed that Wordsworth relied chiefly on Coleridge for philosophical guidance, but more recently scholars have suggested that Wordsworth's ideas may have been formed years before he and Coleridge became friends in the mid-1790s. In particular, while he was in revolutionary Paris in 1792 the 22-year-old Wordsworth made the acquaintance of the mysterious traveler John "Walking" Stewart(1747–1822), who was nearing the end of his thirty years of wandering, on foot, from Madras, India, through Persia and Arabia, across Africa and Europe, and up through the fledgling United States. By the time of their association Stewart had published an ambitious work of original materialist philosophy entitled The Apocalypse of Nature (London, 1791), to which many of Wordsworth's philosophical sentiments may well be indebted.

In 1807 Wordsworth published Poems in Two Volumes, including "Ode: Intimations of Immortality from Recollections of Early Childhood". Up to this point Wordsworth was known only for Lyrical Ballads, and he hoped that this new collection would cement his reputation. Its reception was lukewarm, however.

In 1810, Wordsworth and Coleridge were estranged over the latter's opium addiction, and in 1812, his son Thomas died at the age of 6, six months after the death of 3-year-old Catherine. The following year he received an appointment as Distributor of Stamps for Westmorland, and the stipend of £400 a year made him financially secure. In 1813, he and his family, including Dorothy, moved to Rydal Mount, Ambleside (between Grasmere and Rydal Water), where he spent the rest of his life.

A turn to the elegiac

In the company of Dorothy, Wordsworth spent the winter of 1798–99 in Germany, where, in the remote town of Goslar, in Saxony, he experienced the most intense isolation he had ever known. As a consequence, however, he wrote some of his most moving poetry, including the "Lucy" and "Matthew" elegies and early drafts toward The Prelude. Upon his return to England, Wordsworth incorporated several new poems in the second edition of Lyrical Ballads (1800), notably two tragic pastorals of country life, "The Brothers" and

"Michael." At about this time Wordsworth also wrote the brilliant lyrics that were assembled in his second verse collection, Poems, in Two Volumes (1807), including the enduringly popular "I wandered lonely as a cloud" (also known as "Daffodils"). All of these poems make up what is now recognized as his great decade, stretching from his meeting with Coleridge in 1797 until 1808.

One portion of a second part of The Recluse was finished in 1806, but, like The Prelude, was left in manuscript at the poet's death. This portion, Home at Grasmere, joyously celebrated Wordsworth's taking possession (in December 1799) of Dove Cottage, at Grasmere, Westmorland, where he was to reside for eight of his most productive years. In 1802, during the short-lived Peace of Amiens, Wordsworth returned briefly to France, where at Calais he met his daughter and made his peace with Annette. He then returned to England to marry Mary Hutchinson, a childhood friend, and start an English family, which had grown to three sons and two daughters by 1810.

In 1805 the drowning of Wordsworth's favorite brother, John, the captain of a sailing vessel, gave Wordsworth the strongest shock he had ever experienced. "A deep distress hath humanized my Soul," he lamented in his "Elegiac Stanzas" on Peele Castle. Henceforth he would produce a different kind of poetry, defined by a new sobriety, a new restraint, and a lofty, almost Miltonic elevation of tone and diction. Wordsworth appeared to anticipate this turn in "Tintern Abbey," where he had learned to hear "the still, sad music of humanity," and again in the "Ode: Intimations of Immortality" (written in 1802–04; published in Poems, in Two Volumes). The theme of this ode is the loss of his power to see the things he had once seen, the radiance, the "celestial light" that seemed to lie over the landscapes of his youth like "the glory and freshness of a dream." Now, in the Peele Castle stanzas, he sorrowfully looked back on the light as illusory, as a "Poet's dream," as "the light that never was, on sea or land."

These metaphors point up the differences between the early and the late Wordsworth. It is generally accepted that the quality of his verse fell off as he grew more distant from the sources of his inspiration and as his Anglican and Tory sentiments hardened into orthodoxy. Today many readers discern two Wordsworths, the young Romantic revolutionary and the aging Tory humanist, risen into what John Keats called the "Egotistical Sublime." Little of Wordsworth's later verse matches the best of his earlier years.

In his middle period Wordsworth invested a good deal of his creative energy in odes, the best known of which is "On the Power of Sound." He also produced a large number of sonnets, most of them strung together in sequences.

The most admired are the Duddon sonnets (1820), which trace the progress of a stream through Lake District landscapes and blend nature poetry with philosophic reflection in a manner now recognized as the best of the later Wordsworth. Other sonnet sequences record his tours through the European continent, and the three series of Ecclesiastical Sketches (1822) develop meditations, many sharply satirical, on church history. But the most memorable poems of Wordsworth's middle and late years were often cast in elegiac mode. They range from the poet's heartfelt laments for two of his children who died in 1812—laments incorporated in The Excursion—to brilliant lyrical effusions on the deaths of his fellow poets James Hogg, George Crabbe, Coleridge, and Charles Lamb.

Late Work

In 1808 Wordsworth and his family moved from Dove Cottage to larger quarters in Grasmere, and five years later they settled at Rydal Mount, near Ambleside, where Wordsworth spent the remainder of his life. In 1813 he accepted the post of distributor of stamps for the county of Westmorland, an appointment that carried the salary of £400 a year. Wordsworth continued to hold back from publication The Prelude, Home at Grasmere, The Borderers, and Salisbury Plain. He did publish Poems, in Two Volumes in 1807; The Excursion in 1814, containing the only finished portions of The Recluse; and the collected Poems of 1815, which contained most of his shorter poems and two important critical essays as well. Wordsworth's other works published during middle age include The White Doe of Rylstone (1815), a poem about the pathetic shattering of a Roman Catholic family during an unsuccessful rebellion against Elizabeth I in 1569; a Thanksgiving Ode (1816); and Peter Bell (1819), a poem written in 1798 and then modulated in successive rewritings into an experiment in Romantic irony and the mock-heroic and coloured by the poet's feelings of affinity with his hero, a "wild and woodland rover." The Waggoner (1819) is another extended ballad about a North Country itinerant.

Through all these years Wordsworth was assailed by vicious and tireless critical attacks by contemptuous reviewers; no great poet has ever had to endure worse. But finally, with the publication of The River Duddon in 1820, the tide began to turn, and by the mid-1830s his reputation had been established with both critics and the reading public.

Wordsworth's last years were given over partly to "tinkering" his poems, as the family called his compulsive and persistent habit of revising his earlier poems through edition after edition. The Prelude, for instance, went through four distinct manuscript versions (1798–99, 1805–06, 1818–20, and 1832–39) and was published only after the poet's death in 1850. Most readers find the earliest versions of The Prelude and other heavily revised poems to be the best, but flashes of brilliance can appear in revisions added when the poet was in his seventies.

Wordsworth succeeded his friend Robert Southey as Britain's poet laureate in 1843 and held that post until his own death in 1850. Thereafter his influence was felt throughout the rest of the 19th century, though he was honoured more for his smaller poems, as singled out by the Victorian critic Matthew Arnold, than for his masterpiece, The Prelude. In the 20th century his reputation was strengthened both by recognition of his importance in the Romantic movement and by an appreciation of the darker elements in his personality and verse.

William Wordsworth was the central figure in the English Romantic revolution in poetry. His contribution to it was threefold. First, he formulated in his poems and his essays a new attitude toward nature. This was more than a matter of introducing nature imagery into his verse; it amounted to a fresh view of the organic relation between man and the natural world, and it culminated in metaphors of a wedding between nature and the human mind, and beyond that, in the sweeping metaphor of nature as emblematic of the mind of God, a mind that "feeds upon infinity" and "broods over the dark abyss." Second, Wordsworth probed deeply into his own sensibility as he traced, in his finest poem, The Prelude, the "growth of a poet's mind." The Prelude was in fact the first long autobiographical poem. Writing it in a drawn-out process of self-exploration, Wordsworth worked his way toward a modern psychological understanding of his own nature, and thus more broadly of human nature. Third, Wordsworth placed poetry at the centre of human experience; in impassioned rhetoric he pronounced poetry to be nothing less than "the first and last of all knowledge—it is as immortal as the heart of man," and he then went on to create some of the greatest English poetry of his century. It is probably safe to say that by the late 20th century he stood in critical estimation where Coleridge and Arnold had originally placed him, next to John Milton—who stands, of course, next to William Shakespeare.

The Prospectus

In 1814 Wordsworth published The Excursion as the second part of the three-part work The Recluse, even though he had not completed the first part or the third part, and never did. He did, however, write a poetic Prospectus to "The Recluse" in which he laid out the structure and intention of the whole work. The Prospectus contains some of Wordsworth's most famous lines on the relation between the human mind and nature:

My voice proclaims
How exquisitely the individual Mind
(And the progressive powers perhaps no less
Of the whole species) to the external World
Is fitted:—and how exquisitely, too,
Theme this but little heard of among Men,
The external World is fitted to the Mind.

Some modern critics suggest that there was a decline in his work beginning around the mid-1810s, perhaps because most of the concerns that characterised his early poems (loss, death, endurance, separation and abandonment) has been resolved in his writings and his life. By 1820, he was enjoying considerable success accompanying a reversal in the contemporary critical opinion of his earlier works. Following the death of his friend the painter William Green in 1823, Wordsworth also mended his relations with Coleridge. The two were fully reconciled by 1828, when they toured the Rhineland together. Dorothy suffered from a severe illness in 1829 that rendered her an invalid for the remainder of her life. Coleridge and Charles Lamb both died in 1834, their loss being a difficult blow to Wordsworth. The following year saw the passing of James Hogg. Despite the death of many contemporaries, the popularity of his poetry ensured a steady stream of young friends and admirers to replace those he lost.

Laureateship and other honours

Wordsworth remained a formidable presence in his later years. In 1837, the Scottish poet and playwright Joanna Baillie reflected on her long acquaintance with Wordsworth. "He looks like a man that one must not speak to unless one has some sensible thing to say. however he does occasionally converse cheerfully & well; and when one knows how benevolent & excellent he is, it disposes one to be very much pleased with him."

In 1838, Wordsworth received an honorary doctorate in Civil Law from the University of Durham and the following year he was awarded the same honorary degree by the University of Oxford. In 1842, the government awarded him a Civil List pension of £300 a year.

Following the death of Robert Southey in 1843 Wordsworth became Poet Laureate. He initially refused the honour, saying that he was too old, but accepted when the Prime Minister, Robert Peel, assured him that "you shall have nothing required of you". Wordsworth thus became the only poet laureate to write no official verses. The sudden death of his daughter Dora in 1847 at the age of only 42 was difficult for the aging poet to take and in his depression, he completely gave up writing new material.

Coleridge and Lyrical Ballads

The partnership between Wordsworth and Coleridge, rooted in one marvelous year (1797–98) in which they "together wantoned in wild Poesy," had two consequences for Wordsworth. First it turned him away from the long poems on which he had laboured since his Cambridge days. These included poems of social protest like Salisbury Plain, loco-descriptive poems such as An Evening Walk and Descriptive Sketches (published in 1793), and The Borderers, a blank-verse tragedy exploring the psychology of guilt (and not published until 1842). Stimulated by Coleridge and under the healing influences of nature and his sister, Wordsworth began in 1797–98 to compose the short lyrical and dramatic poems for which he is best remembered by many readers. Some of these were affectionate tributes to Dorothy, some were tributes to daffodils, birds, and other elements of "Nature's holy plan," and some were portraits of simple rural people intended to illustrate basic truths of human nature. Many of these short poems were written to a daringly original programme formulated jointly by Wordsworth and Coleridge, and aimed at breaking the decorum of Neoclassical verse. These poems appeared in 1798 in a slim, anonymously authored volume entitled Lyrical Ballads, which opened with Coleridge's long poem "The Rime of the Ancient Mariner" and closed with Wordsworth's "Tintern Abbey." All but three of the intervening poems were Wordsworth's, and, as he declared in a preface to a second edition two years later, their object was "to choose incidents and situations from common life and to relate or describe them…in a selection of language really used by men,…tracing in them…the primary laws of our nature." Most of the poems were dramatic in form, designed to reveal the character of the speaker. The manifesto and the accompanying poems thus set forth a new style, a new vocabulary, and new subjects for poetry, all of them foreshadowing 20th-century developments.

The Recluse and The Prelude

The second consequence of Wordsworth's partnership with Coleridge was the framing of a vastly ambitious poetic design that teased and haunted him for the rest of his life. Coleridge had projected an enormous poem to be called "The Brook," in which he proposed to treat all science, philosophy, and religion, but he soon laid the burden of writing this poem upon Wordsworth himself. As early as 1798 Wordsworth began to talk in grand terms of this poem, to be entitled The Recluse. To nerve himself up to this enterprise and to test his powers, Wordsworth began writing the autobiographical poem that would absorb him intermittently for the next 40 years, and which was eventually published in 1850 under the title The Prelude, or, Growth of a Poet's Mind. The Prelude extends the quiet autobiographical mode of reminiscence that Wordsworth had begun in "Tintern Abbey" and traces the poet's life from his school days through his university life and his visits to France, up to the year (1799) in which he settled at Grasmere. It thus describes a circular journey—what has been called a long journey home. But the main events in the autobiography are internal: the poem exultantly describes the ways in which the imagination emerges as the dominant faculty, exerting its control over the reason and the world of the senses alike.

The Recluse itself was never completed, and only one of its three projected parts was actually written; this was published in 1814 as The Excursion and consisted of nine long philosophical monologues spoken by pastoral characters. The first monologue (Book I) contained a version of one of Wordsworth's greatest poems, "The Ruined Cottage," composed in superb blank verse in 1797. This bleak narrative records the slow, pitiful decline of a woman whose husband had gone off to the army and never returned. For later versions of this poem Wordsworth added a reconciling conclusion, but the earliest and most powerful version was starkly tragic.

Death

William Wordsworth died at home at Rydal Mount from an aggravated case of pleurisy on 23 April 1850, and was buried at St Oswald's Church, Grasmere. His widow Mary published his lengthy autobiographical "poem to Coleridge" as The Prelude several months after his death. Though it failed to arouse much interest at that time, it has since come to be widely recognised as his masterpiece.

Major works

- Lyrical Ballads, with a Few Other Poems (1798)
- "Simon Lee"
- "We are Seven"
- "Lines Written in Early Spring"
- "Expostulation and Reply"
- "The Tables Turned"
- "The Thorn"

- "Lines Composed A Few Miles above Tintern Abbey"
- Lyrical Ballads, with Other Poems (1800)
- Preface to the Lyrical Ballads
- "Strange fits of passion have I known"
- "She Dwelt among the Untrodden Ways"
- "Three years she grew"
- "A Slumber Did my Spirit Seal"
- "I travelled among unknown men"
- "Lucy Gray"
- "The Two April Mornings"
- "Solitary Reaper"
- "Nutting"
- "The Ruined Cottage"
- "Michael"
- "The Kitten At Play"
- Poems, in Two Volumes (1807)
- "Resolution and Independence"
- "I Wandered Lonely as a Cloud" Also known as "Daffodils"
- "My Heart Leaps Up"
- "Ode: Intimations of Immortality"
- "Ode to Duty"
- "The Solitary Reaper"
- "Elegiac Stanzas"
- "Composed upon Westminster Bridge, September 3, 1802"
- "London, 1802"
- "The World Is Too Much with Us"
- Guide to the Lakes (1810)
- " To the Cuckoo "
- The Excursion (1814)
- Laodamia (1815, 1845)
- The White Doe of Rylstone (1815)
- Peter Bell (1819)
- The Prelude (1850).

7

Literature in the Romantic Age

As we look back today over the literature of the last three quarters of the eighteenth century, here just surveyed, the progress of the Romantic Movement seems the most conspicuous general fact which it presents. But at the death of Cowper in 1800 the movement still remained tentative and incomplete, and it was to arrive at full maturity only in the work of the great writers of the following quarter century, who were to create the finest body of literature which England had produced since the Elizabethan period. All the greatest of these writers were poets, wholly or in part, and they fall roughly into two groups: first, William Wordsworth, Samuel Taylor Coleridge, Robert Southey, and Walter Scott; and second, about twenty years younger, Lord Byron, Percy Bysshe Shelley, and John Keats.

This period of Romantic Triumph, or of the lives of its authors, coincides in time, and not by mere accident, with the period of the success of the French Revolution, the prolonged struggle of England and all Europe against Napoleon, and the subsequent years when in Continental Europe despotic government reasserted itself and sternly suppressed liberal hopes and uprisings, while in England liberalism and democracy steadily and doggedly gathered force until by the Reform Bill of 1832 political power was largely transferred from the former small governing oligarchy to the middle class. How all these events influenced literature we shall see as we proceed. The beginning of the Romantic triumph is found, by general consent, in the publication in 1798 of the little volume of 'Lyrical Ballads' which contained the first significant poetry of Wordsworth and Coleridge. Even during this its greatest period, however, Romanticism had for a time a hard battle to fight, and a chief literary fact of the period was the founding and continued success of the first two important English literary and political quarterlies, 'The Edinburgh Review' and 'The Quarterly Review,' which in general stood in literature for the conservative eighteenth century tradition and violently attacked all, or almost all, the Romantic poets. These quarterlies are sufficiently important to receive a few words in passing. In the later eighteenth century there had been some periodicals devoted to literary criticism, but they were mere un authoritative booksellers' organs, and it was left for the new reviews to inaugurate literary journalism of the modern serious type. 'The Edinburgh Review,' suggested and first conducted, in 1802, by the witty clergyman and reformer Sydney Smith, passed at once to the hands of Francis Jeffrey, a Scots lawyer who continued to edit it for nearly thirty years. Its politics were strongly liberal, and to oppose it the Tory 'Quarterly Review' was founded in 1808, under the editorship of the satirist William Gifford and with the cooperation of Sir Walter Scott, who withdrew for the purpose from his connection with the 'Edinburgh.' These reviews were followed by other high-class periodicals, such as 'Blackwood's Magazine,' and most of the group have maintained their importance to the present day.

JOHN KEATS

No less individual and unique than the poetry of Byron and Shelley is that of the third member of this group, John Keats, who is, in a wholesome way, the most conspicuous great representative in English poetry since Chaucer of the spirit of 'Art for Art's sake.' Keats was born in London in 1795, the first son of a livery stable keeper. Romantic emotion and passionate ness were among his chief traits from the start; but he was equally distinguished by a generous spirit, physical vigour, and courage. His younger brothers he loved intensely and fought fiercely. At boarding school, however, he turned from headstrong play to enthusiastic reading of Spenser and other great English and Latin poets and of dictionaries of Greek and Roman mythology and life. An orphan at fourteen, the mismanagement of his guardians kept him always in financial difficulties, and he was taken from school and apprenticed to a suburban surgeon. After five years of study and hospital practice the call of poetry proved too strong, and he abandoned his profession to revel in Spenser, Shakespeare, and the Italian epic authors. He now became an enthusiastic disciple of the literary and political radical, Leigh Hunt, in whose home at Hampstead he spent much time. Hunt was a great poetic stimulus to Keats, but he is largely responsible for the flippant jauntiness and formlessness of Keats' earlier poetry, and the connection brought on Keats from the outset the relentless hostility of the literacy critics, who had dubbed Hunt and his friends 'The Cockney School of Poetry.'

Keats' first little volume of verse, published in 1817, when he was twenty-one, contained some delightful poems and clearly displayed most of his chief tendencies. It was followed the next year by his longest poem, 'Endymion,' where he uses, one of the vaguely beautiful Greek myths as the basis for the expression of his own delight in the glory of the world and of youthful sensations. As a narrative the poem is wandering, almost chaotic; that it is immature Keats himself frankly admitted in his preface; but in luxuriant loveliness of sensuous imagination it is unsurpassed. Its theme, and indeed the theme of all Keats' poetry, may be said to be found in its famous first line 'A thing of beauty is a joy forever.' The remaining three years of Keats' life were mostly tragic. 'Endymion' and its author were brutally attacked in 'The Quarterly Review' and 'Blackwood's Magazine.' The sickness and death, from consumption, of one of Keats' dearly loved brothers was followed by his infatuation with a certain Fanny Brawne, a commonplace girl seven years younger than himself. This infatuation thenceforth divided his life with poetry and helped to create in him a restless impatience that led him, among other things, to an unhappy effort to force his genius, in the hope of gain, into the very unsuitable channel of playwriting. But restlessness did not weaken his genuine and maturing poetic power; his third and last volume, published in 1820, and including 'The Eve of St. Agnes,' 'Isabella,' 'Lamia,' the fragmentary 'Hyperion,' and his half dozen great odes, probably contains more poetry of the highest order than any other book of original verse, of so small a size, ever sent from the press. By this time, however, Keats himself was stricken with consumption, and in the effort to save his life a warmer climate was the last resource. Lack of sympathy with Shelley and his poetry led him to reject Shelley's generous offer of entertainment at Pisa, and he sailed with his devoted friend the painter Joseph Severn to southern Italy. A few months later, in 1821, he died at Rome, at the age of twenty-five. His tombstone, in a neglected corner of the Protestant cemetery just outside the city wall, bears among other words those which in bitterness of spirit he himself had dictated: 'Here lies one whose name was writ in water.' But, in fact, not only had he created more great poetry than was ever achieved by any other man at so early an age, but probably no other influence was to prove so great as his on the poets of the next generation.

The most important qualities of his poetry stand out clearly:

- He is, as we have implied, the great apostle of full though not unhealthy enjoyment of external Beauty, the beauty of the senses. He once said: 'I feel sure I should write, from the mere yearning and tenderness I have for the beautiful, even if my night's labours should be burnt every morning and no eye ever rest upon them.' His use of beauty in his poetry is marked at first by passionate Romantic abandonment and always by lavish Romantic richness. This passion was partly stimulated in him by other poets, largely by the Italians, and especially by Spenser, from one of whose minor poems Keats chose the motto for his first volume: 'What more felicity can fall to creature than to enjoy delight with liberty?' Shelley's enthusiasm for Beauty, as we have seen, is somewhat similar to that of Keats. But for both Spenser and Shelley, in different fashions, external Beauty is only the outer garment of the Platonic spiritual Beauty, while to Keats in his poetry it is, in appearance at least, almost everything. He once exclaimed, even, 'Oh for a life of sensations rather than of thoughts!' Notable in his poetry is the absence of any moral purpose and of any interest in present day life and character, particularly the absence of the democratic feeling which had figured so largely in most of his Romantic predecessors. These facts must not be overemphasized, however. His famous final phrasing of the great poetic idea 'Beauty is truth, truth beauty' itself shows consciousness of realities below the surface, and the inference which is sometimes hastily drawn that he was personally a fibreless dreamer is as far as possible from the truth. In fact he was always vigorous and normal, as well as sensitive; he was always devoted to outdoor life; and his very attractive letters, from which his nature can best be judged, are not only overflowing with unpretentious and cordial human feeling but testify that he was not really unaware of specific social and moral issues. Indeed, occasional passages in his poems indicate that he intended to deal with these issues in other poems when he should feel his powers adequately matured. Whether, had he lived, he would have proved capable of handling them significantly is one of the questions which must be left to conjecture, like the other question whether his power of style would have further developed. Almost all of Keats' poems are exquisite and luxuriant in their embodiment of sensuous beauty, but 'The Eve of St. Agnes,' in Spenser's richly lingering stanza, must be especially mentioned.

- Keats is one of the supreme masters of poetic expression, expression the most beautiful, apt, vivid, condensed, and imaginatively suggestive. It is primarily in this respect that he has been the teacher of later poets.
- Keats never attained dramatic or narrative power or skill in the presentation of individual character. In place of these elements he has the lyric gift of rendering moods. Aside from ecstatic delight, these are mostly moods of pensiveness, languor, or romantic sadness, like the one so magically suggested in the 'Ode to a Nightingale,' of Ruth standing lonely and 'in tears amid the alien corn.'

- Conspicuous in Keats is his spiritual kinship with the ancient Greeks. He assimilated with eager delight all the riches of the Greek imagination, even though he never learned the language and was dependent on the dull mediums of dictionaries and translations. It is not only that his recognition of the permanently significant and beautiful embodiment of the central facts of life in the Greek stories led him to select some of them as the subjects for several of his most important poems; but his whole feeling, notably his feeling for Nature, seems almost precisely that of the Greeks, especially, perhaps, of the earlier generations among whom their mythology took shape. To him also Nature appears alive with divinities. Walking through the woods he almost expects to catch glimpses of hamadryads peering from their trees, nymphs rising from the fountains, and startled fauns with shaggy skins and cloven feet scurrying away among the bushes.

In his later poetry, also, the deeper force of the Greek spirit led him from his early Romantic formlessness to the achievement of the most exquisite classical perfection of form and finish. His Romantic glow and emotion never fade or cool, but such poems as the Odes to the Nightingale and to a Grecian Urn, and the fragment of 'Hyperion,' are absolutely flawless and satisfying in structure and expression.

ROBERT SOUTHEY

Robert Southey, a voluminous writer of verse and prose who from his friendship with Wordsworth and Coleridge has been associated with them as third in what has been inaptly called 'The Lake School' of poets, was thought in his own day to be their equal; but time has relegated him to comparative obscurity. An insatiate reader and admirable man, he wrote partly from irrepressible instinct and partly to support his own family and at times, as we have seen, that of Coleridge. An ardent liberal in youth, he, more quickly than Wordsworth, lapsed into conservatism, whence resulted his appointment as Poet Laureate in 1813 and the unremitting hostility of Lord Byron. His rather fantastic epics, composed with great facility and much real spirit, are almost forgotten; he is remembered chiefly by three or four short poems 'The Battle of Blenheim,' 'My days among the dead are past,' 'The Old Man's Comforts'

Walter Scott

In the eighteenth century Scotland had contributed Thomson and Burns to the Romantic movement; now, early in the nineteenth, she supplied a writer of unexcelled and marvelous creative energy, who confirmed the triumph of the movement with work of the first importance in both verse and prose, namely Walter Scott. Scott, further, is personally one of the most delightful figures in English literature, and he is probably the most famous of all the Scotsmen who have ever lived.

He was descended from an ancient Border fighting clan, some of whose pillaging heroes he was to celebrate in his poetry, but he himself was born, in 1771, in Edinburgh, the son of an attorney of a privileged, though not the highest, class. In spite of some serious sicknesses, one of which left him permanently lame, he was always a very active boy, more distinguished at school for play and fighting than for devotion to study. But his unconscious training for literature began very early; in his childhood his love of poetry was stimulated by his mother, and he always spent much time in roaming about the country and picking up old ballads and traditional lore. Loyalty to his father led him to devote six years of hard work to the uncongenial study of the law, and at twenty he was admitted to the Edinburgh bar as an advocate. Though his geniality and high spirited brilliancy made him a social favourite he never secured much professional practice; but after a few years he was appointed permanent Sheriff of Selkirk, a county a little to the south of Edinburgh, near the English Border. Later, in 1806, he was also made one of the Principal Clerks of Session, a subordinate but responsible office with a handsome salary which entailed steady attendance and work at the metropolitan law court in Edinburgh during half of each year.

His instinct for literary production was first stimulated by the German Romantic poets. In 1796 he translated Bürger's fiery and melodramatic ballad 'Lenore,' and a little later wrote some vigorous though hasty ballads of his own. In 1802-1803 he published 'Minstrelsy of the Scottish Border,' a collection of Scottish ballads and songs, which he carefully annotated. He went on in 1805, when he was thirty-four, to his first original verse romance, 'The Lay of the Last Minstrel.' Carelessly constructed and written, this poem was nevertheless the most spirited reproduction of the life of feudal chivalry which the Romantic Movement had yet brought forth, and its popularity was immediate and enormous. Always writing with the greatest facility, though in brief hours snatched from his other occupations, Scott followed up 'The Lay' during the next ten years with the much superior 'Marmion,' 'The Lady of the Lake,' and other verse romances, most of which greatly increased both his reputation and his income.

In 1813 he declined the offer of the Poet Laureateship, then considered a position of no great dignity for a successful man, but secured the appointment of Southey, who was his friend. In 1811 he moved from the comparatively modest country house which he had been occupying to the estate of Abbotsford, where he proceeded to fulfill his ambition of building a great mansion and making himself a sort of feudal chieftain. To this project he devoted for years a large part of the previously unprecedented profits from his writings. For a dozen years before, it should be added, his inexhaustible energy had found further occupation in connection with a troop of horse which he had helped to organize on the threat of a French invasion and of which he acted as quartermaster, training in barracks, and at times drilling for hours before breakfast.

The amount and variety of his literary work was much greater than is understood by most of his admirers today. He contributed largely, in succession, to the 'Edinburgh' and 'Quarterly' reviews, and having become a secret partner in the printing firm of the Ballantyne brothers, two of his school friends, exerted himself not only in the affairs of the company but in vast editorial labours of his own, which included among other things voluminously annotated editions of Dryden and Swift. His productivity is the more astonishing because after his removal to Abbotsford he gave a great part of his time not only to his family but also to the entertainment of the throngs of visitors who pressed upon him in almost continuous crowds. The explanation is to be found partly in his phenomenally vigorous constitution, which enabled him to live and work with little sleep; though in the end he paid heavily for this indiscretion. The circumstances which led him to turn from poetry to prose fiction are well known. His poetical vein was really exhausted when in 1812 and 1813 Byron's 'Childe Harold' and flashy Eastern tales captured the public fancy. Just about as Scott was good-naturedly confessing to himself that it was useless to dispute Byron's supremacy he accidentally came across the first chapters of 'Waverley,' which he had written some years before and had thrown aside in unwillingness to risk his fame by a venture in a new field.

Taking it up with renewed interest, in the evenings of three weeks he wrote the remaining two thirds of it; and he published it with an ultimate success even greater than that of his poetry. For a long time, however, Scott did not acknowledge the authorship of 'Waverley' and the novels which followed it, chiefly because he feared that the writing of prose fiction would seem undignified in a Clerk of Session. The rapidity of the appearance of his novels testified to the almost unlimited accumulation of traditions and incidents with which his astonishing memory was stored; in seventeen years he published nearly thirty 'Waverley' novels, equipping most of them, besides, with long fictitious introductions, which the present day reader almost universally skips.

The profits of Scott's works, long amounting apparently to from ten to twenty thousand pounds a year, were beyond the wildest dream of any previous author, and even exceeded those of most popular authors of the twentieth century, though partly because the works were published in unreasonably expensive form, each novel in several volumes. Still more gratifying were the great personal popularity which Scott attained and his recognition as the most eminent of living Scotsmen, of which a symbol was his elevation to a baronetcy in 1820.

But the brightness of all this glory was to be pathetically dimmed. In 1825 a general financial panic, revealing the laxity of Scott's business partners, caused his firm to fail with liabilities of nearly a hundred and twenty thousand pounds. Always magnanimous and the soul of honour, Scott refused to take advantage of the bankruptcy laws, himself assumed the burden of the entire debt, and set himself the stupendous task of paying it with his pen. Amid increasing personal sorrows he laboured on for six years and so nearly attained his object that the debt was actually extinguished some years after his death. But in the effort he completed the exhaustion of his long overtaxed strength, and, a trip to Italy proving unavailing, returned to Abbotsford, and died, a few weeks after Goethe, in 1832.

As a man Scott was first of all a true and thorough gentleman, manly, open hearted, friendly and lovable in the highest degree. Truthfulness and courage were to him the essential virtues, and his religious faith was deep though simple and unobtrusive. Like other forceful men, he understood his own capacity, but his modesty was extreme; he always insisted with all sincerity that the ability to compose fiction was not for a moment to be compared with the ability to act effectively in practical activities; and he was really displeased at the suggestion that he belonged among the greatest men of the age. In spite of his Romantic tendencies and his absolute simplicity of character, he clung strongly to the conservatism of the feudal aristocracy with which he had laboured so hard to connect himself; he was vigorously hostile to the democratic spirit, and, in his later years, to the Reform Bill; and he felt and expressed almost childish delight in the friendship of the contemptible George IV, because George IV was his king. The conservatism was closely connected, in fact, with his Romantic interest in the past, and in politics it took the form, theoretically, of Jacobitism, loyalty to the worthless Stuart race whose memory his novels have done so much to keep alive. All these traits are made abundantly clear in the extended life of Scott written by his son-in-law, J. G. Lockhart, which is one of the two or three greatest English biographies.

Scott's long poems, the best of them, are the chief examples in English of dashing verse romances of adventure and love. They are hastily done, as we have said, and there is no attempt at subtilty of characterization or at any moral or philosophical meaning; nevertheless the reader's interest in the vigorous and picturesque action is maintained throughout at the highest pitch. Furthermore, they contain much finely sympathetic description of Scottish scenery, impressionistic, but poured out with enthusiasm. Scott's numerous lyrics are similarly stirring or moving expressions of the primal emotions, and some of them are charmingly musical.

The qualities of the novels, which represent the culmination of Romantic historical fiction, are much the same. Through his bold and active historical imagination Scott vivifies the past magnificently; without doubt, the great majority of English readers know English history chiefly through his works. His dramatic power, also, at its best, is superb; in his great scenes and crises he is masterly as narrator and describer. In the presentation of the characters there is often much of the same superficiality as in the poems, but there is much also of the highest skill.

The novels may be roughly divided into three classes: first those, like 'Ivanhoe,' whose scene is laid in the twelfth or thirteenth century; second those, like 'Kenilworth,' which are located in the fifteenth or sixteenth; and third, those belonging to England and Scotland of the seventeenth and eighteenth. In the earlier ones sheer romance predominates and the hero and heroine are likely to be more or less conventional paragons, respectively, of courage and tender charm; but in the later ones Scott largely portrays the life and people which he himself knew; and he knew them through and through. His Scottish characters in particular, often especially the secondary ones, are delightfully realistic portraits of a great variety of types. Mary Queen of Scots in 'The Abbot' and Caleb Balderstone in 'The Bride of Lammermoor' are equally convincing in their essential but very personal humanity. Descriptions of scenery are correspondingly fuller in the novels than in the poems and are equally useful for atmosphere and background.

In minor matters, in the novels also, there is much carelessness. The style, more formal than that of the present day, is prevailingly wordy and not infrequently slipshod, though its vitality is a much more noticeable characteristic. The structure of the stories is far from compact. Scott generally began without any idea how he was to continue or end and sent off each day's installment of his manuscript in the first draft as soon as it was written; hence the action often wanders, or even, from the structural point of view, drags.

But interest seldom greatly slackens until the end, which, it must be further confessed, is often suddenly brought about in a very inartistic fashion. It is of less consequence that in the details of fact Scott often commits errors, not only, like all historical novelists, deliberately manipulating the order and details of the actual events to suit his purposes, but also making frequent sheer mistakes. In 'Ivanhoe,' for example, the picture of life in the twelfth century is altogether incorrect and misleading. In all these matters scores of more self-conscious later writers are superior to Scott, but mere correctness counts for far less than genius.

When all is said, Scott remains the greatest historical novelist, and one of the greatest creative forces, in world literature.

SAMUEL TAYLOR COLERIDGE

The poets Wordsworth and Coleridge are of special interest not only from the primary fact that they are among the greatest of English authors, but also secondarily because in spite of their close personal association each expresses one of the two main contrasting or complementary tendencies in the Romantic movement; Coleridge the delight in wonder and mystery, which he has the power to express with marvelous poetic suggestiveness, and Wordsworth, in an extreme degree, the belief in the simple and quiet forces, both of human life and of Nature. To Coleridge, who was slightly the younger of the two, attaches the further pathetic interest of high genius largely thwarted by circumstances and weakness of will. Born in Devonshire in 1772, the youngest of the many children of a self-made clergyman and schoolmaster, he was a precocious and abnormal child, then as always a fantastic dreamer, despised by other boys and unable to mingle with them. After the death of his father he was sent to Christ's Hospital, the 'Bluecoat' charity school in London, where he spent nine lonely years in the manner briefly described in an essay of Charles Lamb, where Coleridge appears under a thin disguise.

The very strict discipline was no doubt of much value in giving firmness and definite direction to his irregular nature, and the range of his studies, both in literature and in other fields, was very wide. Through the aid of scholarships and of contributions from his brothers he entered Cambridge in 1791, just after Wordsworth had left the University; but here his most striking exploit was a brief escapade of running away and enlisting in a cavalry troop. Meeting Southey, then a student at Oxford, he drew him into a plan for a 'Pant isocracy', a community of twelve young couples to be founded in some 'delightful part of the new back settlements' of America on the principles of communistic cooperation in all lines, broad mental culture, and complete freedom of opinion. Naturally, this plan never past beyond the dream stage.

Coleridge left the University in 1794 without a degree, tormented by a disappointment in love. He had already begun to publish poetry and newspaper prose, and he now attempted lecturing. He and Southey married two sisters, whom Byron in a later attack on Southey somewhat inaccurately described as 'milliners of Bath'; and Coleridge settled near Bristol. After characteristically varied and unsuccessful efforts at conducting a periodical, newspaper writing, and preaching as a Unitarian, he moved with his wife in 1797 to Nether Stowey in Somersetshire. Expressly in order to be near him, Wordsworth and his sister Dorothy soon leased the neighbouring manor house of Alfoxden, and there followed the memorable year of intellectual and emotional stimulus when Coleridge's genius suddenly expanded into short-lived but wonderful activity and he wrote most of his few great poems, 'The Ancient Mariner,' 'Kubla Khan,' and the First Part of 'Christabel.' 'The Ancient Mariner' was planned by Coleridge and Wordsworth on one of their frequent rambles, and was to have been written in collaboration; but as it proceeded, Wordsworth found his manner so different from that of Coleridge that he withdrew altogether from the undertaking. The final result of the incident, however, was the publication in 1798 of 'Lyrical Ballads,' which included of Coleridge's work only this one poem, but of Wordsworth's several of his most characteristic ones.

Coleridge afterwards explained that the plan of the volume contemplated two complementary sorts of poems. He was to present supernatural or romantic characters, yet investing them with human interest and semblance of truth; while Wordsworth was to add the charm of novelty to everyday things and to suggest their kinship to the supernatural, arousing readers from their accustomed blindness to the loveliness and wonders of the world around us. No better description could be given of the poetic spirit and the whole poetic work of the two men. Like some other epoch marking books, 'Lyrical Ballads' attracted little attention. Shortly after its publication Coleridge and the Wordsworths sailed for Germany, where for the greater part of a year Coleridge worked hard, if irregularly, at the language, literature, and philosophy.

The remaining thirty-five years of his life are a record of ambitious projects and fitful efforts, for the most part turned by ill health and lack of steady purpose into melancholy failure, but with a few fragmentary results standing out brilliantly. At times Coleridge did newspaper work, at which he might have succeeded; in 1800, in a burst of energy, he translated Schiller's tragedy 'Wallenstein' into English blank verse, a translation which in the opinion of most critics surpasses the original; and down to 1802, and occasionally later, he wrote a few more poems of a high order. For a few years from 1800 on he lived at Greta Hall in the village of Keswick, in the northern end of the Lake Region , fifteen miles from Wordsworth; but his marriage was incompatible, and he finally left his wife and children, who were thenceforward supported largely by Southey, his successor at Greta Hall. Coleridge himself was maintained chiefly by the generosity of friends; later, in part, by public pensions. It was apparently about 1800, to alleviate mental distress and great physical suffering from neuralgia, that he began the excessive use of opium which for many years had a large share in paralyzing his will. For a year, in 1804-5, he displayed decided diplomatic talent as secretary to the Governor of Malta. At several different times, also, he gave courses, of lectures on Shakespeare and Milton; as a speaker he was always eloquent; and the fragmentary notes of the lectures which have been preserved rank very high in Shakespearean criticism. His main interest, however, was now in philosophy; perhaps no Englishman has ever had a more profoundly philosophical mind; and through scattered writings and through his stimulating though prolix talks to friends and disciples he performed a very great service to English thought by introducing the viewpoint and ideas of the German transcendentalists, such as Kant, Schelling, and Fichte. During his last eighteen years he lived mostly in sad acceptance of defeat, though still much honoured, in the house of a London physician. He died in 1834.

As a poet Coleridge's first great distinction is that which we have already pointed out, namely that he gives wonderfully sub tile and appealing expression to the Romantic sense for the strange and the supernatural, and indeed for all that the word 'Romance' connotes at the present day. He accomplishes this result partly through his power of suggesting the real unity of the inner and outer worlds, partly through his skill, resting in a large degree on vivid impressionistic description, in making strange scenes appear actual, in securing from the reader what he himself called 'that willing suspension of disbelief which constitutes poetic faith.' Almost every one has felt the weird charm of 'The Ancient Mariner,' where all the unearthly story centers about a moral and religious idea, and where we are dazzled by a constant succession of such pictures as these:

And ice, masthigh, came floating by,
As green as emerald.
We were the first that ever burst

Into that silent sea.
The western wave was all aflame:
The day was well nigh done:
Almost upon the western wave
Rested the broad, bright sun;
When that strange shape drove suddenly
Betwixt us and the sun.

'Christabel' achieves what Coleridge himself described as the very difficult task of creating witchery by daylight; and 'Kubla Khan,' worthy, though a brief fragment, to rank with these two, is a marvelous glimpse of fairyland.

In the second place, Coleridge is one of the greatest English masters of exquisite verbal melody, with its tributary devices of alliteration and haunting onomatopoeia. In this respect especially his influence on subsequent English poetry has been incalculable. The details of his method students should observe for themselves in their study of the poems, but one particular matter should be mentioned. In 'Christabel' and to a somewhat less degree in 'The Ancient Mariner' Coleridge departed as far as possible from eighteenth century tradition by greatly varying the number of syllables in the lines, while keeping a regular number of stresses. Though this practice, as we have seen, was customary in Old English poetry and in the popular ballads, it was supposed by Coleridge and his contemporaries to be a new discovery, and it proved highly suggestive to other romantic poets. From hearing 'Christabel' read Scott caught the idea for the free and easy meter of his poetical romances. With a better body and will Coleridge might have been one of the supreme

English poets; as it is, he has left a small number of very great poems and has proved one of the most powerful influences on later English poetry.

THE LAST GROUP OF ROMANTIC POETS

Lord Byron

Byron expresses mainly the spirit of individual revolt, revolt against all existing institutions and standards. This was largely a matter of his own personal temperament, but the influence of the time also had a share in it, the time when the apparent failure of the French Revolution had thrown the pronounced liberals back upon their own resources in bitter dissatisfaction with the existing state of society. Byron was born in 1788. His father, the violent and worthless descendant of a line of violent and worthless nobles, was just then using up the money which the poet's mother had brought him, and soon abandoned her. She in turn was wildly passionate and uncontrolled, and in bringing up her son indulged alternately in fits of genuine tenderness and capricious outbursts of mad rage and unkindness. Byron suffered also from another serious handicap; he was born with deformed feet, so that throughout life he walked clumsily a galling irritation to his sensitive pride. In childhood his poetic instincts were stimulated by summers spent among the scenery of his mother's native Scottish Highlands. At the age of ten, on the death of his great-uncle, he succeeded to the peerage as Lord Byron, but for many years he continued to be heavily in debt, partly because of lavish extravagance, which was one expression of his inherited reckless willfulness. Throughout his life he was obliged to make the most heroic efforts to keep in check another inherited tendency, to corpulence; he generally restricted his diet almost entirely to such meager fare as potatoes and soda water, though he often broke out also into periods of unlimited self-indulgence.

From Harrow School he passed to Trinity College, Cambridge, where Macaulay and Tennyson were to be among his successors. Aspiring to be an athlete, he made himself respected as a fighter, despite his deformity, by his strength of arm, and he was always a powerful swimmer. Deliberately aiming also at the reputation of a debauchee, he lived wildly, though now as later probably not altogether so wickedly as he represented. After three years of irregular attendance at the University his rank secured him the degree of M. A., in 1808. He had already begun to publish verse, and when 'The Edinburgh Review' ridiculed his very juvenile 'Hours of Idleness' he added an attack on Jeffrey to a slashing criticism of contemporary poets which he had already written in rimed couplets, and published the piece as 'English Bards and Scotch Reviewers.'

He was now settled at his inherited estate of Newstead Abbey, and had made his appearance in his hereditary place in the House of Lords; but following his instinct for excitement and for doing the expensively conspicuous thing he next spent two years on a European tour, through Spain, Greece, and Turkey. In Greece he traveled, as was necessary, with a large native guard, and he allowed reports to become current that he passed through a succession of romantic and reckless adventures. The first literary result of his journey was the publication in 1812 of the first two cantos of 'Childe Harold's Pilgrimage.' This began as the record of the wanderings of Childe Harold, a dissipated young noble who was clearly intended to represent the author himself; but Byron soon dropped this figure as a useless impediment in the series of descriptions of Spain and Greece of which the first two cantos consist.

He soon abandoned also the attempt to secure an archaic effect by the occasional use of Spenserian words, but he wrote throughout in Spenser's stanza, which he used with much power. The public received the poem with the greatest enthusiasm; Byron summed up the case in his well-known comment: 'I awoke one morning and found myself famous.' In fact, 'Childe Harold' is the best of all Byron's works, though the third and fourth cantos, published some years later, and dealing with Belgium, the battle of Waterloo, and central Europe, are superior to the first two. Its excellence consists chiefly in the fact that while it is primarily a descriptive poem, its pictures, dramatically and finely vivid in themselves, are permeated with intense emotion and often serve only as introductions to passionate rhapsodies, so that the effect is largely lyrical.

Though Byron always remained awkward in company he now became the idol of the world of fashion. He followed up his first literary success by publishing during the next four years his brief and vigorous metrical romances, most of them Eastern in setting, 'The Giaour', 'The Bride of Abydos,' 'The Corsair,' 'Lara,' 'The Siege of Corinth,' and 'Parisina.' These were composed not only with remarkable facility but in the utmost haste, sometimes a whole poem in only a few days and sometimes in odds and ends of time snatched from social diversions.

The results are only too clearly apparent; the meter is often slovenly, the narrative structure highly defective, and the characterization superficial or flatly inconsistent. In other respects the poems are thoroughly characteristic of their author. In each of them stands out one dominating figure, the hero, a desperate and terrible adventurer, characterized by Byron himself as possessing 'one virtue and a thousand crimes,' merciless and vindictive to his enemies, tremblingly obeyed by his followers, manifesting human tenderness only towards his mistress, and above all inscrutably enveloped in a cloud of pretentious romantic melancholy and mystery. Like Childe Harold, this impossible and grandiose figure of many incarnations was well understood by every one to be meant for a picture of Byron himself, who thus posed for and received in full measure the horrified admiration of the public. But in spite of all this melodramatic claptrap the romances, like 'Childe Harold,' are filled with the tremendous Byronic passion, which, as in 'Childe Harold,' lends great power alike to their narrative and their description.

Byron now made a strangely ill judged marriage with a Miss Milbanke, a woman of the fashionable world but of strict and perhaps even prudish moral principles. After a year she left him, and 'society,' with characteristic inconsistency, turned on him in a frenzy of superficial indignation. He shortly fled from England, never to return, both his colossal vanity and his truer sensitive self stung by the injustice to fury against the hypocrisy and conventionalities of English life, which, in fact, he had always despised. He spent the following seven years as a wanderer over Italy and central Europe. He often lived scandalously; sometimes he was with the far more fine spirited Shelley; and he sometimes furnished money to the Italians who were conducting the agitation against their tyrannical foreign governments. All the while he was producing a great quantity of poetry. In his half dozen or more poetic dramas he entered a new field. In the most important of them, 'Manfred,' a treatment of the theme which Marlowe and Goethe had used in 'Faust,' his real power is largely thwarted by the customary Byronic mystery and swagger. 'Cain' and 'Heaven and Earth,' though wretchedly written, have also a vaguely vast imaginative impressiveness.

Their defiant handling of Old Testament material and therefore of Christian theology was shocking to most respectable Englishmen and led Southey to characterize Byron as the founder of the 'Satanic School' of English poetry. More significant is the longest and chief of his satires, 'Don Juan,' on which he wrote intermittently for years as the mood took him. It is ostensibly the narrative of the adventures of a young Spaniard, but as a story it rambles on formlessly without approaching an end, and its real purpose is to serve as an utterly cynical indictment of mankind, the institutions of society, and accepted moral principles. Byron often points the cynicism by lapsing into brilliant doggerel, but his double nature appears in the occasional intermingling of tender and beautiful passages. Byron's fiery spirit was rapidly burning itself out. In his uncontrolled zest for new sensations he finally tired of poetry, and in 1823 he accepted the invitation of the European committee in charge to become a leader of the Greek revolt against Turkish oppression. He sailed to the Greek camp at the malarial town of Missolonghi, where he showed qualities of leadership but died of fever after a few months, in 1824, before he had time to accomplish anything.

It is hard to form a consistent judgment of so inconsistent a being as Byron. At the core of his nature there was certainly much genuine goodness generosity, sympathy, and true feeling. However much we may discount his sacrifice of his life in the cause of a foreign people, his love of political freedom and his hatred of tyranny were thoroughly and passionately sincere, as is repeatedly evident in such poems as the sonnet on 'Chillon,' 'The Prisoner of Chillon,' and the 'Ode on Venice.' On the other hand his violent contempt for social and religious hypocrisy had as much of personal bitterness as of disinterested principle; and his persistent quest of notoriety, the absence of moderation in his attacks on religious and moral standards, his lack of self-control, and his indulgence in all the vices of the worse part of the titled and wealthy class require no comment. Whatever allowances charity may demand on the score of tainted heredity, his character was far too violent and too shallow to approach to greatness.

As a poet he continues to occupy a conspicuous place through the power of his volcanic emotion. It was this quality of emotion, perhaps the first essential in poetry, which enrolled among his admirers a clear spirit in most respects the antithesis of his own, that of Matthew Arnold. In 'Memorial Verses' Arnold says of him:

He taught us little, but our soul
Had felt him like the thunder's roll.
With shivering heart the strife we saw
Of passion with eternal law.

His poetry has also an elemental sweep and grandeur. The majesty of Nature, especially of the mountains and the ocean, stirs him to feeling which often results in superb stanzas, like the well-known ones at the end of 'Childe Harold' beginning 'Roll on, thou deep and dark blue Ocean, roll'! Too often, however, Byron's passion and facility of expression issue in bombast and crude rhetoric. Moreover, his poetry is for the most part lacking in delicacy and fine shading; scarcely a score of his lyrics are of the highest order. He gives us often the blaring music of a military band or the loud, swelling volume of an organ, but very seldom the softer tones of a violin or symphony.

To his creative genius and power the variety as well as the amount of his poetry offers forceful testimony.

In moods of moral and literary severity, to summarize, a critic can scarcely refrain from dismissing Byron with impatient contempt; nevertheless his genius and his in part splendid achievement are substantial facts. He stands as the extreme but significant exponent of violent Romantic individualism in a period when Romantic aspiration was largely disappointed and disillusioned, but was indignantly gathering its strength for new efforts.

Percy Bysshe Shelley

Shelley resembles Byron in his thoroughgoing revolt against society, but he is totally unlike Byron in several important respects. His first impulse was an unselfish love for his fellowmen, with an aggressive eagerness for martyrdom in their behalf; his nature was unusually, even abnormally, fine and sensitive;

and his poetic quality was a delicate and ethereal lyricism unsurpassed in the literature of the world. In both his life and his poetry his visionary reforming zeal and his superb lyric instinct are inextricably intertwined.

Shelley, born in 1792, belonged to a family of Sussex country gentry; a baronetcy bestowed on his grandfather during the poet's youth passed from his father after his own death to his descendants. Matthew Arnold has remarked that while most of the members of any aristocracy are naturally conservative, confirmed advocates of the system under which they enjoy great privileges, any one of them who happens to be endowed with radical ideas is likely to carry these to an extreme. In Shelley's case this general tendency was strengthened by reaction against the benighted Toryism of his father and by most of the experiences of his life from the very outset. At Eton his hatred of tyranny was fiercely aroused by the fagging system and the other brutalities of an English school; he broke into open revolt and became known as 'mad Shelley,' and his schoolfellows delighted in driving him into paroxysms of rage.

Already at Eton he read and accepted the doctrines of the French pre-Revolutionary philosophers and their English interpreter William Godwin. He came to believe not only that human nature is essentially good, but that if left to itself it can be implicitly trusted; that sin and misery are merely the results of the injustice springing from the institutions of society, chief of which are organized government, formal religion, law, and formal marriage; and that the one essential thing is to bring about a condition where these institutions can be abolished and where all men may be allowed to follow their own inclinations.

The great advance which has been made since Shelley's time in the knowledge of history and the social sciences throws a pitiless light on the absurdity of this theory, showing that social institutions, terribly imperfect as they are, are by no means chiefly bad but rather represent the slow gains of thousands of years of painful progress; none the less the theory was bound to appeal irresistibly to such an impulsive and inexperienced idealism as that of Shelley. It was really, of course, not so much against social institutions themselves that Shelley revolted as against their abuses, which were still more flagrantly apparent in his time than in ours. When he repudiated Christianity and declared himself an atheist, what he actually had in mind was the perverted parody of religion mainly offered by the Church of his time; and, as some one has observed, when he pronounced for love without marriage it was because of the tragedies that he had seen in marriages without love. Much must be ascribed also to his sheer radicalism the instinct to fly violently against whatever was conventionally accepted and violently to flaunt his adherence to whatever was banned.

In 1810 Shelley entered Oxford, especially exasperated by parental interference with his first boyish love, and already the author of some crude prose romances and poetry. In the university he devoted his time chiefly to investigating subjects not included or permitted in the curriculum, especially chemistry; and after a few months, having written a pamphlet on 'The Necessity of Atheism' and sent it with conscientious zeal to the heads of the colleges, he was expelled. Still a few months later, being then nineteen years old, he allowed himself to be led, admittedly only through pity, into a marriage with a certain Harriet Westbrook, a frivolous and commonplace schoolgirl of sixteen. For the remaining ten years of his short life he, like Byron, was a wanderer, sometimes in straits for money, though always supported, after some time generously enough, by his father. At first he tried the career of a professional agitator; going to Ireland he attempted to arouse the people against English tyranny by such devices as scattering copies of addresses from his window in Dublin or launching them in bottles in the Bristol Channel; but he was soon obliged to flee the country. It is hard, of course, to take such conduct seriously; yet in the midst of much that was wild, his pamphlets contained also much of solid wisdom, no small part of which has since been enacted into law.

Unselfish as he was in the abstract, Shelley's enthusiast's egotism and the unrestraint of his emotions rendered him fitful, capricious, unable to appreciate any point of view but his own, and therefore when irritated or excited capable of downright cruelty in concrete cases. The most painful illustration is afforded by his treatment of his first wife. Three years after his marriage he informed her that he considered the connection at an end and abandoned her to what proved a few years of a wretched existence. Shelley himself formed a union with Mary Wollstonecraft Godwin, the daughter of his revolutionary teacher. Her sympathetic though extravagant admiration for his genius, now beginning to express itself in really great poetry, was of the highest value to him, the more so that from this time on he was viewed by most respectable Englishman with the same abhorrence which they felt for Byron. In 1818 the Shelley's also abandoned England for Italy, where they moved from place to place, living sometimes, as we have said, with Byron, for whose genius, in spite of its coarseness, Shelley had a warm admiration. Shelley's death came when he was only thirty, in 1822, by a sudden accident he was drowned by the upsetting of his sailboat in the Gulf of Spezia, between Genoa and Pisa. His body, cast on the shore, was burned in the presence of Byron and another radical, Leigh

Hunt, and the ashes were buried in the Protestant cemetery just outside the wall of Rome, where Keats had been interred only a year earlier.

Some of Shelley's shorter poems are purely poetic expressions of poetic emotion, but by far the greater part are documents in his attack on existing customs and cruelties. Matthew Arnold, paraphrasing Joubert's description of Plato, has characterized him as 'a beautiful and ineffectual angel, beating in the void his luminous wings in vain.' This is largely true, but it overlooks the sound general basis and the definite actual results which belong to his work, as to that of every great idealist. On the artistic side the most conspicuous thing in his poetry is the ecstatic aspiration for Beauty and the magnificent embodiment of it. Shelley is the poetic disciple, but a thoroughly original disciple, of Coleridge. His esthetic passion is partly sensuous, and he often abandons himself to it with romantic unrestraint. His 'lyrical cry,' of which Matthew Arnold has spoken, is the demand, which will not be denied, for beauty that will satisfy his whole being. Sensations, indeed, he must always have, agreeable ones if possible, or in default of them, painful ones; this explains his occasional touches of repulsive morbid ness. But the repulsive strain is exceptional. No other poetry is crowded in the same way as his with pictures glorious and delicate in form, light, and colour, or is more musically palpitating with the delight which they create. To Shelley as a follower of Plato, however, the beauty of the senses is only a manifestation of ideal Beauty, the spiritual force which appears in other forms as Intellect and Love; and Intellect and Love as well are equal objects of his unbounded devotion. Hence his sensuousness is touched with a real spiritual quality. In his poetic emotion, as in his social ambitions, Shelley is constantly yearning for the unattainable. One of our best Critics has observed: 'He never shows his full power in dealing separately with intellectual or moral or physical beauty. His appropriate sphere is swift sensibility, the intersecting line between the sensuous and the intellectual or moral. Mere sensation is too literal for him, mere feeling too blind and dumb, mere thought too cold.... Wordsworth is always exulting in the fullness of Nature, Shelley is always chasing its falling stars.'

The contrast, here hinted at, between Shelley's view of Nature and that of Wordsworth, is extreme and entirely characteristic; the same is true, also, when we compare Shelley and Byron. Shelley's excitable sensuousness produces in him in the presence of Nature a very different attitude from that of Wordsworth's philosophic Christian mysticism. For the sensuousness of Shelley gets the upper hand of his somewhat shadowy Platonism, and he creates out of Nature mainly an ethereal world of delicate and rapidly shifting sights and sounds and sensations. And while he is not unresponsive to the majestic greatness of Nature in her vast forms and vistas, he is never impelled, like Byron, to claim with them the kinship of a haughty elemental spirit.

"From the world of imagination the shapes of the old world had disappeared, and their place was taken by a stream of radiant vapours, incessantly forming, shifting, and dissolving in the 'clear golden dawn,' and hymning with the voices of seraphs, to the music of the stars and the 'singing rain,' the sublime ridiculous theories of Godwin. In his heart were emotions that responded to the vision an aspiration or ecstasy, a dejection or despair, like those of spirits rapt into Paradise or mourning over its ruin. And he wrote not like Shakespeare or Pope, for Londoners sitting in a theatre or a coffeehouse, intelligence's vivid enough but definitely embodied in a definite society, able to fly, but also able to sit; he wrote, or rather he sang, to his own soul, to other spirit sparks of the fire of Liberty scattered over the dark earth, to spirits in the air, to the boundless spirit of Nature or Freedom or Love, his one place of rest and the one source of his vision, ecstasy, and sorrow. He sang to this, and he sang of it, and of the emotions it inspired, and of its worldwide contest with such shapes of darkness as Faith and Custom. And he made immortal music; now in melodies as exquisite and varied as the songs of Schubert, and now in symphonies where the crudest of Philosophies of History melted into golden harmony. For although there was something always working in Shelley's mind and issuing in those radiant vapours, he was far deeper and truer than his philosophic creed; its expression and even its development were constantly checked or distorted by the hard and narrow framework of his creed. And it was one which in effect condemned nineteenths of the human nature that has formed the material of the world's great poems

The finest of Shelley's poems, are his lyrics. 'The Skylark' and 'The Cloud' are among the most dazzling and unique of all outbursts of poetic genius. Of the 'Ode to the West Wind,' a succession of surging emotions and visions of beauty swept, as if by the wind itself, through the vast spaces of the world, Swinburne exclaims: 'It is beyond and outside and above all criticism, all praise, and all thanksgiving.' The 'Lines Written among the Euganean Hills,' 'The Indian Serenade,' 'The Sensitive Plant', and not a few others are also of the highest quality. In 'Adonais,' an elegy on Keats and an invective against the reviewer whose brutal criticism, as Shelley wrongly supposed, had helped to kill him, splendid poetic power, at least, must be admitted. Much less satisfactory but still fascinating are the longer poems, narrative or philosophical, such as the early 'Alastor,' a vague allegory of a poet's quest for the beautiful through a gorgeous and incoherent succession of romantic wildernesses; the 'Hymn to Intellectual Beauty'; 'Julian and Maddalo,' in which Shelley and

Byron are portrayed; and 'Epipsychidion,' an ecstatic poem on the love which is spiritual sympathy. Shelley's satires may be disregarded. To the dramatic form belong his two most important long poems. 'Prometheus Unbound' partly follows AEschylus in treating the torture of the Titan who is the champion or personification of Mankind, by Zeus, whom Shelley makes the incarnation of tyranny and on whose overthrow the Golden Age of Shelleyan anarchy succeeds. The poem is a lyrical drama, more on the Greek than on the English model. There is almost no action, and the significance lies first in the lyrical beauty of the profuse choruses and second in the complete embodiment of Shelley's passionate hatred of tyranny.

'The Cenci' is more dramatic in form, though the excess of speech over action makes of it also only a 'literary drama.' The story, taken from family history of the Italian Renaissance, is one of the most horrible imaginable, but the play is one of the most powerful produced in English since the Elizabethan period. That the quality of Shelley's genius is unique is obvious on the slightest acquaintance with him, and it is equally certain that in spite of his premature death and all his limitations he occupies an assured place among the very great poets. On the other hand, the vagueness of his imagination and expression has recently provoked severe criticism. It has even been declared that the same mind cannot honestly enjoy both the carefully wrought classical beauty of Milton's 'Lycidas' and Shelley's mistily shimmering 'Adonais.' The question goes deep and should receive careful consideration.

Bibliography

Abercrombie, D.: *Elements of General Ponetics*, Edinburgh, Edinburgh University Press, 1967.

Ailsby, Christopher: *Roll of Infamy*, Osceola, MBI, 1997.

Ball, M. J. : *Phonetics: The Science of Speech*, London, Arnold, 1999.

Bennett, J. A. W.: *Middle English Literature*, Oxford, Clarendon Press, 1986.

Bentley, Eades: *The Jacobean and Caroline Stage*, Oxford, Clarendon Press, 1941.

Beyond Borders: *An Anthology of SAARC Poetry*, Noida, Rainbow, 2002.

Bhattacharyya, Nath: *Indian Religious Historiography*, New Delhi, Munshiram Manoharlal Publishers, 1996.

Brian L. : *Uniforms and Insignia of the Luftwaffe*, London, Arms and Armor, 1999.

Cavanagh, John: *British Theatre: a Bibliography, 1901 to 1985*, Hampshire, Motley, 1989.

Chambers, Kerchever: *English Literature at the Close of the Middle Ages*, New York: Oxford University Press, 1947.

Classe, A.: *The Rhythm of English Prose*, Oxford, Blackwell, 1939.

Couper-Kuhlen, E.: *An Introduction to English Prosody*, London, Edward Arnold, 1986.

Courthope, John: *A History of English Poetry*, London, MacMillan and Co., 1903.

Crystal, D.: *Prosodic Systems and Intonation in English*, Cambridge, Cambridge University Press, 1969.

Dobree, Bonamy: *English Literature in the Early Eighteenth Century, 1700-1740*, Oxford, Clarendon Press, 1959.

Edmund Spenser: *A Critical Study*, New Delhi, Anmol Pub., 2005.

Edmund, Kerchever: *English Literature at the Close of the Middle Ages*, New York: Oxford University Press, 1947.

Ferrence, G.: *Deadly Fashion: the Rise and Fall of Cigarette Smoking in North America*, New York, Garland, 1989.

Francis, Russell: *The Scottish Novel: from Smollett to Spark*, Cambridge, Harvard University Press, 1978.

Gerald, Eades: *The Jacobean and Caroline Stage*, Oxford, Clarendon Press, 1941.

Gladstone, William : *Early English Stages, 1300 to 1660*, London, Routledge and Paul; 1959.

Glynne, William Gladstone: *Early English Stages, 1300 to 1660*, London, Routledge and Paul; 1959.

Harivansh R.B.: *In the Afternoon of Time: An Autobiography*, New Delhi, Penguin, 2001.

Hart, Russell: *The Scottish Novel: from Smollett to Spark*, Cambridge, Harvard University Press, 1978.

Hogan, Robert Goode: *The Modern Irish Drama: a Documentary History*, NJ: Humanities Press, 1975.

Jack, Ian Robert James: *English Literature, 1815-1832*, Oxford, Clarendon Press, 1963.

James Baldwin: *Protest and Beyond: A Study of Afro-American Fiction*, New Delhi, Rajat Pub., 2005.

James, Ernest: *Principles of Textual Criticism*, San Marino, Huntington Library, 1972.

Jhumpa Lahiri: *The Master Storyteller: A Critical Response to Interpreter of Maladies*, New Delhi, KPH, 2002.

John Milton: *A Critical Study*, New Delhi, Anmol, 2005.

Knowles, G.: *Patterns of Spoken English: An Introduction to English Phonetics*, London, Longman, 1987.

Matricardi, Paolo: *Complete Book of World War II Combat Aircraft*, NY, Military Press, 1988

Naipaul, V.S. : *A House for Mr. Biswas: With an Introduction by Ian Buruma*, New Delhi, Penguin, 1992.

Nath, Narendra: *Indian Religious Historiography*, New Delhi, Munshiram Manoharlal Publishers, 1996.

Neil Bissoondath: *Indo-Caribbean-Canadian Diaspora*, New Delhi, Rawat, 2005.

Pierre, Turner: *Uniforms and Insignia of the Luftwaffe*, London, Arms and Armor, 1999.

Raja Rao: *The Fictionist*, Delhi, B.R. Publishing, 2003.

Salzman, Paul: *English Prose Fiction, 1558-1700: a Critical History*, Oxford, Clarendon Press, 1985.

Seidlhofer, B.: *Pronunciation, Oxford*, Oxford University Press, 1994.

Seth, Vikram : *Multiple Locations, Multiple Affiliation*, New Delhi, Rawat, 2001.

Terence, P.: *The Later Jacobean and Caroline Dramatists*, Lincoln, University of Nebraska Press, 1978.

Terence, P.: *The Later Jacobean and Caroline Dramatists*, Lincoln, University of Nebraska Press, 1978.

Thorpe, Ernest: *Principles of Textual Criticism*, San Marino, Huntington Library, 1972.

Vikram Seth: *Multiple Locations, Multiple Affiliation*, New Delhi, Rawat, 2001.

Walter, Ernest: *Tradition and Dream : the English and American Novel from the Twenties to Our Time*, London: Hogarth Press, 1986.

Wearing, J. P.: *The London Stage, 1890-1899: a Calendar of Plays and Players*, NJ, Scarecrow Press, 1976.

Wickham, Gladstone: *Early English Stages, 1300 to 1660*, London, Routledge and Paul; 1959.

Wilmeth, Don : *American and English Popular Entertainment: a Guide to Information Sources*, Detroit, Gale Research Co., 1980.

Yonah, A.: *Combating Terrorism: Strategies of Ten Countries*, Mich., University of Michigan Press, 2002.

Index

❑❑❑